UNDER CONSTANT SUPERVISION

Under Constant Supervision
C.J. Thomson

Copyright © BookRefine publishing, 2020

First published 2020
ISBN: 9798633845419

Published by BookRefine Publishing, Australia

Contact@bookrefine.com
Bookrefine.com
Design by *CJCreative.design*

All rights reserved. Without limiting the rights under copyright reserved above, no part of this publication may be reproduced, stored in or introduced into a database and retrieval system or transmitted in any form or any means (electronic, mechanical, photocopying, recording or otherwise) without the prior written permission of both the owner of the copyright and the above publishers. Every effort has been made to ensure that this publication contains accurate and current information at the time of its publication; however, the publisher and the author(s) shall not be liable for any loss, damage or liability as a result of the information contained herein. The views and opinions expressed in this book are those of the author(s) and do not necessarily reflect the position of the publisher. Any content provided or opinions are not intended to malign any religious or ethnic group, club, company, individual or government entity. All content is for educational and informational purposes only. The author(s) and publisher are not liable or responsible for any damages resulting from or related to your use of content featured within including -- but not limited to -- any suggestions or suspected encouragement that breaches local and international law.

All trademarks mentioned within the published works are acknowledged as belonging to their respected owners. This book may contain copyrighted material the use of which has not been specifically authorised by the copyright owner. We believe making such material available to advance understanding of user privacy, surveillance, censorship and technologies constitute 'fair use'

This work is creator endorsed under a strict set of guidelines aiming for a better copyright system and therefore all fairness between publisher and author(s) has been insured under the hope that these guides are respected by the consumer of such works.

UNDER CONSTANT SUPERVISION

BookRefine
PUBLISHING

This book contains footnotes and citations. Any links referenced are listed using archived links in case of the original content being removed.

For additional longevity, mirrored files, and additional resources such as leaked documents, location data and high-resolution images are available at GitHub: *bookrefine.github.io*

We cannot guarantee that all links will work and cannot take responsibility for any changes to live pages.

UNDER
CONSTANT
SUPERVISION

INTRODUCTION: THE SPY WHO LOVES YOU 15
PART ONE: GAINING SERVICES, LOSING CONTROL 19
THE RISE OF GOOGLE THANKS TO EMAIL 31
PART TWO: EVER FEEL LIKE YOU'RE THE PRODUCT? 41
PART THREE: A RESTRICTED TECHNOLOGY FOR ALL TO ENJOY 65
A RESTRICTED INTERNET 67
COPYRIGHT ENFORCEMENT OR RESTRICTION? 87
FORCED PIRACY / FORCED BOYCOTTS? 115
PART FOUR: GLOBAL SURVEILLANCE 119
SPYING ALLIANCES: AN OVERVIEW 121
UNITED STATES AND UNITED AUSTRALIA 123
COMMUNICATIONS 129
CABLE TAPPING 133
THE EDWARD SNOWDEN REVELATIONS 141
THE ESPIONAGE AND INTERVENTION OF FVEY THROUGHOUT HISTORY 151
MULTIPLE ACTS OF ABUSE 155
GLOBAL REACTIONS TO GLOBAL SURVEILLANCE 169
SURVEILLANCE IN NUMBERS 173
THE SPY PROGRAMS 175
ECHELON 183
SPECIAL COLLECTION SERVICE / STATEROOM 195
PRISM 200
RAMPART 203
STELLARWIND 205
TEMPORA 209
TAO AND THE ANT CATALOGUE 211
XKEYSCORE 221
MUSCULAR 225
INTELLIPEDIA 227
NSA LOCATIONS 229
OTHER LOCATIONS: 237
GCHQ SURVEILLANCE AND SIGNAL TRACKING LOCATIONS 238
AT&T: INTERNET SURVEILLENCE PROVIDER 245

WITH UFED, IT'S EASY TO DOWNLOAD EVERYTHING..255
THEY'RE WATCHING YOU 272
PART FIVE: SMART AND ALWAYS CONNECTED 276
SMART FEATURES IN A SMART WORLD – BUT WHO BENEFITS MOST?................278
SMART CONSUMPTION...280
SMART VIEWING BUT WHO IS THE VIEWER?...288
SMART AUTOMOTIVE...295
IN CONCLUSION... 305
GLOSSARY...309

UNDER CONSTANT SUPERVISION

He sees you when you're sleeping
He knows when you're awake
He knows if you've been bad or good
So be good for goodness sake!

Santa Claus is Comin' To Town,
Published 1934 by Leo Feist, Inc.

INTRODUCTION: THE SPY WHO LOVES YOU

One day you are enjoying yourself. You decide to go out shopping. You visit a clothing retailer and try on a nice leather jacket. It suits you and you like it, but it's quite expensive so you decide you'll think. You continue to another clothing shop. There's an awful-looking hat. Something you wouldn't be seen dead in!

There's a man following you into each shop, documenting your every move. When you decide it's time to look at the new release movies, you begin to forget about ever wanting new clothes. Suddenly, you walk past a shop that has the perfect jacket, much like the one you saw previously, but this one suits your budget and comes in your favourite colour. Your new stalker has successfully planted this jacket and knows you're likely to at least try it on.

This strange creepy fellow has been watching you every time you've gone out. He has seen the photos you have uploaded; he knows what you like to do with your friends, and he knows just how much you enjoy playing puzzle games on your phone.

When you drive home after work, he's there watching where you go, the speed you do, and the time you usually get back. He thinks about how if you'd simply leave a little while earlier, you'd save 5 minutes in traffic jams. Then he hangs around while you relax and enjoy the fun side. As you scroll through various news articles and watch a few funny videos, he takes his diary out and notes down the videos you watched and the ones you skipped.

When his job is complete for the day, he returns to his office located thousands of miles away from where he collaborates with other spies just like him. He matches your activity with those just like you before setting out to see you the next time you go shopping, watch a movie or chat with your friends.
His job is to adapt the world around you to your preferences. Deep down he wants you to see the things you like, all while getting paid each time you see what he's put in front of you. If you go take a closer look at that thing, whether it be a video or item of clothing, his company gives him a bonus.
When you decide it's time for a clear out, you unknowingly kill your personal spy. He does not return to bother you and everything he has ever taken note of is gone forever.

Within a few minutes of doing this, a new inexperienced personal spy comes along and learns all about you from that moment.
This spy is known as a tracking cookie. He works for various companies like Google, Facebook, Yahoo and his goal is to learn as much as he can about you for the purpose of analysis and mapping you to advertisers. Looking for love? Well, he is cupid – only instead of mapping you to potential love interests, he maps your personality with those who pay to promote their products to you.

When you are tracked online, it is for targeted advertising and improvement of company services with many major online businesses profiting from the sale of your personal or anonymised information.

When you are tracked as part of a global surveillance system, proven time and time again by whistleblowers and top-secret documents, it is justified as for your safety and security. There's no doubting that your rights to a private life are slowly dissipating.

When you are tracked by a major manufacturer, you are given two simple options: disable the features or surrender to the restrictions and surveillance we have set.

For businesses – especially those offering 'free' services – your data is their biggest asset which will be a focus in the book alongside the mass surveillance that has grown by industry. At the end of it all, it's up to you to decide if such surveillance is protecting our society or if it's unnecessary snooping and whether or not personalised advertising and the sale of your information – no matter how little it provides about you – is a small trade-off for a decent product.

TOP SECRET//UNDER//CONSTANT//SUPERVISION//REL TO READER

There will come a time when it isn't *'They're spying on me through my phone'* anymore. Eventually, it will be *'My phone is spying on me'*

- Philip K. Dick
  Author

PART ONE: GAINING SERVICES, LOSING CONTROL

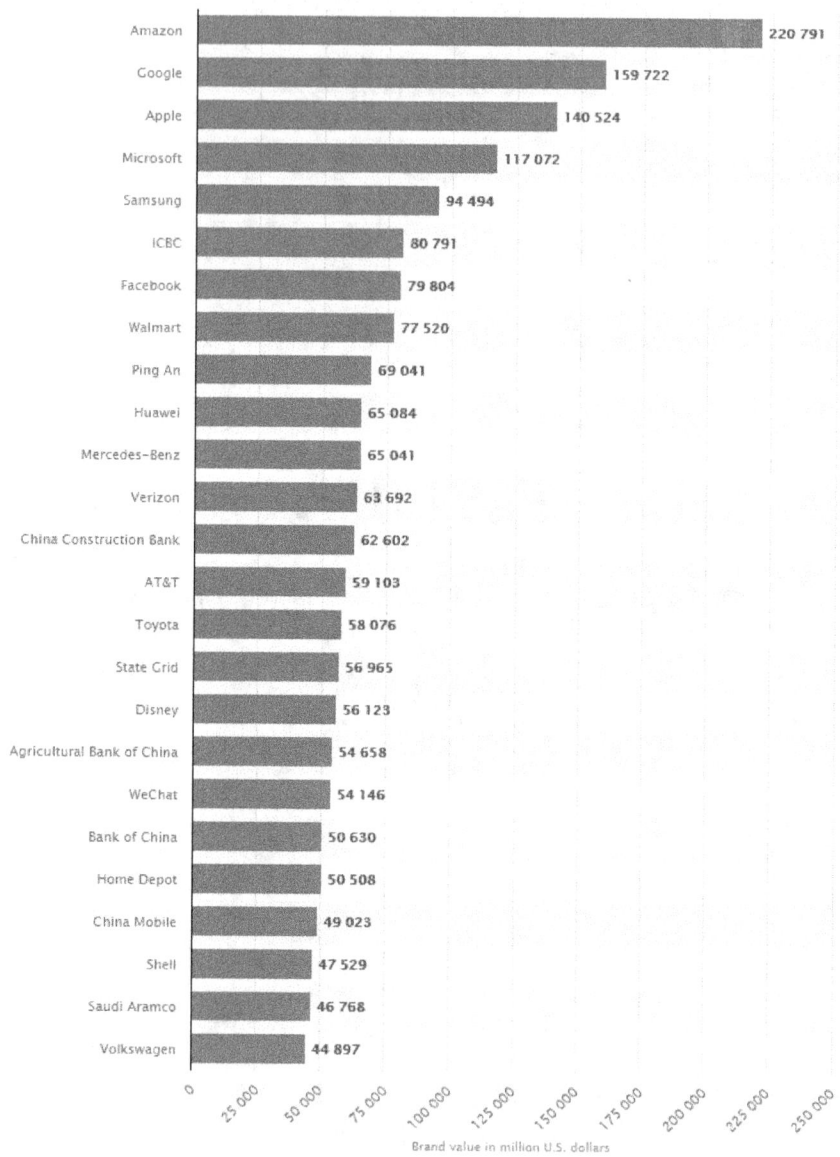

Source: Brand value of the 25 most valuable brands in 2020, Statista © Statista.com

Look at the chart on the previous page and you'll notice many of them all have one thing in common: Internet services. We're not talking about online banking, selling physical goods through an online shop or subscription video-on-demand streaming services such as the ones operated by Amazon, Apple and Disney. We are talking about online advertising networks, digital "cloud" storage solutions, Software-as-a-Service (SAAS) and, to some extent, the sale of personal information to analytics companies.

Whilst Amazon may initially be known for their e-commerce website around the world, the majority of their $280 billion US dollar profits in 2019 came from the sale of digital services including one of their biggest products: Amazon Web Services or AWS, which is one of the largest providers of storage for website and application owners in the world. Major companies publicly recorded as using AWS include the likes of giants AOL, Adobe, Disney, European Space Agency, ESPN, Johnson & Johnson, Netflix, Reddit, Spotify, The Weather Company, Ticketek, Yelp and even governmental agencies such as the United Kingdom Ministry of Justice and US Department of State.

The data storage and bandwidth are handled by millions of data servers with AWS Vice President James Hamilton even stating in a 2016 presentation that at least three of Amazon's many global data centres contain over 300,000 servers within the building.[1]

Cloud computing is a growing necessity with AWS, Microsoft Azure, Google Cloud and IBM Cloud being the most profitable and expansive divisions of the technology giants in recent years.

---

[1] https://www.youtube.com/watch?v=AyOAjFNPAbA

Another thing you may notice on the graph is the major technology providers are predominantly American. Amazon, Apple, Google, Facebook and Microsoft are considered "the big five" tech companies with users all around the world consuming computer hardware, mobile technology, operating systems (for both computer and mobile devices), online search, digital downloads and streaming and personal cloud storage. It should be very little surprise then that these companies are also featured on the list of worst abusers of digital privacy.

Often, these companies are pressured into handing over data and conforming to legal demands served by government agencies.
 This creates a problematic matter of blame for surveillance and censorship: Are the company, who willingly allows it for fear of ostracization, to blame? Or is it the governments and lawmakers who remove the liberty of consumers and Internet users?

Market capitalisation statistics from 2019 show 37 of the 50 largest Internet companies are headquartered in the United States. These companies are subject to surveillance and compliance with the intelligence companies and media monopolies that have been exposed to large-scale surveillance across the globe. Whilst often touted as necessary for the security of our nations', this is not always the case with millions of unnecessarily collected phone and Internet records captured and stored with numbers that can often seem unimaginable.

The best way to maintain privacy in our digital era is to destroy all of your devices, never go outside and try to seek comfort in a safe cave where you can rebuild your life and live as our ancestors did millions of years ago, but it doesn't have to be that way. Many steps can be taken to ensure your privacy without having to abandon each one of your favourite services or without having any alternatives.

The atomic bomb, satellite technology, aerospace and more: all the result of collaboration by intelligence communities and scientists.

In 1958, President Dwight Eisenhower established a subdivision of the Department of Defense, the Advanced Research Projects Agency (ARPA) in retaliation to the Soviet Union's launching of Sputnik 1 the year before.
The interconnected network – Internet – was developed by connecting four supercomputers that could handle massive transfers of data.

The Advanced Research Projects Agency Network (ARPANET) was handed down to the National Science Foundation (NSF) which propagated the new network across thousands of universities to share knowledge and communications. Eventually, the network was shared with the public. This seeded the Internet we know and depend on today. When these basic principles were commercialised, the 'Modern Internet' was born.

Sergey Brin and Larry Page, two young PhD students at Stanford University, made their breakthrough on the first automated web crawling and page ranking application. The project was funded from the Digital Library Initiative – an organisation program of the NSF and DARPA.[2]
This innovation led to Google Search, which launched in 1997.

---

[2] https://www.nsf.gov/discoveries/disc_summ.jsp?cntn_id=100660 **OR** https://archive.vn/HapEA

LifeLog was a DARPA project that would be used to gather the information that a user shared with friends, family and even strangers. From phone calls to television shows and movies to relationships and personal experiences, LifeLog would be a research project that would give computer scientists and researchers the ability to see into the lives of Internet users. Submissions to DARPA were opened in 2003[3].

A 2003 article from in the New York Times[4] reads:

> The Pentagon is shopping for ways to capture everything a person sees, says and hears, as part of a project it says is meant to help create smarter robots. The Defense Advanced Research Projects Agency, or DARPA, the Pentagon's cradle for new technologies, is sponsoring a competition for proposals to set up such a system.
>
> The project could result in more effective computers capable of building on a user's past and interpreting his or her commands, said Jan Walker, a DARPA spokeswoman.
>
> The goal of LifeLog is to create a searchable database of human lives, initially those of the developers, to promote artificial intelligence, the agency said. The technology would advance a new class of systems able to reason in a number of ways, learn from experience and "respond in a robust manner to surprises," the agency's Information Processing Technology Office said.
>
> To do so, the office said, the system must index the details of daily life and make it possible "to infer the user's routines, habits and relationships with other people, organizations, places and objects, and to exploit these patterns to ease its task."

On the 4th of February 2004, the Pentagon cancelled their project over privacy concerns.[5]
On the 4th of February 2004, Mark Zuckerberg launched Facebook[6]
I'll leave you to decide if that's just coincidence.

---

[3] https://web.archive.org/web/20030603173339/http://www.darpa.mil/ipto/Solicitations/PIP_03-30.html
[4] https://www.nytimes.com/2003/05/30/us/pentagon-explores-a-new-frontier-in-the-world-of-virtual-intelligence.html **OR** https://archive.vn/A0m92
[5] https://archive.vn/wJ26p
[6] http://time.com/3686124/happy-birthday-facebook/ **OR** https://archive.vn/CnvwR

UNDER CONSTANT SUPERVISION

The Information Awareness Office (IAO) – of which was created by DARPA –was born in 2002 to apply surveillance and technology to terrorists and threats to national security. Under new plans, computer databases would gather and store personal information of everyone in the United States without the requirement of surveillance.

One project, Genisys, was aimed at developing software which would provide intelligence agencies with *"Ultra-large, all-source information repositories"* TIA was meant to compare detailed information about people to prevent terrorism. Predictions would lead to prevention – or, at least, that's how the government saw it. The program launched less than six months after the September 11 attacks.

An All-seeing eye and the latin words for "Knowledge is Power" - - not exactly subtle

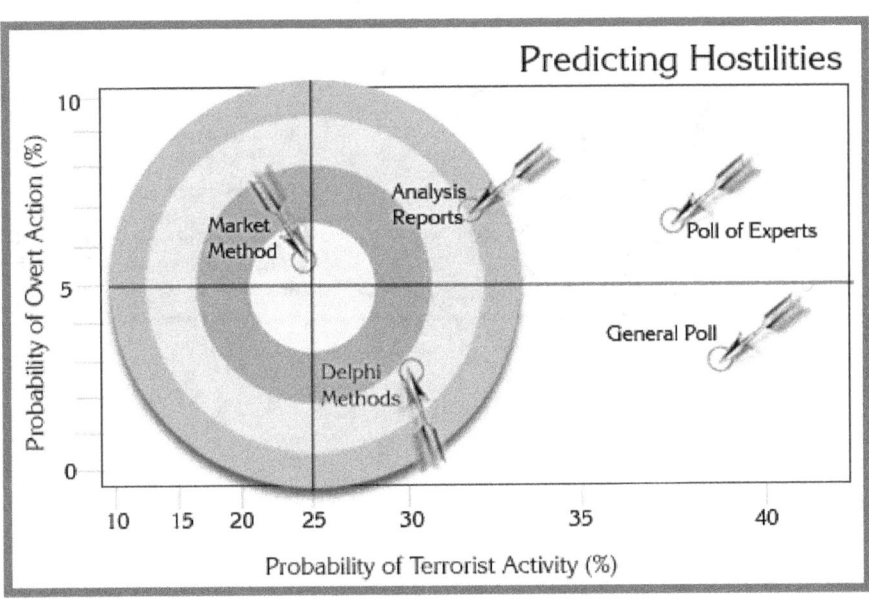

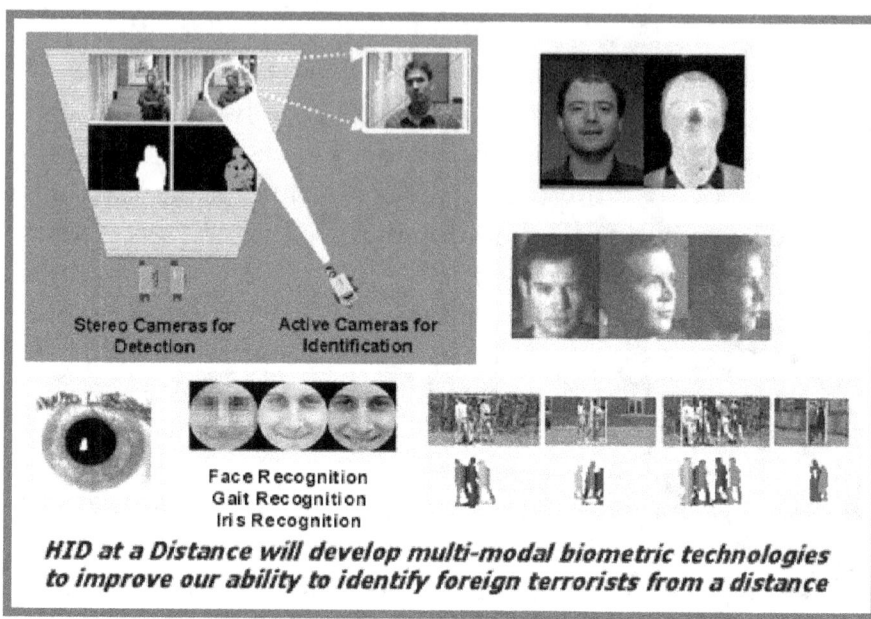

HID at a Distance will develop multi-modal biometric technologies to improve our ability to identify foreign terrorists from a distance

Communicator creates dialog-based user interfaces for Warfighters to obtain information in the battle space

The IAO was abandoned in 2003 over privacy concerns, but as will be made clear in this book, it would continue to be funded and operated under different names over the decade that followed.

DARPA claimed LifeLog was entirely unrelated to the *Total Information Awareness* (TIA) program, later named Terrorism Information Awareness.

TIA was endorsed by Information Awareness Office director and former national security adviser to President Ronald Reagan, John M. Poindexter.

Poindexter was previously convicted in April 1990 of numerous misdemeanours relating to the *Iran–Contra affair* that occurred during Reagan's second term. His convictions were reversed on appeal in 1991. He was recalled to service to work under Secretary of State Donald Rumsfeld after 9/11.

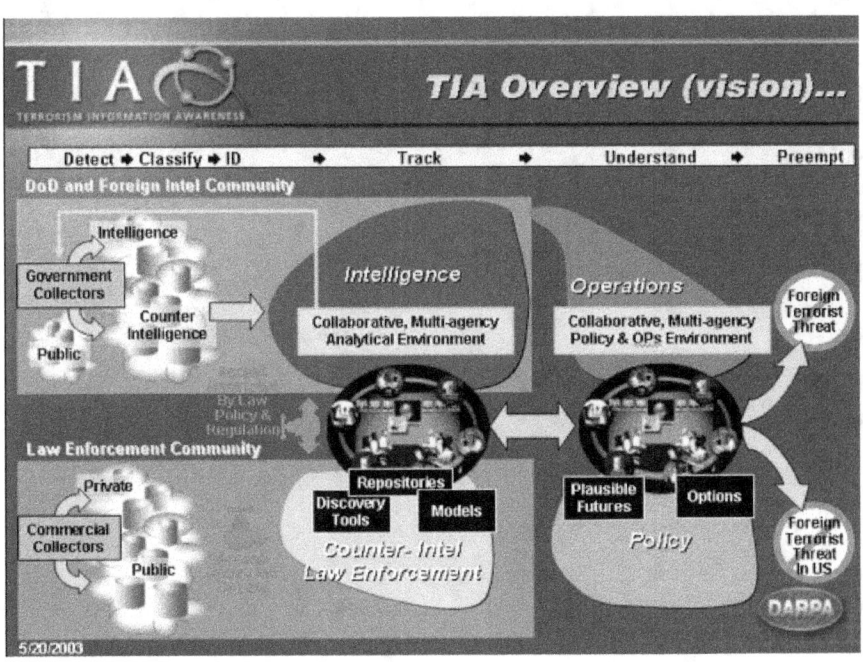

Various slides from the now-defunct website showed the development of biometric identification technologies, one of which even led to the development of *MALINTENT*.

MALINTENT was a system created by the U.S. Department of Homeland Security that would detect potential terrorist suspects using test scans for blood pressure, increased heart rates and sensors that would detect and evaluate a person's facial expressions to gauge whether or not they were planning on committing a crime.[7]

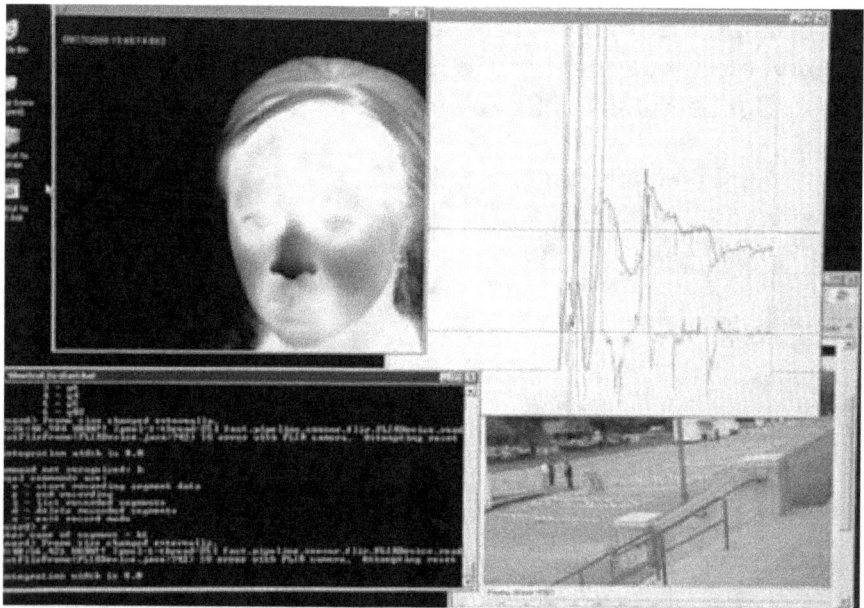

Promotional Material for MALINTENT released by Department of Homeland Security in 2008.

---

[7] https://archive.vn/F1Rv

UNDER CONSTANT SUPERVISION

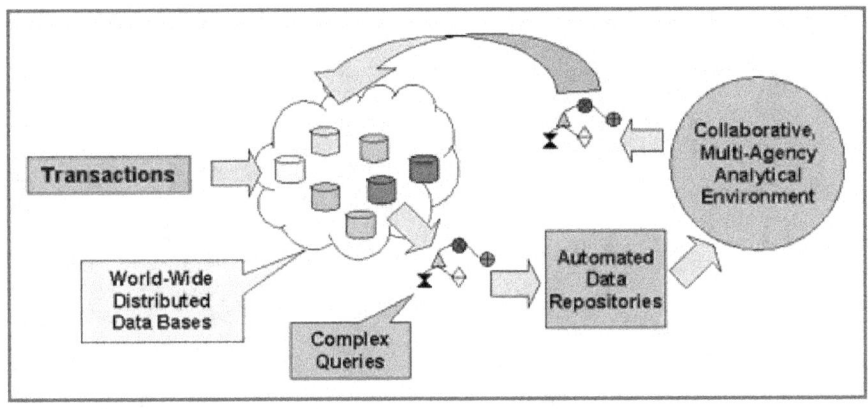

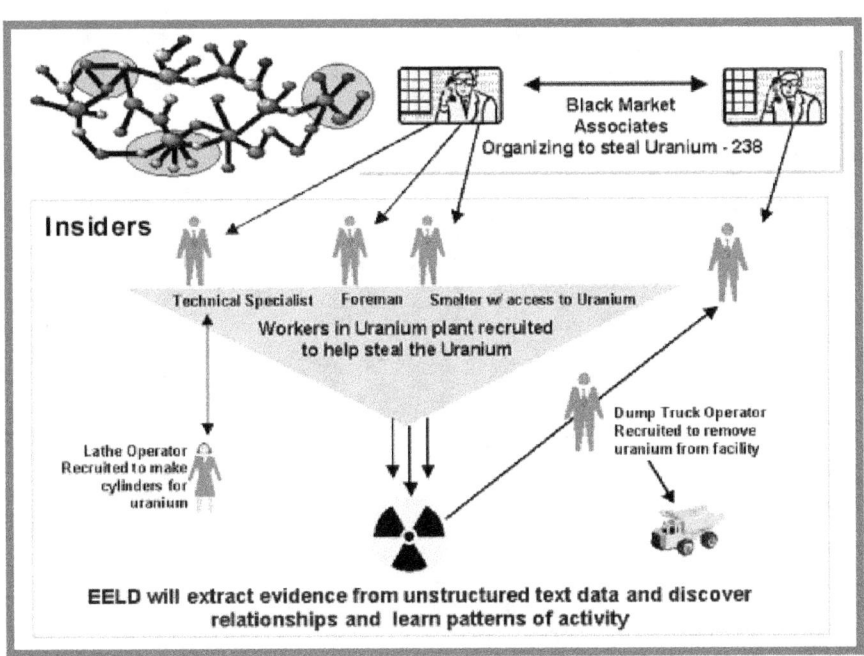

TOP SECRET//UNDER//CONSTANT//SUPERVISION//REL TO READER

Arguing that you don't care about the right to privacy because you have nothing to hide is no different than saying you don't care about free speech because you have nothing to say.

- Edward Snowden
  Ex-NSA whistleblower

THE RISE OF GOOGLE THANKS TO EMAIL

With Yahoo And MSN Hotmail leading the webmail revolution, to see a company that essentially only provided a search engine give you an email account, free from smileys and terrible advertisements crammed into the signature field, was exciting – especially given that Google would offer what Hotmail would sell for $29.95USD annually (known as Hotmail Plus – this was, however, ad-free). There was a concern, however, that this was all a joke. After all, it was announced on April 1st, 2004. Google had already garnered a reputation for April Fool's pranks.

Based on the belief that founders Sergey Brin and Larry Page had that searching the Internet was the second step to online activity, with checking emails being the first, the goal was to provide a free service which would allow users to worry less about having to empty their inbox of various chain mail and irrelevant Nigerian scams simply to receive communications from work, friends and family. The promises of "no pop-up ads. No banners" were enough to convert many to the new service.

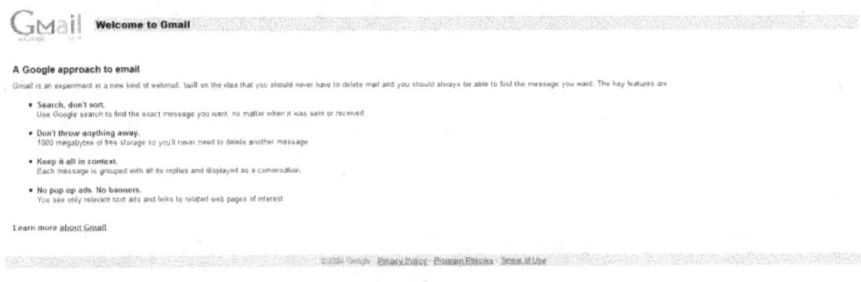

Gmail as it appeared on April 1st, 2004

Larry Page (centre) and other Google executives, (from left) CFO George Reyes, CEO Eric Schmidt, Omid Kordestani, and David Drummond (far right), join NASDAQ president Robert Greifeld (second from right) (PHOTO: NASDAQ)

Google's "experiment" would turn out to be invite-only, with each user receiving a small number of invites to share.

It came of no surprise that invites would soon appear for sale on auction sites like eBay, fetching generous amounts exceeding $100.
Google would become a listed company, with an Initial Public Offering of $85US per share leading Google to have a compatible market of over $23 billion.

Supposedly Gmail users weren't to replace their main accounts with the service as it was still strictly a beta offering. As the market for invites increased, Google would give out more invites per account. This didn't stop people from selling the invites on eBay.

Eventually, Google brought out rules prohibiting the sale of invites and accounts. Websites such as *Gmail Swap* would give Gmail account holders the ability to be charitable with their invites.

One service, *Gmail Invite Spooler,* was taken down in 2005 with the developer told that his website was "threatening the quality of Gmail" and that by the service being more and more available, Google was susceptible to higher amounts of spam and abuse. In 2006, the developer revealed on his personal blog that "Google felt as it too many spammers were gaining access to invites" and that it was due to applications like his.[8]

The frustrated developer concluded with:

> "In the end, insistence on keeping the spooler open would have certainly summoned the massive lawyering machine deep within the "don't be evil" company and I don't think reasonable person wants that fight."

As the service grew, so did the questions regarding its privacy. The very thought of a company using the analysis to read emails and match them with relevant advertisements was new and frightening to advocates of online privacy around the world. Several civil rights and privacy groups attacked Google's service, calling it a threat to the freedom of the individuals using the service. Larry and Sergey compiled a group of influential professionals to calm the outrage – even enlisting the help of former US Vice president Al Gore. Google introduced a highly visible delete button to assure users that Google wouldn't keep and retain emails forever. The company also agreed to delete all unwanted accounts and to permanently destroy any deleted emails, though an exact timeframe of erasure wasn't provided.

---

[8] https://isnoop.wordpress.com/2006/03/23/gmail-invite-spooler-post-mortem/ **OR** https://archive.vn/RSoYF **OR** https://git.io/Jv5d0

As the roll-out continued, Gmail became a common address and the hype died down. In the months that would follow, Google would practically provide unlimited invitations to users and by 2005 upgraded accounts to a total of 2GB storage – which was referred to as "2GB Plus"

It wasn't until September 2009, five years after launching, that Gmail would officially exit beta. By this time, Google had become so much more than a search engine website. They had acquired video-sharing site YouTube, Internet advertising provider DoubleClick and built an empire upon the rise of online marketing.

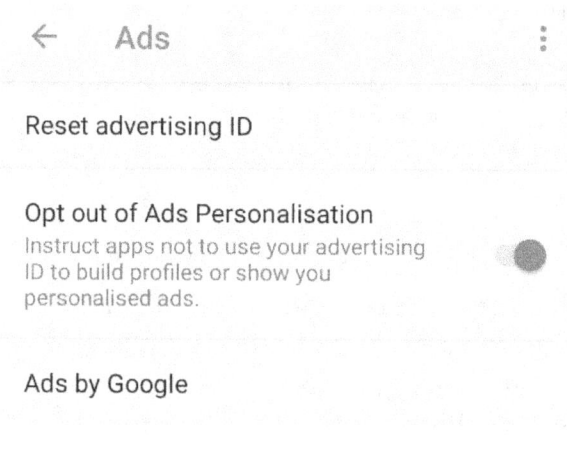

The collection of data from user email continued until 2017 when the European Union announced proposals that would restrict emails being scanned without the users' permission. Google would conveniently release an announcement that it would not cease the scanning of emails for targeted advertisements. This simply meant that the advertisements would be based on account-wide settings that could be toggled in account settings. Today, users are allocated an "Advertising ID" and are given the ability across Google products such as the Android operating system to deselect the feature "Ads Personalisation"

UNDER CONSTANT SUPERVISION

In March 2020, Florida man Zachary McCoy was listed as a suspected in a home robbery. Google's legal investigation team contacted him to make him aware that local police had requested information relating to his Google accounts. He was informed that they would hand over the data unless he had the request blocked by the local court within 7 days of receiving the letter. McCoy went to see his parents who agreed to use their savings to hire a lawyer.

Lawyer Caleb Kenyon discovered that a police surveillance tool had been used and that all GPS, Bluetooth, Wi-Fi and cellular data had linked him to the scene of the crime as he had been riding his bicycle past the house in question on the day of the burglary. Fortunately for Zachary, the very same data confirmed he could not have committed the crime. A simple mistake or a sign of things to come?

An equally strange use of Google's information was the release of the "COVID-19 Community Mobility Report" during the stages of the global pandemic. The reports, released on the Google website, used information from location history collected and sorted by country showing the use of transit stations, grocery stores and parks – all detailed for each state and territory of the country.[9] Whilst the data collection can easily be stopped, many comments on various websites reporting the statistics show how unaware users are to the tracking that takes place on applications hiding away in their pockets

---

[9] https://www.google.com/covid19/mobility/

TOP SECRET//UNDER//CONSTANT//SUPERVISION//REL TO READER

And thus, the pendulum must swing right to correct what is wrong so that it can in turn swing back when all that is wrong will be blamed on those who are right.

   - Volker G Fremuth
      Author

AND WHAT ABOUT THE CHILDREN?

Classrooms all around America are no-doubt benefiting from the multitude of services Google has provided, however at what cost to the children themselves? A lawsuit filed by New Mexico's Attorney General Hector Balderas in February 2020 claims that Google uses its supremacy to "spy" on masses of their future potential customers by tracking the lives of children using Google's services for learning. Often, it's a concern that children, parents and education staff especially haven't considered the risks of.

The suit claims *"The consequences of Google's tracking cannot be overstated: Children are being monitored by one of the largest data-mining companies in the world, at school, at home, on mobile devices, without their knowledge and without the permission of their parents"* and that within the past several years' Google has *"infiltrated more than half the nation's primary and secondary schools by offering a 'free' web-based service"*

Google's Education tool (Google Education) is used by nearly 100 million educators and students, giving the company access to their digital lives and personal data.
As many of the students are under the age of 13, Google's tracking allegedly breaches the Children's Online Privacy Protection Act (COPPA) in America.

The Federal Trade Commission and New York Attorney General required Google and YouTube to develop and implement a system that would permit any YouTube channel owners to identify child-targeted content so that moderators could ensure the content met the COPPA standards. The fine was one of the highest in FTC history.

In 2014, Google was demanded by the FTC to refund unauthorised in-app charges. The complaint which can be read on the FTC website[10] reads:

> Google offers thousands of apps for free or a specific dollar amount, including games that children are likely to play. In many instances, after installation, children can obtain virtual items within a game, many of which cost money. Google bills charges for items that cost money within an app—"in-app charges"—to the parent. Although the issue of unauthorized charges in kids' apps had received media scrutiny before Google introduced in-app charges to its app store in March 2011, Google began billing for such charges without any password requirement or other method to ensure account holder authorization. In fact, just weeks after it began billing for in-app charges, Google began receiving complaints from parents and other consumers about being billed for unauthorized charges by children. Yet Google took no steps to require account holder involvement within an app prior to in-app charges being incurred by children until mid- to late 2012.

---

[10] https://www.ftc.gov/enforcement/cases-proceedings/122-3237/google-inc

In September 2019, Google was fined $170 million for breaching COPPA as it was deemed Google's service YouTube was collecting children's personal information without parental or guardian consent. [11]

It's certainly unlikely that companies such as Google can be tamed by fines and demands that barely dent their total revenue. According to market analysers Statista, Google's total income in 2019 was $160.74 billion.[12]
Nearly 71% of this revenue came from Google's various advertising platforms. That's almost $114 billion. Overall, the FTC fines make up roughly 0.125% of Google's total income.

Google's 2019 figures don't end there. Still topping the list as the worlds' biggest online search provider, Google was responsible for nearly 90% of desktop search traffic and held a 90% market share in digital service offerings.

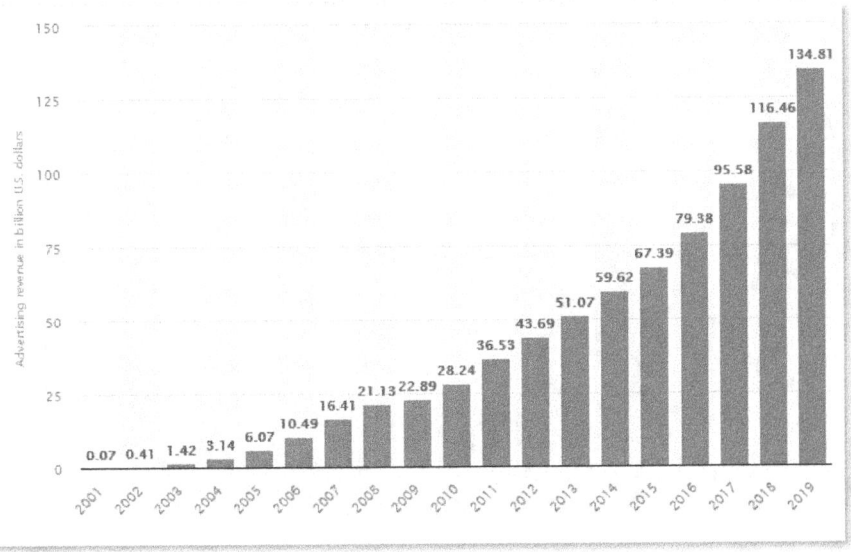

Source: Statista

---

[11] https://www.ftc.gov/enforcement/cases-proceedings/172-3083/google-llc-youtube-llc **OR** https://git.io/Jv5do

[12] https://www.statista.com/statistics/266249/advertising-revenue-of-google/

TOP SECRET//UNDER//CONSTANT//SUPERVISION//REL TO READER

I Disapprove of What You Say, But I Will
Defend to the Death Your Right to Say It

  - Voltaire (François-Marie Arouet) /
    Evelyn Beatrice Hall [disputed]

UNDER CONSTANT SUPERVISION

PART TWO:
EVER FEEL LIKE <u>YOU'RE</u> THE PRODUCT?

Google Data Center in St. Ghislain, Belgium (source: Google)

UNDER CONSTANT SUPERVISION

Since the very beginning of connectivity, the right to privacy has been fought, debated, revoked and renewed throughout every nation with government entities, businesses and users having their say for or against.

> **Cookie / web cookie / Internet cookie / browser cookie/ HTTP cookie etc.**
>
> The Founding engineer of Netscape Communications, Lou Montulli, coined the term 'cookie' deriving it from the term *"magic cookie"* which is a packet of data a program receives and sends back. It is based on the analogy of a token being provided when a coat is cloaked in a cloakroom. The token has no real value or meaning, and yet its uniqueness ensures the correct coat is returned.
>
> Montulli is one of the few people in the world to be inducted into the World Wide Web Hall of Fame.

During the 1980s most countries began to include personally identifiable information – or PII, as it is known in nations such as the United States – to their Privacy Acts or general regulations. With targeted advertising on the rise throughout the early 2000s, it was becoming normal to collect, utilise and sometimes sell data that had been captured from consumers. This information includes the likes of your race, class, gender, age, education, income and online interests.

Have you ever searched for some lovely furniture online, only to find that you'd see an advertisement on a completely different website potentially showing you something that may be the perfect solution? It's not mind-reading and it's not a coincidence. This is the result of tracking cookies and behavioural targeting.

Cookies are sort-of like small text files that note down various options, much like the presets you have set on your washing machine or microwave oven. "Regular cookies" simply remember your preferences.

When you tell a search engine that you want it to show you results from your country, this is stored in a cookie on your computer. You won't have to worry about having to tick that "show results from" checkbox again until you clear your cookies or access the site from a different device. You may have noticed that "clearing" your cookies has led to you having to log in to your accounts again and update websites with your preferences. With this, you know that not all cookies are bad.

A tracking cookie, on the other hand, is a different type of fish altogether. Tracking cookies not only add your preferences, but they add things like your IP address, rough location, computer Operating System and the web browser your using – and that's just to name a few. Instead of storing this information on your computer like a normal cookie, this data – usually free from personally-identifiable information – is sent off to a database and used for marketing assessment. Your device is one of many millions connecting to this network. You may be visiting a local website that only exists to serve a few hundred people in your community, but your collected information is one tiny star in a vast ever-expanding universe. If a website successfully recognises you from your cookie data, it will link you to a set of advertisements that represent what the networks think you'd like to see – whether that be slightly relevant or uncannily relevant depends on how much tracking has been done.

Most popular browsers have a feature called "Do Not Track" which one can select. Whilst it sounds as though it does exactly what the name implies, not all websites honour the request and therefore tighter measures are required to maintain that tiny bit of privacy that is deserved.

Cookies are a treasure trove to all advertising networks.

A single visit and/or search on a website can create a paper trail that will be shared with multiple companies such as Facebook, Google, Yahoo, Microsoft and Amazon just to name a few. With each of these companies having ties to a product, advertiser or solution to your query, this information can be shared with hundreds upon hundreds of other websites, all linking back to advertising networks both large and small to target you with something you may be interested in. Like a dragnet cast along the ocean floor, the more that is collected, the better the understanding. One methodology applied is psychographic profiling. As your interests are swiftly spread from site to site, your psychographic profile paints a much more accurate picture of who you are and what you are interested in. The more accurate the profile, the more relevant the advertisements become. And that's where relevant advertising comes into play.

The general business consensus is that if you are going to see advertisements on their free service, you may as well see ones that relate to you. If you are a butch male who loves fast cars; why would you want to be on websites with side banners covered in bridal gowns and top fashion tips from young celebrities aimed at improving the skincare of pre-pubescent girls? Whilst most of us would simply think that it's extraneous as we won't be clicking on said advertisements anyway, companies feel that your experience would be better if they show what they prove to matter to you.

Operating System Windows 10, for example, will install tracking cookies within certain applications to "personalise your experience". When it was made clear that Windows 10 would do this by default, Microsoft received a great backlash and spent years attempting to make things a little more transparent to their users. Many – including myself – felt as though this was a gross disrespect to the customer who had already purchased a license and entered their personal information into a computer that would potentially be left connected to the Internet for several hours at a time.

Nowadays, it's not only your connected computer and web browser that can track you for analysis or "improving their service" with Smart TV's, home automation devices and even appliances like fridges and toasters collecting information to upload to their servers. Whilst it is predominantly expected that you as a user have the right to opt-out of such services, many major corporations have been ousted for collecting data unbeknownst to the user.
Let's save that for later.

UNDER CONSTANT SUPERVISION

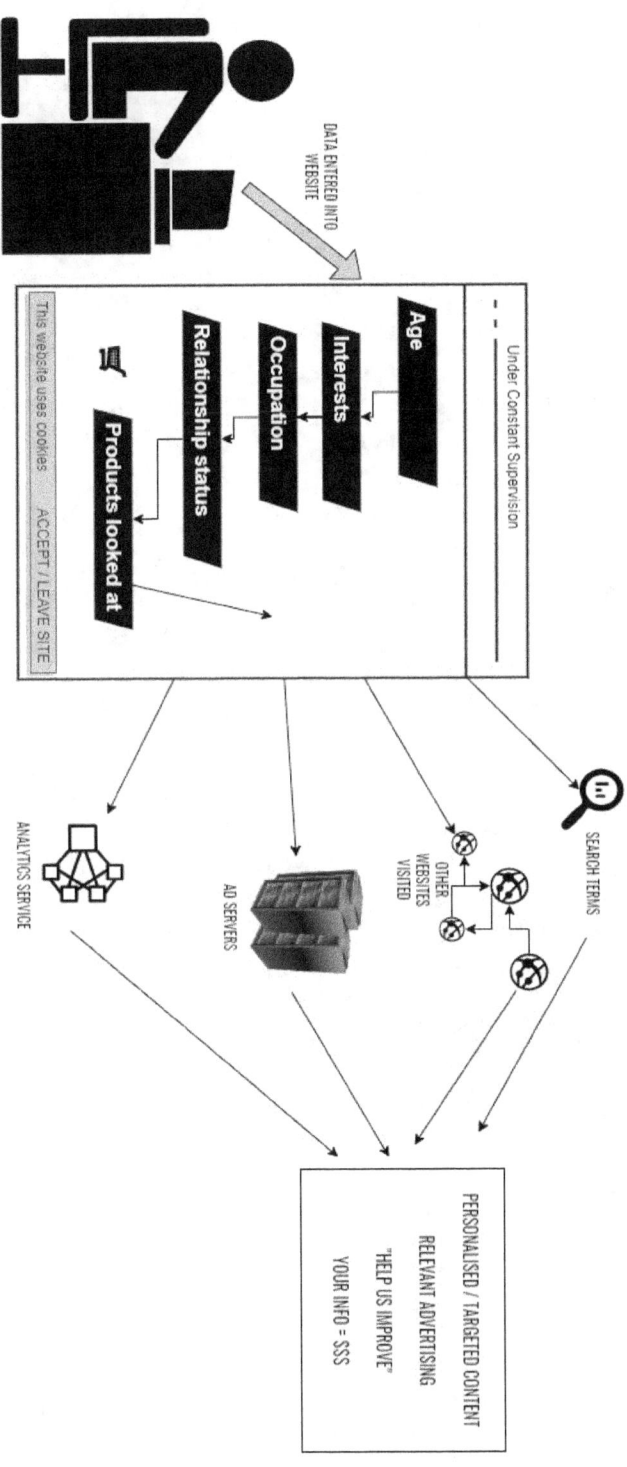

TOP SECRET//UNDER//CONSTANT//SUPERVISION//REL TO READER

If you have something that you don't want
anyone to know, maybe you shouldn't be
doing it in the first place.

   - Eric Schmidt
      Google CEO 2001-2011 / Defense Chair

The many pro-surveillance advocates I have
debated since Snowden blew the whistle have
been quick to echo Eric Schmidt's view that
privacy is for people who have something to
hide. But none of them would willingly give
me the passwords to their email accounts or
allow video cameras in their homes.

   - Glenn Greenwald

DATA PROTECTION LAWS

On May 25, 2018, the European Union implemented the General Data Protection Regulation – or GDPR – which was introduced to bring control to individuals over their personal data. Whilst not exclusive to users within the European Union (EU), it would set a standard for many national laws that would follow. Argentina, Brazil, Chile, South Korea, Kenya and Japan would all adopt similar approaches to the laws. The California Consumer Privacy Act – or CCPA – would almost mirror the terms within the GDPR. The proposal for the GDPR was first released in 2012 and would take several years before being adopted by the European Parliament.

Any company offering "goods or services" would be required to oblige to the terms and obey the data protection policies that were put in place, regardless of the business' main location of business.

The GDPR brought about debate and concern, with just over 3000 amendments to the act suggested. Several websites found it easier to shut down than to fulfil the new requirements – especially small websites unable to afford legal advice should ever an issue over data collection arise.

Many leaders voted against the privacy regulations with Spain, Sweden, Finland, Poland, Romania, Italy and the United Kingdom among those in opposition.

Just after the GDPR was implemented at midnight, None of Your Business (NOYB), a non-profit organisation based in Austria, filed complaints against Google as well as Facebook and subsidiaries WhatsApp and Instagram. The focus was placed especially on Google's Android operating system for violation of Article 7(4) which states:

> When assessing whether consent is freely given, utmost account shall be taken of whether, inter alia, the performance of a contract, including the provision of a service, is conditional on consent to the processing of personal data that is not necessary for the performance of that contract.

Put in plain English; this act prevents a company from attempting to block use of services if a user refuses to accept all data processing. Privacy campaigner Max Schrems, who filed the complaints, accused Google of "coercing" its users into agreeing to company policies that were not necessary to make the service usable. With major companies offering free services in exchange for user profiling and data collection to transmit to advertisers, the landmark complaints saw potential fines of up to 4 billion euros for both major technology companies.

Schrems claimed that Facebook was blackmailing their users into accepting their rules or deactivating their account. He claimed that Facebook would require more data than was necessary to continue serving users with the new GDPR laws in place.

Within a year of the GDPR being enacted, Google was fined half a billion Euros for failing to comply. France's data protection office CNIL found Google guilty of breaking the rules by failing to obtain enough consent from consumers regarding Google's targeted advertising.

Operating in the EU would essentially become impossible for any company failing to conform. One thing that certainly did make a difference for consumers overseas was the ability to download their data. Companies like Google, Twitter, Facebook and Apple all implemented or improved systems for users worldwide to download everything a company had stored. For those not interested in such things, the irritating consent windows that would pop up on pages all over the Internet were there to remind them of what they were agreeing to.

> This website uses cookies to improve our website, provide more personalised services to you and analyse our traffic
>
> To find out more information about our use of cookies please read our Cookies Policy
>
> ☐ I consent to the use of cookies

Ironically, websites who did not use cookies of any kind would be expected to implement a cookie that would remember the checked consent form.

TOP SECRET//UNDER//CONSTANT//SUPERVISION//REL TO READER

It is no longer the Seventies! We live in another age. The world has become a more dangerous place, and there is a need to name things. During the intermission in the show, I display the words "Resist Mark Zuckerberg!" on the LED screen, because I believe the collaboration of Facebook and Google with the US government is dangerous. They control, censor, and manipulate. We are surrounded by propaganda, and that is why I take the opportunity to spread messages like, "Do not allow the bastards to silence Julian Assange."

— Roger Waters
    Musician (best known for Pink Floyd)

CAMBRIDGE ANALYTICA

One of the major turning-points in online privacy was the scandal involving Facebook and UK political consulting firm Cambridge Analytica.

This is how the scandal played out:

- Moldavian-born American Data scientist Aleksandr Kogan developed an application titled "This is Your Digital Life"
- Cambridge Analytica arranged an informed consent process for research in which several hundred thousand Facebook users would agree to complete a survey for academic use only.
- Facebook's design allowed this app not only to collect personal information of the users who agreed to take the survey but of all the people (friends) connected to the user, despite those social networking connections being unaware their data was collected.

The result? A dataset that included the information of over 85 million users.

The claims were initially published in 2015, 2016 and 2017 respectively. Facebook refused to comment and stated they were investigating. The illegitimate collecting of user data was not fully ousted until March 2018 when ex-Cambridge Analytica employee Christopher Wylie blew the whistle.

On March 22nd, Facebook CEO Mark Zuckerberg released a statement on his personal Facebook page:

> *I want to share an update on the Cambridge Analytica situation -- including the steps we've already taken and our next steps to address this important issue.*

We have a responsibility to protect your data, and if we can't then we don't deserve to serve you. I've been working to understand exactly what happened and how to make sure this doesn't happen again. The good news is that the most important actions to prevent this from happening again today we have already taken years ago. But we also made mistakes, there's more to do, and we need to step up and do it.

Here's a timeline of the events:

In 2007, we launched the Facebook Platform with the vision that more apps should be social. Your calendar should be able to show your friends' birthdays, your maps should show where your friends live, and your address book should show their pictures. To do this, we enabled people to log into apps and share who their friends were and some information about them.

In 2013, a Cambridge University researcher named Aleksandr Kogan created a personality quiz app. It was installed by around 300,000 people who shared their data as well as some of their friends' data. Given the way our platform worked at the time this meant Kogan was able to access tens of millions of their friends' data.

In 2014, to prevent abusive apps, we announced that we were changing the entire platform to dramatically limit the data apps could access. Most importantly, apps like Kogan's could no longer ask for data about a person's friends unless their friends had also authorized the app. We also required developers to get approval from us before they could request any sensitive data from people. These actions would prevent any app like Kogan's from being able to access so much data today.

In 2015, we learned from journalists at The Guardian that Kogan had shared data from his app with Cambridge Analytica. It is against our policies for developers to share data without people's consent, so we immediately banned Kogan's app from our platform, and demanded that Kogan and Cambridge Analytica formally certify that they had deleted all improperly acquired data. They provided these certifications.

Last week, we learned from The Guardian, The New York Times and Channel 4 that Cambridge Analytica may not have deleted the data as they had certified. We immediately banned them from using any of our services. Cambridge Analytica claims they have already deleted the data and has agreed to a forensic audit by a firm we hired to confirm this. We're also working with regulators as they investigate what happened.

This was a breach of trust between Kogan, Cambridge Analytica and Facebook. But it was also a breach of trust between Facebook and the people who share their data with us and expect us to protect it. We need to fix that.

In this case, we already took the most important steps a few years ago in 2014 to prevent bad actors from accessing people's information in this way. But there's more we need to do and I'll outline those steps here:

First, we will investigate all apps that had access to large amounts of information before we changed our platform to dramatically reduce data access in 2014, and we will conduct a full audit of any app with suspicious activity. We will ban any developer from our platform that does not agree to a thorough audit. And if we find developers that misused personally identifiable information, we will ban them and tell everyone affected by those apps. That includes people whose data Kogan misused here as well.

Second, we will restrict developers' data access even further to prevent other kinds of abuse. For example, we will remove developers' access to your data if you haven't used their app in 3 months. We will reduce the data you give an app when you sign in -- to only your name, profile photo, and email address. We'll require developers to not only get approval but also sign a contract in order to ask anyone for access to their posts or other private data. And we'll have more changes to share in the next few days.

Third, we want to make sure you understand which apps you've allowed to access your data. In the next month, we will show everyone a tool at the top of your News Feed with the apps you've used and an easy way to revoke those apps' permissions to your data. We already have a tool to do this in your privacy settings, and now we will put this tool at the top of your News Feed to make sure everyone sees it.

Beyond the steps we had already taken in 2014, I believe these are the next steps we must take to continue to secure our platform.

I started Facebook, and at the end of the day I'm responsible for what happens on our platform. I'm serious about doing what it takes to protect our community. While this specific issue involving Cambridge Analytica should no longer happen with new apps today, that doesn't change what happened in the past. We will learn from this experience to secure our platform further and make our community safer for everyone going forward.

> *I want to thank all of you who continue to believe in our mission and work to build this community together. I know it takes longer to fix all these issues than we'd like, but I promise you we'll work through this and build a better service over the long term.*

The political and commercial domino effect caused severe unrest with Zuckerberg agreeing to testify in front of the United States Congress over the handling of the data. The United States Congress argued that the data had been used to intentionally sway the votes of the 2016 Presidential Campaign.

Candidate Ted Cruz, who partnered with Cambridge Analytica, was questioned by the media over allegations that CA had collected and analysed data on American voters. It was alleged that strategic communication was used to manage voter behaviour. Some critics saw this as a form of political warfare.

Further political fallout was raised over CA's data analysis services used by Donald Trump for his presidential campaigning and one of the organisations (Leave.EU) lobbying for voters in the United Kingdom to vote "leave" in the referendum on European Union membership – commonly referred to as Brexit. In April 2018 the Information Commissioner's Office (ICO) was revealed to have been investigating unrelated data sharing offences against the latter.

As Facebook and Cambridge Analytica's data protection violations occurred in 2015 – 3 years before the implementation of the GDPR – the maximum possible fine the ICO could impose was a mere 500,000 pounds (roughly $640,000 US) which is approximately a percentage of Facebook's revenue for that year. Had the violations been carried out whilst the GDPR was in-effect, Facebook could have been expected to pay roughly 4% of their annual revenue in fines. Cambridge Analytica and its parent company filed for insolvency and ceased operations following the scandal.

Mark Zuckerberg attempted to win back the love of millions of users with promises to launch a "clear history" feature during damage control over Facebook's handling of the situation. Multiple advertisements were televised throughout the world apologising for the mishap and pledging that the company would make amends for the mistrust.

On paper, the tool seemed useful to anyone hoping to 'disappear' from Facebook altogether. However, when the tool finally launched it simply anonymised the data Facebook had collected. Facebook claimed that the data of user actions would still be collected but would not match the interactions of users. According to Facebook, this data was crucial to advertisers and application developers. Facebook stated: "We can do this without storing the information in a way that's associated with your account" and "We don't tell advertisers who you are"

Instagram, which was acquired by Facebook in 2012, is also a harvester of data when it comes to the things you view, "like", comment on or upload photos of.

For example, my personal Instagram profile shows the following information under the "Ads Interests" section of their privacy & security dashboard. Most of these items, however, seem completely unrelated to the information I may have looked at or uploaded during my use of the service. As a musician, I predominantly upload promotional material relating to promoting my music, and so the targeting is certainly doing its job but there are multiple car manufacturers and subjects such as meditation, self-care and Christian music that seem entirely out of place to me. Unlike Facebook, it appears that Instagram does not give users the ability to clear this data without deactivating their account.

Tattoos	Pets	Tattoo ink
Physical fitness	Concerts	PRS Guitars
Physical exercise	Personal development	Instrumental
Yoga	Toyota	Bass guitar
Hip hop music	Arts and music	Indian rock
Pop music	Happiness	Kemper Amps
Rock music	CrossFit	Berklee College of Music
Health & wellness	Spotify	Mammal
Running	Nissan	Album
Dogs	Motorsport	Art rock
Electronic music	Psychology	Sound reinforcement system
TV reality shows	Singing	Digital art
Fitness and wellness	Guitar	Epiphone
Rhythm and blues music	Mindfulness	Shred guitar
Music	Popular music	Chicago blues
Motorcycles	Christian music	Spiritual (music)
Meditation	Drums	Guitar amplifier
Heavy metal music	Animal welfare	IK Multimedia
Blues music	Emotion	orange amplifiers
Cats	Self care	Audio Engineering Society
Jazz music	Empowerment	Musical instrument
Automotive industry	Motorcycle racing	Madchester
Theatre	Alternative rock	Acid rock
Music festivals	Animal	Extreme metal
Classical music	Tattoo artist	
	Fender Stratocaster	

SPOTIFY

In 2015 music streaming service Spotify was pulled into the privacy spotlight after their privacy terms were updated to introduce comprehensive new permissions for both free and paid users. On top of already collecting information on what its users were listening to, the service would collect authentication information from connected applications like Facebook:

> *If you connect to the Service using credentials from a Third Party Application (as defined in the Terms and Conditions of Use) (e.g., Facebook), you authorise us to collect your authentication information, such as your username and encrypted access credentials. We may also collect other information available on or through your Third Party Application account, including, for example, your name, profile picture, country, hometown, email address, date of birth, gender, friends' names and profile pictures, and networks.*
>
> *Depending on the type of device that you use to interact with the Service and your settings, we may also collect information about your location based on, for example, your phone's GPS location or other forms of locating mobile devices (e.g., Bluetooth). We may also collect sensor data (e.g., data about the speed of your movements, such as whether you are running, walking, or in transit).*

Free and premium users were given a period of thirty days to agree to the terms or have their service cancelled. Premium members who did not agree to the terms were unable to use Spotify but were still charged the subscription fee unless they had cancelled it on their own.

The Terms of Service states simply "if you don't agree with the terms of this privacy policy, then please don't use the service"

In response to the bad publicity, Spotify's founder and CEO *Daniel Ek* claimed in a blog post that the updates were simply misinterpreted and poorly written. Despite some clearing up over the years, the privacy policy still makes it very clear that Spotify is harvesting the data of their users for reasons unclear.

Many "free" services take a similar approach to Google, Yahoo, Microsoft, and Spotify by essentially trading information in exchange for providing a free service. In April 2020 Twitter slyly presented any user who accessed the website or application that they'd have less control over their data as of that moment[13]. Like Spotify, Twitter provides a nice way of suggesting you have no choice if you want to continue using the service:

An update to your data-sharing settings

The control you have over what information Twitter shares with its business partners has changed. Specifically, your ability to control mobile app advertising measurements has been removed, but you can control whether to share some non-public data to improve Twitter's marketing activities on other sites and apps. These changes, which help Twitter to continue operating as a free service, are reflected now in your settings. Learn more.

OK

---

[13] https://archive.vn/kdKDC **OR** https://help.twitter.com/en/safety-and-security/data-through-partnerships

KEEP DANCING

Video sharing application **TikTok** has grown to be one of the largest social networking platforms in recent years thanks to various short comedy, dance and talent videos being created and shared by celebrities around the world. Miniature clips have made many users viral with young adults, teenagers and even minors among the applications' one billion downloaders.

TikTok has come under fire for multiple issues since its inception in 2012. Leaked documents[14] reveal moderators are directed to suppress any video created by or featuring "poor" and "ugly" users, LGBTQ users and disabled users. This is supposedly to deter cyberbullying[15].

New rules	Reason
Abnormal body shape, chubby, have obvious beer belly, obese, or too thin (not limited to: dwarf, acromegaly)	Unlike diversified videos of which the content itself is the mainly focus, in the non-diversified content, the character himself/herself is basically the only focus of the video, therefore, if the character's appearance or the shooting environment is not good, the video will be much less attractive, not worthing to be recommended to new users.
Ugly facial looks (not limited to: disformatted face, fangs, lack of front teeth, senior people with too many wrinkles, obvious facial scars) or facial deformities (not limited to: eye disorders, crooked mouth disease and other disabilities)	
The shooting environment is shabby and dilapidated, such as, not limited to: slums, rural fields (rural beautiful natural scenery could be exempted), dilapidated housing, construction sites, etc. (For internal housing background which has no obvious slummy character, only those cases as specified should be labelled: crack on the wall, old and disreputable decorations, extremely dirty and messy)	This kind of environment is not that suitable for new users for being less fancy and appealing.

---

[14] https://git.io/JfaLl
[15] https://git.io/JfaLZ

TikTok's parent company *ByteDance* claims that the application and its content is is stored outside of China. The privacy policy reserves the right to share collected information with Chinese authorities. The company's founder CEO Zhang Yiming issued a letter in 2018 that states his business would "further deepen cooperation" with authorities from the Communist Party of China. TikTok's collects information on usage alongside personally identifiable data such as IP addresses, mobile network carriers, device identifiers, keystroke patterns, and location specifics.

Despite assurances that the data is not stored in China, a class action was filed in California claiming TikTok harvested and transferred personal information to servers in China owned by Chinese multinationals Alibaba and Tencent.[16]

The United States prohibits all federal employees from using or downloading TikTok. The Australian Defence Force prohibits use of the application. The Australian Strategic Policy Institute released an extensive report revealing that the Chinese Communist Party and TikTok were strategically linked[17]. The Institute's China Tech Map voices concern over ByteDance's cooperation with the Chinese government in Xinjiang[18]:

> *In April 2019, the Ministry of Public Security's Press and Publicity Bureau signed a strategic cooperation agreement with ByteDance to promote the "influence and credibility" of the police department nation-wide.*
> *Under the agreement, all levels and divisions of police units from the Ministry of Public Security to county-level traffic police would have their own Douyin account to disseminate propaganda.*
>
> *The agreement also reportedly says ByteDance would increase its offline cooperation with the police department, however it is unclear what this offline cooperation is.*

---

[16] https://archive.vn/lHk67 OR https://git.io/JfaLc

[17] https://www.aspi.org.au/report/mapping-chinas-tech-giants

[18] https://chinatechmap.aspi.org.au

GIVE US YOUR BLOOD, GIVE US YOUR IDENTITY

Sometimes we are handing over our data with the assumption that it won't be used for anything other than a medical test. This has been seen in recent years with medical testing. DNA testing has become a huge business in recent years with customers sending samples of their saliva to labs eager to learn something new about their family background, health and ethos.

Ancestry.com, myDNA and 23andMe to name but a few can somewhat-accurately tell you many things about your family tree – but they're not telling you alone, they are telling the world. Your results can be used for research to help scientists learn more about health and curing hereditary conditions – which sounds great, but there is often a bigger picture. 23andMe boasted[19] about their deal with medical company GlaxoSmithKline which would see 5 million people's data shared for "new medicine and cures" and whilst the press release ensured customers there would be plenty of *"stringent security protections in place when it comes to collecting, storing and transferring information about research participants"* this doesn't ensure anonymous data simply because DNA can never be anonymous. Research participants are given the option to opt-out of handing over the information, but it's not exactly mentioned in the press release and there's the possibility it's too late.

The deal made 23andMe a cool $300 million US dollars. Oh, and guess who the company are affiliated with? Calico Life Sciences. Never heard of them? Well, they are owned by Alphabet, Inc. – Google's parent company.[20]

---

[19] https://mediacenter.23andme.com/press-releases/gsk-and-23andme-sign-agreement-to-leverage-genetic-insights-for-the-development-of-novel-medicines/ **OR** https://archive.vn/1Nb1E **OR** https://git.io/Jv5Fx

[20] https://www.theatlantic.com/science/archive/2018/07/big-pharma-dna/566240/ **OR** https://archive.vn/wk6p7

The company has a rather vague retention policy that says they'll store your sample for between 1 and 10 years and this may change otherwise.[21] It also states they may contact you to re-analyse your sample in the future.

---

[21] https://www.23andme.com/en-eu/about/biobanking/ **OR** https://archive.vn/Pfuqe **OR** https://git.io/Jv5Fh

PART THREE:
A RESTRICTED TECHNOLOGY FOR ALL TO ENJOY

TOP SECRET//UNDER//CONSTANT//SUPERVISION//REL TO READER

Personally, I think people need to get over this 'being offended' thing. Being offended does not give you the right to silence people. I get offended by things all the time - it's just part of life. The right not to be offended is not a human right, especially in a democracy.

- Ben Miller
  Actor / Comedian

A RESTRICTED INTERNET

Tim Berners-Lee in 1994. Image: CERN

When Sir Tim Berners-Lee invented the Internet as we know it (the World Wide Web) in 1989, he never expected that the release of the first website and web browser would influence current and future generations the way that it has. As one of the most prominent advocates of net neutrality, Berners-Lee has been critical of companies and governments disrespecting a free and open Internet and undermining the wonderful resource we have.

The threat of online censorship is perhaps one of the biggest concerns of a *free* Internet. Governments of the world have restricted access, interfered with or filtered the Internet in many ways. From pornographic content to violent videos and news archives; the fundamental value of freedom of speech has been a debate throughout the Internet's growth. Online freedom is also majorly influenced by how illegal it is to bypass the censorship laws of a country.
For example, some countries have severe consequences for using Virtual Private Networks (VPN) to circumvent suppressed content.

It probably comes as no surprise that countries like China, North Korea and Saudi Arabia rank as some of the worst offenders of restricting Internet access.

Despite the world wide web being a worldwide system – hence *interconnected network* – content providers, government organisations and national regulators can rule the net to within their country of jurisdiction to protect their political, business or personal interests.

Whilst each country and related telecommunication provider have their methods and reasons for control, the extremes of such measures and the effect it has on society will be a discussion that lasts until the end of time.

Whilst a country can *physically* restrict the Internet by disconnecting the cables or satellites, most of the restrictions placed on a country's Internet is implemented by Internet Service Providers (ISPs) whether voluntary or enforced by government order.

The OpenNet Initiative[22] (ONI), was a group devoted to informing the public about content filtering and net-utilised surveillance worldwide. Made up of an international team of investigators they used several methods to test and document the censorship of the Internet per country and report on how the net was used to spy on a country's citizens. A conclusive study of 74 countries revealed that 42 had been found to engage in some form of filtering and 21 had been engaging in 'substantial' content blocking. The ONI did not test for the filtering of material related to child exploitation and any country filtering such material was excluded – essentially considered 'not filtering' – from the 42 countries. According to the results, the following countries were the worst for restricting access to major parts of the web: Armenia, Bahrain, China, Ethiopia, Gaza and the West Bank, Indonesia, Iran,

---

[22] https://opennet.net/

Kuwait, Burma/Myanmar, Oman, Pakistan, Qatar, Saudi Arabia, South Korea, Sudan, Syria, Turkmenistan, United Arab Emirates, Uzbekistan, Vietnam and Yemen.

Non-profit organisation *Reporters Sans Frontières* (RSF) or *Reporters with Borders* who focus on freedom of the press echoed these countries in their violations of press freedom ranking. Despite covering 180 countries, rather than ONI's 74, The World Press Freedom Index provided by RSF almost mirrors the list.
It's no surprise then, that countries who restrict the Internet are restricting press freedom.

The web is made up of many intricate factors, one of which is Content Delivery Networks (CDN)
CDN providers serve Internet content like text, graphics, scripts, media, software, documents, and applications including live streaming closer and faster to the user sitting in front of the screen.
Akamai Technologies is responsible for providing 20-30% of all web traffic. Like AWS, Akamai has a huge client base relying on their services including multiple government agencies around the world which puts them in the direct firing line for censorship.

In 2001, Arabic news network Al Jazeera – of whom is funded by Qatar – became the only channel to cover the eruption of war in Afghanistan live. The network distributed exclusive footage of the war from the front lines and a series of videos featuring Osama bin Laden which would become the Western world's first vision of 21st-century terrorism.
In 2003, Al Jazeera launched its first English-language website. The website's controversial launch was faced with backlash

and subsequently hacked to replace the site with an American flag. Three days after the attack, Al Jazeera signed a contract with Akamai who would provide hosting and cybersecurity services.

Within 14 days of providing their service, Akamai decided to terminate the contract[23] over what Joanne Tucker, the managing editor of the web site, said was due to *"nonstop political pressure"* by the United States government on companies dealing with the site.

Although the company never commented on the cancellation, the Acceptable Use Policy found on Akamai's website stated:

Al Jazeera's English-language website as seen in 2004

"Akamai takes no responsibility for any content created, accessible or delivered on or through the Akamai Network and Services. Akamai does not monitor or exercise any editorial control over such content...Material deemed unacceptable includes anything that is illegal, indecent, obscene, pornographic, defamatory, libellous, or inconsistent with the generally accepted practices of the Internet community"

Companies like Akamai are well within their rights to terminate the service of customers as stated in almost every terms and conditions. Officials from the U.S. Defense Department criticised the network for showing uncensored images of the war, including captured and deceased American soldiers.

Ms Tucker called the hacking attempts *"a narrow, pro-censorship attempt to silence a news site"*

---

[23] http://tech.mit.edu/V123/N17/17aljazeera.17n.html **OR** https://archive.vn/Ed1lD

UNDER CONSTANT SUPERVISION

Although possibly entirely unrelated to Akamai's decision, it should be stated that the company was co-founded in 1998 by Daniel M. Lewin, an American-Israeli who had served in the *Sayeret Matkal* or *General Staff Reconnaissance Unit* – of the Israel Defence Forces. Under the intelligence-gathering unit, he would earn the rank of captain before moving to America in the mid-1990s where he'd soon generate great wealth at the height of the '*Internet boom*'. Lewin was Chief Technical Officer of the company and lived with his family in Boston. In 2001, Lewin was murdered aboard *American Airlines Flight 11* during its hijacking and subsequent crash into the North Tower of the World Trade Center.

A Federal Aviation Administration report leaked in 2002 states that a frantic phone call received from a flight stewardess revealed Lewin was shot by one of the hijackers, possibly sitting behind him in business class at the front section of the plane. [24]

The report generated controversy of its own due to the FAA and FBI's strong denial of firearms smuggled onto the plane. The final 9/11 Commission report mentions Lewis was stabbed. [25]

> "...passenger Daniel Lewin, who was seated in the row just behind Atta and Omari, was stabbed by one of the hijackers-probably Satam al Suqami, who was seated directly behind Lewin..."

Lewin's name, along with other passengers of Flight 11, can be seen on panel N-75 at the North Pool of the National September 11 Memorial.

U.S. and U.K. government intelligence analysts reportedly intercepted communications between Facebook and its CDN

---

[24] https://archive.vn/uqLaY
[25] https://www.9-11commission.gov/report/911Report_Ch1.htm

provider Akamai with mass data collection being denied by the company, stating *"there was no vulnerability on the Akamai CDN"*

Akamai may have had no direct involvement in surveillance targeting.

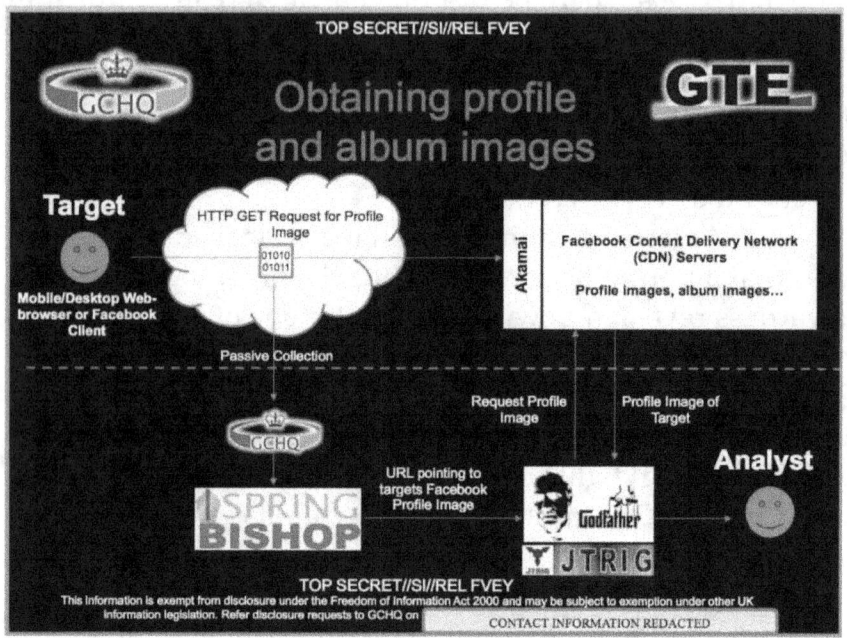

One of the most common methods of enforced online restriction is the use of filters. This is known as DNS blocking (or DNS filtering)

Domain Name System (DNS) blocking is intended to make it difficult for users to reach certain websites without having to change their computer or modem's configuration. Perhaps the easiest form of censorship to implement and circumvent, DNS blocks are almost-always enforced by Internet service providers attempting to limit access to copyright-infringing websites. Government and law agencies can also attempt to encourage ISPs to filter domains "voluntarily" in-place of or before legislation being introduced.

One of the reasons for DNS blocking is to contain information which is a form of news suppression.

Perhaps the biggest example of such process in recent years is the 2019 Christchurch Mosque Shooting in New Zealand which saw 50 people killed by a gunman. Within a day of the footage being streamed online many governments around the world demanded websites remove the videos, photos or offending material. With websites such as Archive.is containing archived mirrors of the content; the Australian and New Zealand ISPs individually decided to restrict access to a selection of websites in their entirety to prevent the spread of the crime. Many websites such as news website ZeroHedge and video-sharing platform LiveLeak refused to remove the videos and details, citing public transparency and the right to know what had taken place. These websites were added to a blacklist and inaccessible to Internet users shortly after the attacks.

Australia's largest ISP Telstra voluntarily blocked an unnamed list of websites that had hosted the footage or screenshots which lead to many other providers following the suspensions.

Telstra News ✓
@Telstra_news

We've started temporarily blocking a number of sites that are hosting footage of Friday's terrorist attack in Christchurch. We understand this may inconvenience some legitimate users of these sites, but these are extreme circumstances and we feel this is the right thing to do.

4:19 PM · Mar 18, 2019 · Twitter Web Client

This effort was criticised by many advocates of a free Internet, with many demanding legal basis for the censorship rather than personal morals. Criticism was also directed at the companies and governments for not restricting social media giants like Facebook and Twitter where the content could still be viewed freely. Many residents took to the Internet to express their irritation that content featuring extremist groups executing innocent persons were never affected by the same moral decisions.

UNDER CONSTANT SUPERVISION

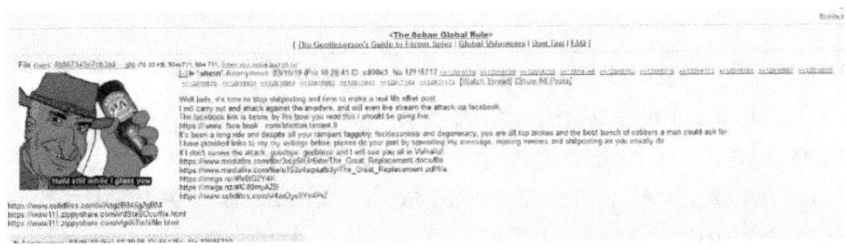

The post on message board 8chan, allegedly by the shooter, featured links to the manifesto and the shooters personal Facebook profile in which the live footage was streamed in its entirety.
Note: the links displayed were removed almost immediately following the attacks, as was the post itself.

Minutes before the attacks a user uploaded a manifesto titled "The Great Replacement" on imageboard website 8chan stating he would carry out the attacks. The manifesto was emailed to more than 30 addresses, including to the office of the New Zealand Prime Minister. The post linked to his personal Facebook profile. Simply uploading a screenshot of this post was enough to have your website temporarily blocked. Forums discussing the content were also blocked, with users accessing the websites given a notice stating that URL had been deactivated for security reasons. Many residents explained they felt they had the right to read the shooter's manifesto to understand what led the gunman to carry out such a violent attack. Some journalists claimed the manifesto was filled with content designed to troll – or '*shitpost*', as the 8chan message would back up – the media and create outrage for fame.[26][27]

Various media outlets were accused of spreading misinformation about both the manifesto and video stream, either intentionally or otherwise, with verification of the document and video's content impossible without breaking the law.

---

[26] https://www.nytimes.com/2019/03/15/world/asia/new-zealand-gunman-christchurch.html **OR** https://archive.vn/CC8WO
[27] https://www.theatlantic.com/technology/archive/2019/03/the-shooters-manifesto-was-designed-to-troll/585058/ **OR** https://archive.vn/gZwdN

Whilst YouTube and Facebook stated they were using automated tools to identify and remove violent content uploaded to their platforms, many sites took the stance that there were no legally enforceable actions against the hosting of such content – especially when operated and hosted outside of the country requesting the removals. The live stream on Facebook lasted roughly 17 minutes before it cut out due to network connectivity issues or camera battery depletion.

Reactance is a psychological motivation to do something one is told not to. The reaction occurs when people feel as if their liberty to choose or to do something is being eradicated. Within moments of the news breaking, headlines like "think twice about watching it" and warnings that simply viewing the video or storing it could land you in jail were bound to raise conspiracy theories. *Something must be amiss if they want to censor it that badly!*
Another example of such behaviour is **the Streisand effect** named after performer Barbra Streisand. Streisand's attempt to conceal online photographs of her residence in California led to the unplanned consequence of having it shared even more.
In short: by attempting to remove something from the Internet, you're almost guaranteed to have it shared more than if you'd simply left it.

As a result of the mainstream media and governments urging people not to share the footage or to even view the footage, there was an increase in attempts to upload it to various websites including YouTube and Facebook. Facebook claimed the video was uploaded 1.5 million times while YouTube confirmed that at one point it was removing one video per second, with tens of thousands of uploads removed within 24 hours of the stream.

American Internet forum *Kiwi Farms* republished the livestream footage and manifesto. New Zealand Police requested the website operators voluntarily hand over the information of users who posted or commented concerning the shooting. The request for IP addresses, email addresses and other information was aggressively denied by the website's owner.

At least eight people were arrested for storing or sharing the video and/or manifesto. The New Zealand Office of Film and Literature Classification (OFLC) classified the footage as 'objectionable' which made it a criminal offence in New Zealand to distribute, copy or exhibit the video. A week later the manifesto was also given the same classification. Researchers, journalists and academics can apply for an exception should they wish to analyse the manifesto but are unable to view or store the footage. Those without a written exception can face up to 14 years in prison and or a fine of $10,000 – the same sentence as viewing, sharing or having a copy of the video.

The OFLC classification decision page remarks why the content was illegal for public reading:

> **Why not give everyone access so we can all see how insane those ideas are and deconstruct them?**
> *We appreciate people may be curious about the attacker's motives, and interested in reading the publication for that purpose. This document has not been produced in order to inform New Zealanders. It is a document with a specific purpose – to radicalise those who may be persuaded by it, to carry out further attacks. Most people won't be influenced by its ideology and calls to attack identified groups and targets. Some may be. This raises the real possibility of further attacks inspired by this document.*

The OFLC application to *"access or hold a copy or copies of the banned document THE GREAT REPLACEMENT"* incurs a fee of $102.20. This led several critics to accuse New Zealand's Classification board of profiting from the attack by licensing a document which was released publicly by the author.

Website security company Cloudflare terminated the account of right-wing news website the *Daily Stormer* and ceased processing their domains with CEO Matthew Price reminding people in a Cloudflare blog post that the *"terms of service reserve the right for us to terminate users of our network at our sole discretion."*

The decision was made by the company as they did not want to be seen condoning the actions and promoted beliefs of the website which is considered neo-Nazi and does not remove comments in its discussion board that express hatred towards Jews and accusations that U.S. Italian-Palestinian comedian Dean Obeidallah was involved in the 2017 Manchester Arena bombing. The website's editor Andrew Anglin was ordered to pay $4.1 million in damages to the comedian. Whilst some believe the website is intentionally sparking controversy to generate income, it has been defended as a site for freedom of speech.

Cloudflare's CEO claimed in 2017 that he considered himself a "free-speech absolutist" and that he hated terminating the website's use, but pressure from other customers mounted against the company which would have lost more money had the other customers cancelled their accounts. Some Twitter users cancelled their accounts because of the decision to remove the *Daily Stormer*, fearing it would snowball into more website bans and go against freedom of speech.

Before the disconnection, Cloudflare had maintained they would not police content published by customers. As part of their transparent approach, Cloudflare even published a page of criticism against their actions which stated the page was intended to "recognise and memorialise" the criticism whilst still having the rather-biased reference to the *Daily Stormer* as a "repugnant" website.[28]

In response to the termination, the EFF published an article warning that the Internet was in jeopardy when major content providers block websites with one paragraph reading:[29]

> "All fair-minded people must stand against the hateful violence and aggression that seems to be growing across our country. But we must also recognize that on the Internet, any tactic used now to silence neo-Nazis will soon be used against others, including people whose opinions we agree with."

And another saying:

> "Protecting free speech is not something we do because we agree with all of the speech that gets protected. We do it because we believe that no one—not the government and not private commercial enterprises—should decide who gets to speak and who doesn't."

Despite Matthew Prince's proclamation that he didn't want to have to censor another website, Cloudflare terminated the services of website *8chan*.[30]
The decision was based on evidence that the El Paso gunman had posted on the message board website just moments before opening fire and killing 20 people.

---

[28] https://www.cloudflare.com/cloudflare-criticism/ **OR** https://archive.vn/7oKGH

[29] https://www.eff.org/deeplinks/2017/08/fighting-neo-nazis-future-free-expression **OR** https://archive.vn/fbHhX

[30] https://blog.cloudflare.com/terminating-service-for-8chan/ **OR** https://archive.md/Yq0PT

Echoing the Christchurch shooter's use of the site just months before; the gunman published a manifesto titled *The Inconvenient Truth* on the message board. The manifesto even proclaims his support of the Christchurch shooter.

The content was removed within minutes of being uploaded, but as with all Internet content, it was too late. Matthew Prince published a blog post comparing his decision to the termination of the *Daily Stormer* whilst maintaining his belief that *"the Daily Stormer is still available and still disgusting"* before ending the paragraph with *"They are no longer Cloudflare's problem, but they remain the Internet's problem."*

Whilst many praised the decision to cease the website's services, it was also seen as a total backflip to blog entries[31] written by Matthew Prince that declare:

> *"A website is speech. It is not a bomb. There is no imminent danger it creates and no provider has an affirmative obligation to monitor and make determinations about the theoretically harmful nature of speech a site may contain"*

and perhaps more conflictingly state:

> *"There are lots of things on the web I find personally distasteful. I have political beliefs, but I don't believe those beliefs should color what is and is not allowed to flow over the network."*

And:

> *"One of the greatest strengths of the United States is a belief that speech, particularly political speech, is sacred. A website, of course, is nothing but speech,"*

---

[31] https://blog.cloudflare.com/cloudflare-and-free-speech/ **OR** https://archive.md/gNlx5

Prince ended his post with the claim that after his email was hacked by a Cloudflare user – who even used a Cloudflare-powered website to publish details of the attack – he did not terminate the user and believed he had no right to. The post ends with the assertion Cloudflare would *"hold consistently to a belief that our proper role is not that of Internet censor."*
Below the blog entry is the **RELATED POSTS** section that directs users to the multiple entries contradicting his view that Cloudflare would not use their power to filter the Internet.

Cloudflare revealed its intentions to become a publicly traded company just two weeks after banning 8chan[32]. The companies' Initial Public Offering, or IPO, took place just a month later with the company raising $385 million at $10 to $12 per share.

With the consistently-changing structure of the Internet, it is often important to preserve a web page by using an archive site in case a website is taken down, accountability if a news article is changed or removed or to simply make a 'snapshot' of a page that could have future significance.

Whilst many online services like digital library *The Internet Archive's* **Wayback Machine**[33] will automatically preserve pages on the Internet for later reference, the service *archive.today* is a popular site that can take a snapshot of any page at the moment a user submits a link. This is also useful for content comparison and downloading the cached view of the submitted website.

---

[32] https://www.sec.gov/Archives/edgar/data/1477333/000119312519222176/d735023ds1.htm **OR** https://archive.vn/a4mOd

[33] https://web.archive.org

After the New Zealand shooting, Australian and New Zealand Internet providers blocked access to archive.today in response to the service having snapshots of pages relating to the shooting.

Whilst the manifesto had been quickly scrubbed from the Internet, several media outlets and opposing political parties claimed the removed document was proof that President Donald Trump was responsible for inspiring the shooters' bigotry.

Political consultant Kellyanne Conway (of whom popularised the term *Alternative Facts* during Trump's first term as President) suggested people read the manifesto to make up their own minds about its contradictions, claiming the media scoured the document for any mention of President Trump to lay blame. Again, Reactance comes into play.

For this book, the webmaster of Archive.today agreed to answer a few questions regarding the archival of links relating to such cases. For sake of anonymity, we will refer to the person as **_Archive._**

Archive stated that their role was 'passive' in the censorship of the offending links.

EU criminal intelligence agency Europol *(European Union Agency for Law Enforcement Cooperation)* and Russian censorship body Roskomnadzor[34] would often contact webmasters to perform the content blocks with minimal impact to the rest of the website. Australia and New Zealand blocked the entire website, hoping that Archive would respond by removing the offending content and perhaps requesting access be restored.

---

[34] The Federal Service for Supervision of Communications, Information Technology and Mass Media

UNDER CONSTANT SUPERVISION

The UK Metropolitan Police Service CTIRU *(Counter Terrorism Internet Referral Unit)* contacted Archive with a list of links they wanted removing. Archive complied by hiding the sites from UK visitors.

Like myself, Archive reiterates the opinion that had the website been hosted in Australia, the hardware would have been ceased and the website disconnected.

Archive noted that the business community were to blame for the censorship of multiple websites nationwide saying *"The most effective way to shut down something on the Internet is to annoy business contacts of the target with messages like **please take them offline or be our next target**"*.

With the Daily Stormer, Archive received the following email:

> *"Archives from 8chan/8kun need to be removed as it is a bastion for white supremacists, terrorists, and mass shooters."*

Archive also told me they believed that anthropologically, businesses like Cloudflare are concerned about being the scapegoat and therefore take the law into their own hands without any requests from authorities due to their political disposition or the worry that failure to censor right-wing content would end up with the company being labelled the same way.

Along with *Wayback Machine, Archive.today* cannot be viewed from a Russian or Chinese service provider.

Despite the mass censorship of websites promoting white supremacy and hateful content, Cloudflare still allows websites run by Islamic State terrorists, the Taliban, Hamas and Islamic extremist sympathisers to be protected by their service.[35]

In response to a Huffington Post article that questioned the morals of providing services to "at least 7 terror groups"[36], the company's general counsel Doug Kramer told UK technology news website *The Register* that *"taking an anti-censorship stance was a long-term decision by Cloudflare to keep itself from becoming an arbiter of what is acceptable speech and what should be censored."*[37]

Cloudflare also provides its services to website *Chimpmania* which pokes fun at photos of black people and mocked the appearance of a black baby born with severe medical problem *Gastroschisis*.

The website featured comments on photos of the baby calling him a *"mutant male nigfant"* and calling the white father a *"race traitor"*

Cloudflare responded to an online petition with nearly half a million signatures[38] that they had no power to remove the website or terminate it from using the services. The website explicitly states in the rules they don't advocate violence or the bashing of humans with one moderator responding to a new user saying *"tell your friends and family about us and invite them to join us in bashing the nigger beasts"*[39] Whether this website constitutes freedom of speech, satire or political motivation; there have been no linked cases of violence inspired by or pre-empted by *Chimpmania*. Strange, considering the same can be said for *Daily Stormer* and a large

---

[35] https://www.theepochtimes.com/anti-terrorist-hacker-group-reveals-40-isis-websites-protected-by-us-tech-firm_1892477.html **OR** https://archive.vn/gy4lU

[36] https://archive.vn/viOjf

[37] https://www.theregister.co.uk/2018/12/19/cloudflare_terror_groups/ **OR** https://archive.vn/ljo4i

[38] https://archive.vn/7RwfO

[39] https://archive.vn/CQDwg

majority of anonymous message boards like 8chan – of whom almost immediately removed offending content that landed it in such hot water.

The EFF recommended that in-order to protect net neutrality, companies should adopt the *Manila Principles on Intermediary Liability*[40] which outline the example of six possible principles as an alternative to – what EFF refers to as – *acting on the headlines.*

> I. Intermediaries should be shielded from liability for third-party content
>
> II. Content must not be required to be restricted without an order by a judicial authority
>
> III. Requests for restrictions of content must be clear, be unambiguous, and follow due process
>
> IV. Laws and content restriction orders and practices must comply with the tests of necessity and proportionality
>
> V. Laws and content restriction policies and practices must respect due process
>
> VI. Transparency and accountability must be built into laws and content restriction policies and practices.

---

[40] https://www.manilaprinciples.org/
https://www.eff.org/files/2015/10/31/manila_principles_1.0.pdf

TOP SECRET//UNDER//CONSTANT//SUPERVISION//REL TO READER

Since real spies are so good, you never really know what actual spying is. But I do think spying is a lot more dangerous than we are led to believe.

- Richard C. Armitage
  Actor

COPYRIGHT ENFORCEMENT OR RESTRICTION?

Copyright Infringement laws are a dangerously misused tool in online censorship. In the United States, United Kingdom and Australia; governments have ordered ISPs block multiple websites deemed to be hosting or sharing copyrighted content. In 2010 studios Twentieth Century Fox, Universal, Warner Bros., Paramount Pictures, Disney and Columbia Pictures all took legal action against British Usenet website Newzbin, a website that indexed files that infringed the copyright of the pursuing parties. After a successful judgement, British Telecommunications (BT) and later Sky Broadband were ordered to block access to the website.[41]

The studios' combined efforts paid off. Newzbin shut down shortly after. A short-lived successor, Newzbin2, was launched but closed after a lengthy battle with the MPAA (Motion Picture Association) who are known for continuously seeking ways to remove pirated content from the Internet. Their long anti-piracy stance – alongside UK trade organisation Federation Against Copyright Theft or FACT – goes back a long way with perhaps the most influential campaign "Piracy, it's a crime" which featured as an unskippable video on thousands of purchased DVDs throughout the 2000s with the classic line "You Wouldn't Steal a Car" preceding visuals depicting multiple crimes which were equated to the unauthorised copying and circulation of movies through the Internet. Ironically, the MPA has been accused of copyright infringement several times, even making illegal copies of a 2006 documentary exploring the MPA and its classification system.

---

[41] https://www.bailii.org/ew/cases/EWHC/Ch/2011/2714.html

These copies were made when the film was submitted to the MPA to obtain a classification. The association justified the infringement claiming that the privacy of their members had been breached. The MPA never made a legal complaint against the director of the film for such accusations.

The MPA have played a major role in the attempted – and often successful – removal of piracy websites from the web. As stated before, DNS blocking can often be influenced by related businesses and organisations before legally mandated. Companies like the MPA, FACT and The Recording Industry Association of America (RIAA) have consistently lobbied for the United States government to block infringing websites and track down the owners and 'enablers' of any website that they claim facilitates unauthorised downloading. The complex argument is that many of these sites do not store the allegedly infringing content but provide a means for users to download from others.

This is known as Peer-to-Peer transfer or file sharing and has seen multiple websites and application developers attacked. P2P sharing increased in notoriety with the establishment of file sharing applications such as Napster, Morpheus and Kazaa.

In recent years, protocols such as BitTorrent have become increasingly common, with most torrent hosting sites targeted by major corporations for allowing users to download small files that can connect them to a large userbase of peers. In 2006 the MPA persuaded the Swedish government to conduct a raid of torrent site The Pirate Bay. Sweden's decision to authorise roughly 65 police officers to raid multiple locations including the data centres owned by ISP *PeRiQuito AB* was considered by the MPA themselves as "highly successful" despite the site's traffic increasing by almost double thanks to media coverage of the event. The raid and trials of Pirate Bay founders would go on to be immortalised in documentaries *Good Copy Bad Copy* and *Steal This Film*. A similar raid took place in 2014 when Stockholm police stormed The Pirate Bay and confiscated multiple computers.

Whilst there have been several high-profile cases that have led to the closure of many websites; online piracy is still rampant. The MPA claimed that college pirates were responsible for nearly 50% of movie studio losses. These claims were met with scepticism due to the Associations' calculations kept private with no credible evidence to back up the claim. Two years later after much scrutiny, the MPA claimed they had miscalculated the results and blamed "human error". Turns out 44% meant roughly 14%.

Since 2010 more than 200,000 copyright infringement lawsuits have been filed against BitTorrent websites alone. In Australia, roughly 500 web domains have been blocked after Federal Court cases by Roadshow Films and Foxtel.[42]

---

[42] http://www8.austlii.edu.au/cgi-in/viewdoc/au/cases/cth/FCA/2016/1503.html

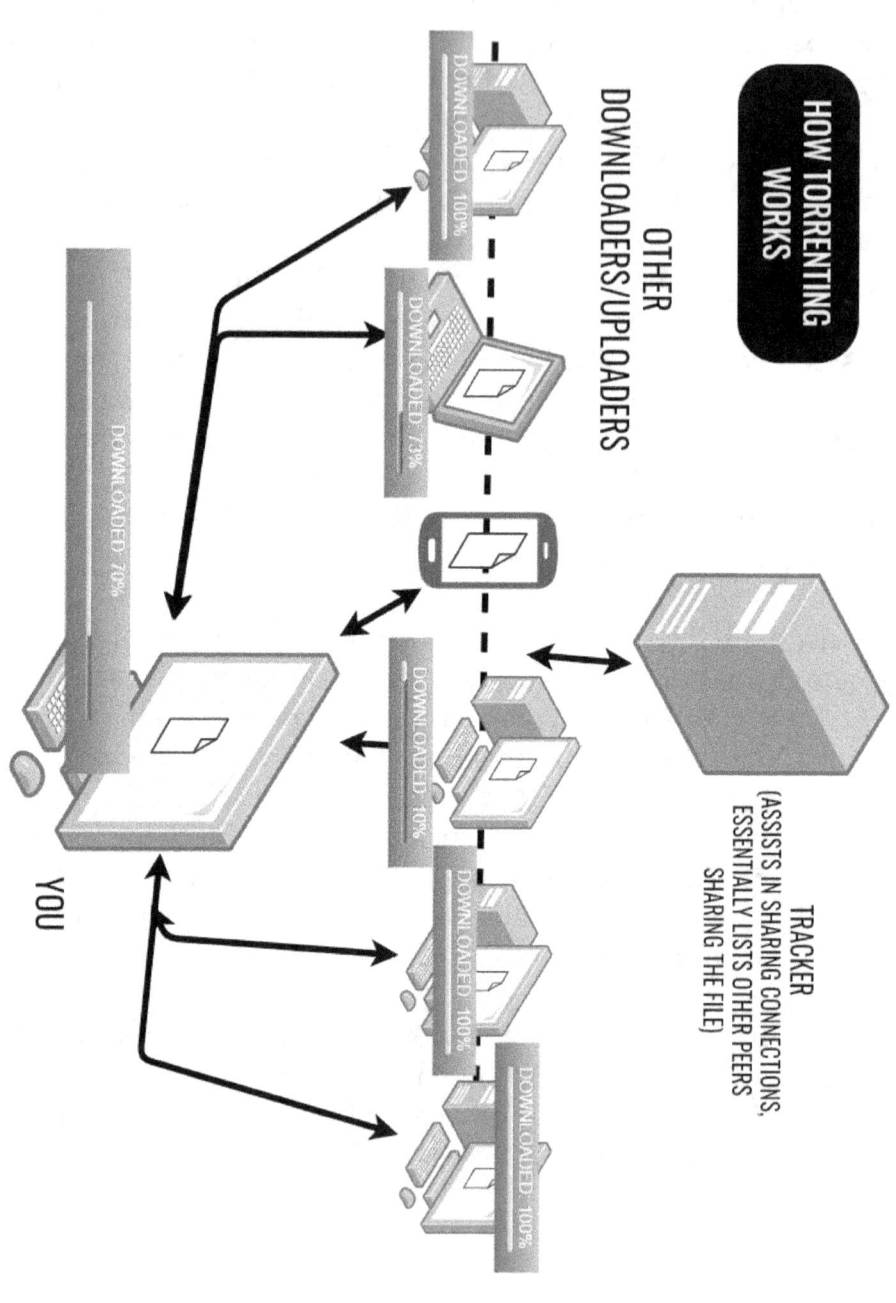

Foxtel, Australia's dominating pay-tv subscription provider is partially owned by News Corp and telecommunications monopolising[43] company Telstra. With Foxtel costing an average of 600 Australian dollars per year for a basic package and double that for the platinum subscription (with a majority of the channels featuring paid advertisements) Australia often ranks as one of the biggest contributors to digital piracy. Foxtel's delayed content and maintaining exclusive rights to broadcast many popular TV shows are also cited as a reason many choose to download. As these blocks are mostly DNS-based, any benefit to the restrictions remains to be seen with statistics from the organisations in support of the rulings giving numbers of visitors to the redirection rather than any increased sales. The source code of the block site reveals a Google Analytics tracking code.

What Australians using default DNS see when visiting a blocked site

---

[43] Telstra own a majority of Australian telecommunications and lease the network to other providers. They have long been accused of monopoly due to due to their extensive ownership and control over networking infrastructure within the country.

The *Digital Content Guide* website[44] that you're told to see for more information doesn't educate the visitor why they blocked you or what effect piracy has on the Australian economy. There is no comprehensive list of services available, nor is there any encouragement as to how cheap the 'legal and safe digital content' is. If I was pirating, I'd think it was pathetic and if I was a content owner genuinely irritated by the loss of sales, I'd think it was a wasted opportunity. For example: when you click that you were looking for music on your pirating quest, the website lists Google Play and Apple iTunes.

If you go to the directory for music videos, it links to five sites, one of which no longer exists and another – a blog on popular music – that doesn't let you view any music videos. The eBooks page lists a total of three providers most people have never heard of. There are no references to Kindle (or Google Play) or even any authors or publishing companies who self-publish and sell online.

Reading the poorly-worded *"why can't I get what I want from that site?"* paragraph advises you that *"you can source the content you wanted from this website.* No, you probably can't. Amazingly, nearly every answer in the FAQ section repeats that phrase.[45] Ironically, pirating sites make it easier to find what it is you're looking for.

Despite little information about the effectiveness of site blocking in Australia, the MPA described it as highly effective to the United States Senate[46]

---

[44] https://digitalcontentguide.com.au/
[45] https://digitalcontentguide.com.au/about/
[46] https://advanced-television.com/2020/03/12/mpa-supports-pirate-site-blocking/ **OR** https://archive.vn/IszfD

So why defend the piracy of copyrighted work? Surely it is better for the economy and professionals involved to dismantle and block access to the websites that help pirates continue their pursuit?

Nothing is safe from the copyright trolls. Not even a flag. Indigenous artist and land rights activist Harold Thomas copyrighted the Aboriginal flag[47]
An Australian health organisation selling merchandise to fund community programs was issued with a cease and desist notice and given three days to comply[48].

Harold Thomas has even refused Google the right to publish one of their logos *'doodles'* drawn by an 11-year-old girl featuring the flag.[49]
Harold Thomas wanted Google to pay an unspecified fee to use the drawing on their homepage:

> "They didn't give me a straight-out offer, and with all their money and machinery and know-how, they should have known what to do - it's as simple as that... I said well you can use it but there's a fee component and the [Google] person said: 'Oh we can't do that, we can't pay for it, we'll have to ask the girl to change it [the logo] if we have to pay for it,'"

Chocolate manufacturer Cadbury even fought a lengthy battle to trademark the colour purple, insisting that a specific shade - *Pantone 2685C* – formed part of their identity and should not be used by other companies.[50]

---

[47] https://github.com/BookRefine/references/blob/master/supervision/Copyright%20Australia%20Aboriginal%20Flag.pdf
[48] https://www.abc.net.au/news/2019-06-11/new-licence-owners-of-aboriginal-flag-threaten-football-codes/11198002 **OR** https://archive.vn/BhAXi
[49] https://www.smh.com.au/technology/oh-dear-google-flagged-over-logo-dispute-20100126-mvhd.html **OR** https://archive.vn/4noWb
[50] https://www.telegraph.co.uk/news/2019/02/02/chocolate-wars-break-colour-purple/ **OR** https://archive.vn/9cGv0

People choose to pirate for a whole number of reasons. Most of these extend far beyond the idea of wanting something for nothing. According to various surveys conducted online, the top reasons people pirate is:

- The content is not affordable
- The content isn't available worldwide
- The content is delayed in the country
- Lack of accessible or easy payment options
- The content won't be used again after purchased
- "content makers don't need my money"
- "I own a physical copy; I don't want to purchase a digital copy too" (it's much easier to download the media than to convert from the physical)

Rather than compile a long list of references for these claims, a simple Internet search for piracy surveys reveals thousands of statistics collected over the past 20 years all give the same reasons. (ironic suggestion: do not use Google)

The last entry is perhaps the best way to justify illegal downloads. Digital Rights Management (DRM) restricts the ability to transfer content from device-to-device. Imagine if you removed your CD from your home stereo and tried to continue listening on the way to work in your car but were refused the ability. As Defective by Design[51] puts it: *When a program is designed to prevent you from copying or sharing a song, reading an eBook on another device, or playing a single-player game without an Internet connection, you are being restricted by DRM.*

The rise in online piracy is with no doubt a damaging worry for content creators everywhere, so is censorship the solution? Or do we need better educating?

---

[51] https://www.defectivebydesign.org

The assumption that every famous person lives in a large mansion with no financial issues is part of the reason parts of society are so blasé about the consequences.

Many good reasons exist for copyright infringement. For example, the 20th anniversary of *E.T. the Extra-Terrestrial* in was released with altered effects and even police and FBI agents' guns replaced with walkie-talkies. Those looking for the "true" version would resort to piracy. Many re-released television shows and movies also have changes in soundtrack due to licensing issues, these changes can easily influence a person viewing. An example of this is the film adaptation of *Nineteen Eighty-Four* which multiple versions exist; Some featuring the soundtrack by pop duo Eurythmics and other releases featuring only the original score.

You fork out your hard-earned cash and buy yourself a new device. Surely, seeing as it is yours, you can modify it, repair it and tweak it to your heart's content? You don't have to take it to their authorised repairer and seeing as it's yours, you can do whatever you want right?
The Digital Millennium Copyright Act (DMCA) has been used to argue otherwise. Manufacturers have cited section 1201 of the act to contend that the user does not have the right to repair or modify the application software in any way:

> *No person shall circumvent a technological measure that effectively controls access to a work protected under this title.*
>
> *- 17 U.S. Code Section 1201 (a)(1)(A)*

The DMCA is a 1998 United States copyright law that forbids production and propagation of technology, devices, or services that circumvent access to copyrighted works…DRM.

YOU BOUGHT IT; YOU OWN IT‹ THAT DOESN'T MAKE IT YOURS.

DRM doesn't just apply to software – there are hundreds of physical devices that use the same pretence to lock users into their product.

As such, the law can be manipulated to force consumers to upgrade the technology they otherwise wouldn't. This leads to environmental consequences and the revocation of user rights.

The *Right to Repair* is intentionally removed when manufacturers make it difficult to access genuine parts and service, thus forcing the consumer to use the manufacturers' authorised repair services rather than an independent – and in most cases cheaper – repairer.

In 2017 a farmer from Nebraska challenged John Deere over the right to repair his tractor[52]. The tractor sounded an alert warning every ten minutes warning him of a failed feature he had no use for. Only an authorised technician could clear the fault code, costing several hundred dollars. The Nebraskan farmer was not the only one who'd experienced such issues with attempts to fix or diagnose errors. After multiple complaints, the company defended their proprietary requirements with a proposal for an exemption to the U.S. copyright office[53], claiming that repair could *"make it possible for pirates, third-party developers, and less innovative competitors to free-ride off the creativity, unique expression and ingenuity of vehicle software."*

The company also argued that by allowing users to modify entertainment systems, one opens the floodgates to pirating music through their technology. Yes, really.

---

[52] https://www.theguardian.com/environment/2017/mar/06/nebraska-farmers-right-to-repair-john-deere-apple **OR** https://archive.vn/xulM0

[53] http://copyright.gov/1201/2015/comments-032715/class%2021/John_Deere_Class21_1201_2014.pdf **OR**

Despite calls for action from multiple organisations, including a petition by the EFF featuring thousands of signatures, the request to amend section 1201 was denied[54] with the Copyright Office advising it could "*severely weaken the right of copyright owners to exercise meaningful control over the terms of access to their works online*"

The EFF claims *"if you can't fix it, you don't own it"*

Beverage brewing system Keurig found themselves sitting in a pile of lawsuits after introducing a new coffee machine with a proprietary lock that would only accept their K-Cup system. The company were accused of violating anti-competition laws for attempts to stop cheaper alternatives from being used in the machine[55].

The extent of forcing users into continuous purchase has even hit the pet market with a technological cat litter box that features sensors preventing the user from replacing the sanitation lining with products a third-party product[56]

---

[54] https://www.copyright.gov/policy/1201/section-1201-full-report.pdf
[55] https://www.canadianbusiness.com/companies-and-industries/keurig-2-single-serve-coffee-pod-drm/ OR https://archive.vn/qOPjS
[56] https://archive.vn/nkVO6

As with the regional locking technology, printer ink also uses DRM. HP has been caught releasing a software update claiming to be a security patch. The patch was in-fact a new 'feature' that would check for and block third-party inks from being used[57]. It should be of little surprise that companies like Lexmark sued ink manufacturer *Static Control Components, Inc.* for selling the product that could bypass the printers' verification mode so that you could refill the cartridge with another, often cheaper and better quality, ink. The court case accused Static Control of reverse-engineering their product which, they claimed, was... against Section 1201 of the Digital Millennium Copyright Act.

Electric car manufacturer *Tesla* is one of the many companies using things like DRM to protect their mass-data collection. Later in the book, I'll go into the consequences of transmitting data from vehicles which involves an experiment performed by an anonymous white-hacker known as *greentheonly*.

I managed to get in touch with greentheonly and asked for his or hers opinion on the security of the car and implications of the firmware and the possibilities the car would become obsolete with its locked firmware should Tesla decide to stop releasing updates.
They believed the proprietary firmware wasn't as dangerous as the proprietary hardware – specifically, their proprietary charging network. Greentheonly stated: *"Take that away and the use of the car is greatly diminished."*

Tesla's Supercharger network is a subscription-based vehicle charge station found in multiple locations across the drivers' city.

---

[57] https://boingboing.net/2016/09/19/hp-detonates-its-timebomb-pri.html **OR** https://archive.vn/P5has

Most Tesla's sold have a fair-use policy such as 1500km worth of charge per year given free, with additional costs when the user goes over that tier.

If you're not close to a Tesla Supercharger, you may need to resort to a privately-run charging station that has much higher fees or slower charging capabilities. Supercharger stations cannot be used by rideshare drivers or delivery drivers.

Electric cars do not (yet) have a universal power adapter. If every manufacturer had a proprietary petrol and petrol pump station; the result would be a nightmare. Charger stations may or may not have the ability to charge your particular vehicle connector your car requires.

Throughout the 1990s, nearly every new mobile phone had its own type of phone charger. Drawers would be filled with power supplies with different shapes and even voltages, all of which would sooner-or-later end up in landfill. The European Parliament introduced a new regulatory action to standardise USB-C by July of 2020[58]. This would help the EU reduce electronic waste and ensure maximum compatibility between devices. In recent years, Apple is one of the biggest companies accused of intentionally deprecating adapters and requiring new accessories to be used for their devices.

Apple charges roughly $20US for a USB-C to Lightning cable whilst most comparable USB-C cables can be found for a

---

[58] https://www.europarl.europa.eu/news/en/press-room/20200128IPR71205/parliament-wants-binding-rules-on-common-chargers-to-be-tabled-by-summer

fraction of the price. Apple patented their lightning cable to ensure only genuine licenced cables would work, with cheaper non-Apple cables giving the warning *"This cable or accessory is not certified and may not work reliably with this iPhone"*
The company have also implemented features to prevent new non-genuine batteries from being installed in iPhones[59]. Installing a new battery gives users the message *"unable to verify this iPhone has a genuine Apple battery"*
In 2019, Apple's 'innovation' was discovered to be blocking third-party screen replacements giving users a similar error.[60]

DRM/DMCA is suggested to contribute to illegal activity by manufacturers. For example, in the 2015 Volkswagen emissions scandal (referred to as Dieselgate or Emissionsgate) VW were found to have violated the multiple international environmental acts by programming vehicle computers to only conform to emission standards when being tested in laboratories. The vehicles manufactured between 2009 and 2015 (which would possibly have continued if not discovered) used DMCA to prevent access to the software.

If an independent researcher, white-hat hacker or programming enthusiast had managed to circumvent the software, they could have alerted authorities to the changes in code and evasive features much sooner. On an environmental scale, this would have ensured Volkswagen conformed to the emissions standards and sliced a good amount of the nearly 350,000 affected vehicles in "VW graveyards" around the world.

---

[59] https://www.ifixit.com/News/32343/apple-is-locking-batteries-to-iphones-now **OR** https://archive.vn/dlepR
[60]   https://www.ifixit.com/News/33147/apple-is-discouraging-screen-repair-with-an-iphone-11-genuine-warning   **OR** https://archive.vn/BHrFO

Right to Repair laws are slowly being implemented around the world, but with plenty of resistance from manufacturers who can persuade governments that it can cause more harm than good, or that it could lead to other laws being broken (as we've seen with the John Deere music piracy claim)
And what about those large WARRANTY VOID IF SEAL REMOVE/DAMAGED warning labels that cover every access point of your device? Believe it or not, there are no issues with repairing consumer electronics that can affect your warranty. It's illegal for companies to void the warranty because of your repair or modification and a company would be required to prove that any issue your device has in the future is related to your repair.

Breaking the seal does not void the warranty – it simply proves that you may have caused another failure or made an issue worth should a company suggest so.
The *Magnuson–Moss Warranty Act* in the United States is a federal law that was developed to prevent manufacturers using false or misleading disclaimers suggesting the device wouldn't be covered if modified by anyone other than authorised technicians. The FTC has clarified the warnings are not legally enforceable:

> "Provisions that tie warranty coverage to the use of particular products or services harm both consumers who pay more for them as well as the small businesses who offer competing products and services."
>
> - Thomas B. Pahl, Acting Director of the FTC's Bureau of Consumer Protection

In conclusion, the EFF put it best:

> "The end result: users are disempowered, trained to go hat in hand to the Apple store just to change a battery (rather than doing it themselves). Medical clinics must waste scarce resources on expensive repair contracts rather than patient care. Independent repair shops are driven out of business. And the electronic waste piles up, as users discard their devices rather than fixing them or donating them for re-use."

Seized websites/domain names feature this graphic replacing all content.

DRM is also a privacy issue. Many products that require online activation force the consumer to create an account, hand over their details and even use specific software to play the purchased media. In many cases, this then gives a company the ability to learn your watching habits and interests. Just as the often-unskippable anti-piracy announcements do, consumers are punished for doing the right thing.

In 2005 Sony BMG were investigated for implementing protection methods on audio CDs. When inserted into a computer, the CDs in question would install software to prevent copying. The *SunnComm MediaMax copy-protection technology* unintentionally exposed users to malicious attacks due to software weaknesses. Sony responded to the criticism by releasing an uninstallation package. It was then discovered the software was not being uninstalled but hidden. The software itself was deeply embedded into the users Operating System meaning it was difficult to trace (the very definition of a *rootkit*)
Ironically, the code was revealed to have used free and open-source materials without meeting the credit and acknowledgement requirements set by the licenses they were released under.

Logically, developers did not attempt to sue for copyright infringement as it would not be in their best interests, but it highlighted the hypocritical nature of companies like Sony BMG and their attempts to enforce surveillance tactics on audio consumers who would not have been affected had they pirated the content and consequentially cost artists and businesses millions of dollars. In the wake of the scandal, the United States Computer Emergency Readiness Team released advice "*[not to] install software from sources that you do not expect to contain software, such as an audio CD.*"

The Electronic Frontier Foundation released a list of affected albums[61] and highlighted that the fine print was barely visible on the back of CD's featuring MediaMax due to limits in printing. Despite mass recalls of the albums, many American lawmakers alleged the affected CD's could still be purchased in multiple stores. In 2008 Sony released a list of the albums and barcodes affected as well as information on the ordeal. The website has since been taken down and can only be accessed by archive[62]

Rather than outright acknowledge the software did not collect information, the FAQ has a dubiously worded assurance that the _**installer**_ would not collect information:

> Will personal information be collected from my computer during the installation process?
> No, none of your personal information will be collected during the installation process.

The controversy did very little to tackle the DRM issue and despite the bad publicity, Sony maintained the stance they were serving the interest of the artists whose content is frequently subject to unauthorised duplication and replication.

---

[61] https://www.eff.org/IP/DRM/Sony-BMG/mm_3.0_titles.php
[62] https://web.archive.org/web/20071012024250/http://cp.sonybmg.com/xcp/english/titles.html

The popularity of DVD – and later Blu-Ray – media was also affected by a form of DRM known as regional locking. These formats were not the first to feature such restrictions with cartridge video games and VHS tapes also victim to the locks. Even printers are subject to the locks with companies like Canon, Epson, Lexmark, Xerox and Hewlett-Packard among just a few of the many companies that enforce blocks against ink cartridges from different regions. Some mobile phones also feature the implementation to encumber grey market imports.

Regional locking prevents the owner of the media from playing it elsewhere in the world without the use of a hacked or unlocked media player. Strategically designed to discourage people from buying their media from overseas; this is yet another restriction put in place by the very companies opposing online piracy.
Users would sometimes be given a limited number of times to change the region of the DVD to play it on their computer. Some DVD drives subsequently disable the changing of the region number after the limit has been reached. Modern approaches to region locking include geolocation restriction which limits customers outside a particular region from visiting a website or playing media.

DRM also prevents users from making copies of the media they have purchased. Those who wish to convert their DVD to a video file they can watch on their computer or mobile device must jump through multiple hoops to make a copy for personal use.

UNDER CONSTANT SUPERVISION

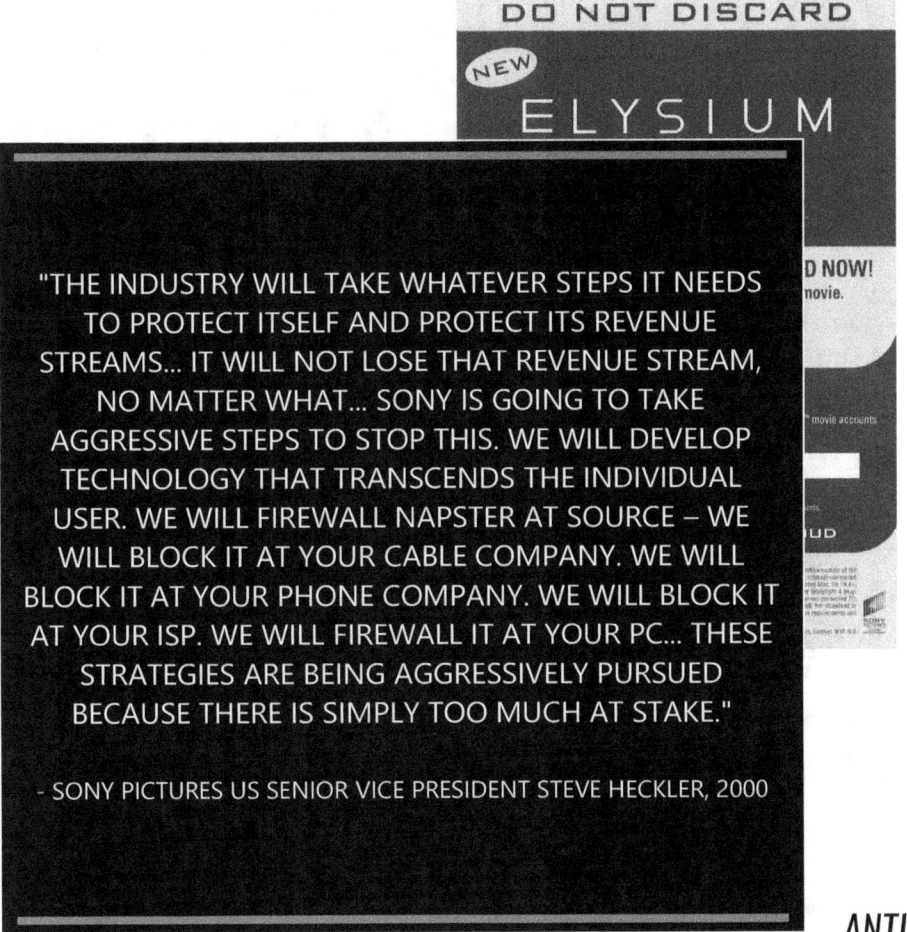

"THE INDUSTRY WILL TAKE WHATEVER STEPS IT NEEDS TO PROTECT ITSELF AND PROTECT ITS REVENUE STREAMS... IT WILL NOT LOSE THAT REVENUE STREAM, NO MATTER WHAT... SONY IS GOING TO TAKE AGGRESSIVE STEPS TO STOP THIS. WE WILL DEVELOP TECHNOLOGY THAT TRANSCENDS THE INDIVIDUAL USER. WE WILL FIREWALL NAPSTER AT SOURCE – WE WILL BLOCK IT AT YOUR CABLE COMPANY. WE WILL BLOCK IT AT YOUR PHONE COMPANY. WE WILL BLOCK IT AT YOUR ISP. WE WILL FIREWALL IT AT YOUR PC... THESE STRATEGIES ARE BEING AGGRESSIVELY PURSUED BECAUSE THERE IS SIMPLY TOO MUCH AT STAKE."

- SONY PICTURES US SENIOR VICE PRESIDENT STEVE HECKLER, 2000

ANTI-PIRACY CAN LEAD TO ANTI-PRIVACY‹ AND A HEADACHE:

Cloud-based rights system *UltraViolet* was brought in to curb the excuse that it was too much hassle to convert video files and often not worth the attempt thanks to stringent DRM. A limited number of DVD and Blu-Ray titles were released with an UltraViolet code that you could redeem to watch the movie anywhere.

When the *Digital Entertainment Content Ecosystem* (DECE) – a consortium of over 80 film studios, content providers, retailers and Internet providers – *announced* UltraViolet as a brand-new way of having digital access to your new purchase. The platform made sure that all content had to be streamed or downloaded in a proprietary video format and only playable through a proprietary application on devices.

If you downloaded a video to your Android phone, you couldn't play it through your computer – despite using the software intended. Once again, genuine customers punished for trying to view what they purchased.
A planned file format was planned so that an authorised device such as a smartphone, media player and computer could play the content, but this was seemingly abandoned in 2015 – likely when DECE realised how difficult it would be to encourage software and hardware companies to support yet another file format particularly when the file format offered no new benefits and would require additional measures to read and verify any digital licensing.

But how did you redeem your UltraViolet code and authorise a device with your digital stream or download? Well, of course, you had to register your information. If you purchased a movie and wanted to watch it without the disc, you'd need to 'upgrade' your video for $5 with the **Disc-to-Digital** platform. Would you like a HD version of that proprietary file? That will be another $2, please!

UltraViolet technically wasn't a DRM system, it was a *digital locker* that tied you into proprietary hardware, software and file formats. That description alone makes it sound like DRM doesn't it?

Amusingly, in 2011 when movies were released giving users a code to redeem the digital version of the film, a Wikipedia discussion arose arguing that UltraViolet was not a DRM. The user, *JimTheFrog*, who started the argument to have the article updated posted the following:

> "UltraViolet is many things, including an entitlements clearinghouse with a common file format that uses standard DRMs, but it's not a DRM. Unless there are substantive objections I will change the title and change the link."

Clicking on the users Wikipedia page revealed a bit more about the user:

> "Jim Taylor is Head of Technology and Product Development for UltraViolet/DECE, the online entertainment equivalent to DVD and Blu-ray."

A little silly, considering editing a Wikipedia article that you are closely affiliated with is against the online encyclopedia's terms and conditions.
Furthermore, making it so blatantly obvious was bound to lead to ridicule. Mr Taylor's website[63] continued his defence in the FAQ saying:

> "Snide note: For years, people have complained that one of the biggest problems with DRMs is they aren't interoperable. That is, if you buy content protected by one DRM you can't play it in a player that uses a different DRM. UltraViolet made huge advances in solving the DRM compatibility problem, yet some people are now griping —inaccurately— that UltraViolet is another DRM."

Okay, we get it. It's not a DRM.

Despite being touted as a digital copy of your purchase, the paper insert found with the redemption code had some lovely small print:

---

[63] https://archive.vn/jviiz

> "If offer redeemed prior to deadline, delivery of streaming and downloads available at no additional charge for 3 years from date of redemption."

This was backed up by DECE Director Mark Teitell telling Reuters[64]:

> "Consortium members have agreed to offer the content for unlimited streaming and downloading from the cloud for at least a year...but after that time studios reserve the right to levy additional service fees"

So not only were you locked into file formats and software, you were potentially going to end up buying your video again.
I'd have loved to ask him if squeezing the customer for 'service fees' meant any benefit for the content's creators.

In July 2019, UltraViolet was shut down.
30 million users and 300 million films and TV shows stored in a digital locker, and the solution to piracy was yet another failure.
To maintain access to your digital library, you had to move your content which involved registering with another provider such as the service *Vudu*, *Flixster Video* or *Movies Anywhere*.
The end.

But wait, there's more!

Vudu was only available to users in the United States, as was the ironically named Movies Anywhere. This meant you had no choice but to move to register a Flixster Video account and migrate your digital library. I did just that.

---

[64] https://archive.vn/IJbi2

UNDER CONSTANT SUPERVISION

Then on the 23rd of January 2019, 38 days before the UltraViolet service was to shut down, I received the following email:

> *Our records indicate that your purchases and redemptions were all made at Flixster, which no longer provides UltraViolet service in your country.*
>
> *If you do not link your UltraViolet Library to a current retailer, you risk losing access to all of your movies and TV shows following UltraViolet's closure.*
>
> *We urge you to link to FandangoNOW and/or Vudu right away.*

So, I decided to move my content over to Flixster Video. *The end...?*

But then guess what?

Flixster Video announced they would be shutting down by the end of 2019[65]. My only option to maintain access was to move my collection to Google Play[66]. For the sake of it, I linked my accounts and shifted the collection over. I had about ten films, and I never used the service but figured I'd see where my voyage took me.

During the transfer, I was struck by this message on four of the ten movies:

> *Title not available in Google Play*
> *Read More*

I clicked the link and scanned through the FAQ page it led me to and was presented with this question and answer[67]:

> *Why is my video listed as unavailable for migration to Google Play?*
> *Unfortunately, a relatively small number of titles will not be available.*

---

[65] https://archive.vn/UJ15k
[66] https://archive.vn/knmuG
[67] https://archive.vn/7yHh0

I went back to the now-abandoned UltraViolet website and saw the support page with the sentences:

> Ultraviolet users who followed the directions in emails sent by Ultraviolet from January to July 2019 and linked to one or more retailers before UltraViolet shut down should be able to access some or all of their movies and TV shows.

I then saw the claim:

> "Some movies and TV shows that were in your UltraViolet Library may not be available, in which case you may wish to contact the studio or distribution company for help"

So, for a laugh, I decided I'd contact Warner Brothers, who had distributed the film. After advising me to use Movies Anywhere – still not available in my country – I requested another solution only to be told that they could not provide access to the movies in question and that I could access them on Amazon Video. When I requested an access code to Amazon Video, I was, of course, informed that this would not be possible, and that Amazon Video required a subscription. So, I gave up and downloaded the movies illegally and can now be arrested for copyright infringement. Thanks, Hollywood!

The end.
... Or at least, it is for me.

ALSO...

While researching the old UltraViolet website, I noticed the following lines in the now-defunct websites' privacy policy in relation to anyone submitting their original content – which it defines as ideas, samples, marketing plans and so on – to DECE for consideration:

[you] grant us a royalty-free, unrestricted, worldwide, perpetual, irrevocable, non-exclusive and fully transferrable, assignable and sublicensable right and license to use, reproduce, modify, translate, edit, distribute, create derivative works from, publish, perform, display, translate, syndicate, and transmit the whole or any part of your Submission (including without limitation any of the information, details, ideas, concepts and/or formats and all intellectual property rights contained within it) in any manner and in any format, media and/or technology now known or later developed (including, without limitation, archiving and making such material available on the Services); and (iv) represent and warrant that the Submissions are original to you, that no other party has any rights (including without limitation copyright or contractual rights) thereto, and that the Submissions do not violate any applicable law, regulation, or code of practice. To the extent permissible by law, you waive all moral rights subsisting in your Submissions anywhere in the world.

Does such a clause suggest that you sending them unsolicited content will lead them to making your movie and screwing you out of the rights? How ironic.

TOP SECRET//UNDER//CONSTANT//SUPERVISION//REL TO READER

The easiest way to stop piracy is not by putting antipiracy technology to work. It's by giving those people a service that's better than what they're receiving from the pirates.

- Gabe Newell
  Game developer, co-founder of Valve and Steam

FORCED PIRACY / FORCED BOYCOTTS?

Much of today's bandwidth is used for streaming services. Many people are renting content and subjecting themselves to the restrictions that come with the service they're paying for. As explored in Part Two – despite it being a little plainer when using a digital content service – convenience not only costs a small amount of money but a major part of privacy.

Streaming services like Netflix and Spotify maintain complete control over what you can watch or listen to. At any given time, the service can remove your favourite content. When companies like Disney begin their streaming services, they take their content off third-party streaming platforms to entice users to move over or subscribe to their own service on top. Users are simply renting access to the streaming service rather than owning any of the content outright. Whilst this still seems to be financially beneficial – after all, a Blu-Ray movie costs the same as 30 days of Netflix – it can be argued that companies can use their commercial, political or moral motivations to determine what can and cannot be viewed.

An example of this is the music of Michael Jackson. Streaming services threatened to remove movies, documentaries and music from the late singer after multiple posthumous allegations arose suggesting he had abused several children surfaced in the HBO documentary *Leaving Neverland*.

Some radio stations around the world ceased playing Jackson's music and online petitions were started to have his content removed from digital content providers. Some retailers reported the noticeable increase in sales of Michael Jackson's albums on vinyl, CD and DVD/BD with fans focusing on his artistic career and fearing they'd no longer be able to listen through their digital devices. Many people held the view that by boycotting Michael Jackson's music, you were devaluing the talent of everyone involved or that you were convicting a deceased artist who was not proven guilty.

The documentary was scrutinised by critics and lawmakers for its biasedness and queried the accuracy of the evidence presented. The backlash over the documentary combined with the resurgence of Michael Jackson's music led to increased digital and physical sales.

"Stark Raving Dad", an episode of the animated sitcom *The Simpsons*, in which Michael Jackson lends his voice, was pulled from syndication with writer Al Jean claiming he believed Michael Jackson had used the episode to entice young boys despite the lack of accusations against Jackson by his accusers.

When Disney – who had since acquired 21st Century Fox thus owning the rights to The Simpsons – launched their video streaming platform *Disney+* they opted to exclude the episode. It is the only episode of the sitcom that is not available to stream.

The decision was based purely on the episode's writers and Disney executives who thought *Leaving Neverland* was proof of the late singers' wrongdoing.

Jackson was accused of sexual assault in the early 1990s and settled out of court with several involved in the case defending the singer and suggesting the father of the accuser had sought excessive financial damages. The son never testified against Jackson. In 2005 Jackson went on trial for allegedly sexually assaulting a minor according to a documentary released two years prior. He was acquitted of all charges.

As you can probably guess, his albums became increasingly popular on torrent sites, as did the episode.

TOP SECRET//UNDER//CONSTANT//SUPERVISION//REL TO READER

Money spent by Hollywood to fight piracy: hundreds of millions of dollars.

- Lexi Alexander
  Director

PART FOUR:
GLOBAL SURVEILLANCE

TOP SECRET//UNDER//CONSTANT//SUPERVISION//REL TO READER

No system of mass surveillance has existed in any society that we know of to this point that has not been abused.

— Edward Snowden

SPYING ALLIANCES: AN OVERVIEW

International Surveillance Alliances have operated since the Second World War. In 1941 to an alliance known as the United Kingdom-United States of America Agreement (UKUSA) which some publications refer to as the Quadripartite Agreement or Pact.

The UKUSA agreement (*pronounced you-koo-sah*) is a multiparty arrangement for the cooperation of signals intelligence between Australia, Canada, the United Kingdom and the United States known as **Five Eyes** or **FVEY**

The extent of the initial agreement is comprehensive and includes the:
- collection of traffic.
- acquisition of communications documents and equipment.
- traffic analysis.
- cryptanalysis.
- decryption and translation; and
- acquisition of information regarding communications organisations, procedures, practices and equipment.

A draft of the original UKUSA agreement, declassified in 2010, explains that the exchange of the above-listed information:

> "will be unrestricted on all work undertaken except when specifically excluded from the agreement at the request of either party to limit such exceptions to the absolute minimum and to exercise no restrictions other than those reported and mutually
> agreed upon."

The leaks led to the formation of a U.S. Senate select committee in 1975 known as the *Church Committee*, headed by lawyer and Idaho senator Frank Church. The committee inspired the enactment of the *Foreign Intelligence Surveillance Act* which would prevent the spying on American citizens and would establish measures for physical and electronic surveillance. and the creation of the *Senate Select Committee on Intelligence.* Henry Kissinger, who was in Germany on September 11, 2001, told the media that the controls imposed on U.S. intelligence operations over the years facilitated the rise of international terrorism.

The legislations were consistently amended after the attacks. The first revelations of the Five Eyes alliance were revealed by National Security Agency (NSA) analyst Perry Fellwock in 1971 under the pen name Winslow Peck. Fellwock, or *Peck*, lifted the lid on the existence of the NSA and its worldwide covert surveillance network. At the time, the NSA was almost unknown and were among the most secretive of the US intelligence agencies. Fellwock blew the whistle on **ECHELON**, a government code name operated by the UKUSA Security Agreement's signatories.

UNITED STATES AND UNITED AUSTRALIA

In December of 1972, Gough Whitlam led the Australian Labor Party to power for the first time in 23 years. Terrorism potential was still on many people's minds, with the Summer Olympics terrorist attacks in Munich – referred to as the Munich Massacre – having taken place just a few months before.

One of Whitlam's priorities was to assist the US to neutralize the increase of politically motivated violence, with conflicts between the Yugoslavian government and Croatian ultranationalists firing up leading to the bombing of the *Yugoslav General Trade and Tourist Agency* building in Sydney. The scheduled official visit by Yugoslavian Prime Minister Džemal Bijedić created anxiety after Yugoslavian president Josip Tito stated before the visit *"We will send more agents to Australia. We will crush these people"* referring to the Croatian terrorist groups.

It was believed ASIO was involved in surveillance operations against Croatian extremists which led to Lionel Murphy, the new attorney general, prompting a raid on the headquarters of the Australian Security Intelligence Organisation (ASIO). Murphy was suspicious that ASIO was concealing information that related to Bijedić's visit.

In the aftermath of the raids, Whitlam was informed of the security alliance between Australia and the U.S. and the existence of a secret satellite station in the town of Alice Springs, Northern Territory known as Pine Gap. It was originally presented as a space research facility in 1966 called the *Joint Defence Space Research Facility*. In leaked NSA documents, the classified name is *Australian Mission Ground Station*.

Whitlam was informed that it had been operated by the Central Intelligence Agency (CIA) – something he strongly opposed.

Whitlam established a royal commission – the Royal Commission on Intelligence and Security – in August 1974 to reach findings and make suggestions to the Australian Intelligence Community (AIC)

Australia's political system was thrown into chaos in 1975 which saw Whitlam removed from office by then-Governor-General of Australia, Sir John Kerr of whom had previously joined the Association for Cultural Freedom – a conservative group that had received funding from the CIA.

The commission was conducted by Justice Robert Hope who continued the work under new Prime Minister Malcolm Fraser. The Secretary of the Department of Defence, Arthur Tange, ordered that the Commission "*should not be told too much*"

In January 1977, Yugoslav Government Learjet 25B crashed into Inac Mountain near Sarajevo killing Prime Minister Džemal Bijedić and his wife and six others. The accident was deemed pilot error which has been disputed by many conspiracy theorists.

In 1977 the commission concluded with the recommendation that ASIO should continue to be overseen by the Australian government. Hope believed that the intelligence-sharing system was too close for comfort and that the arrangement did not guarantee the intelligence information Australia requested would be received. With this suspicion, Hope asserted that Australia should develop its own SIGINT (Signals intelligence) without the five eyes partners and not modelled on British intelligence agencies MI5 and MI6. In the 1980s further commissions were put forward under Prime Minister Bob Hawke.

Hope died in 1999 at 80 years of age. He conducted an interview with the National Library of Australia that was to be released after his death. Hope revealed that he was unhappy about many of his main proposals, claiming ASIO to be an incompetent and extremely biased organisation. He claimed the Whitlam Government had used Pine Gap to spy on Japanese delegates during 1973 trade negotiations. During the 1980s commission, he found that the Hawke Government was handing raw intelligence to major Australian corporations. He claimed that ASIO was controlled by Cold War-obsessed conservatives and that "*the whole system was substantially directed to the left-wing of politics*" and that the organisation was "*deliberately designed to shield from external (and internal) scrutiny*"
Classified supplements to Hope's reports state he believed that ASIO had been "*penetrated by a hostile intelligence agency*"

According to columnist and author Brian Toohey, James Angleton, the CIA's head of counterintelligence, sought to initiate the removal of Gough Whitlam from office in 1974. Angleton asked the CIA station chief in Canberra, John Walker to request ASIO head Peter Barbour make a false declaration stating Whitlam had lied. Barbour refused.

Further details came from Christopher Boyce – a former CIA contractor who sold secret intelligence to the Soviet Union in the 1970s.
Boyce – whose life was detailed in the book and subsequent film *The Falcon and the Snowman* – claimed that Whitlam was removed from power over fears that he would close the U.S. bases in Australia, including Pine Gap.

He pointed to the U.S. government as a major factor in Whitlam's dismissal and claimed Sir John Kerr had a very close relationship with the CIA who referred to him as *"our man Kerr"*.[68]

Boyce escaped from prison in the early 1980s and carried out a string of bank robberies, hoping to pay for passage to the Soviet Union. He was returned to prison and sentenced for the escape and seventeen bank robberies.

He appeared on Australia's *60 Minutes* and discussed Whitlam's dismissal. After the interview, Boyce was beaten by inmates – an attack he claims was orchestrated by prison guards. He was released from prison on parole in September of 2002.

Pine Gap still functions today and is featured in many recent leaks as both a defence location and mass surveillance hub – for both protecting members of FVEY and otherwise.

The *Nautilus Institute for Security and Sustainability*, led by Australian defence academic Desmond Ball, released a series of reports[69] that described the facility as a ground control and processing station for geosynchronous satellites involved in signals intelligence collection.

The report claims that there are 400 Australian employees and 400 Americans. The report further states that despite being a joint effort, Pine Gap is a U.S. facility. Australian personnel do not have access to the US National Cryptographic Room. Desmond Ball remained a "person of interest" for ASIO following his inquiries into the tracking facilities. He died in 2016.

---

[68] https://archive.vn/4PZBJ

[69] https://nautilus.org/napsnet/napsnet-special-reports/australias-participation-in-the-pine-gap-enterprise/ OR
https://archive.vn/jQHak

Leaked documents reveal U.S. military satellites in stationary orbit 36,000 kilometres above Earth are commanded by operators at Pine Gap and a base in the UK. Communications are absorbed by the satellites and transferred to Pine Gap. More on this will be explored later in the chapter.

Pine Gap as seen in 2020 by satellite (image: Landsat/Copernicus © Maxar Technologies)

TOP SECRET//UNDER//CONSTANT//SUPERVISION//REL TO READER

We are rapidly entering the age of no privacy, where everyone is open to surveillance at all times, where there are no secrets from government.

- William O. Douglas
    Associate Justice of the Supreme Court of the United States (1939 - 1975)

COMMUNICATIONS

For most of us, the Internet is just *there*. We often don't sit down to appreciate the complexity of connecting to a website or the fantastic voyage that a simple '*like*' or text message goes on before reaching its destination. Whilst satellites do carry a lot of our connections, roughly 99% of the Internet is all thanks to physical cables running under the ocean. In the same vein, we often consider network maintenance to involve long lines of computer code and data servers, not large cable ships travelling across the water the world, picking up gigantic reinforced wires and inspecting the overall structural integrity for what is essentially a mass of spaghetti telephone wires, each strand rising to the surface connecting to a giant phone. The cables reach land points across the world known as *cable landing stations* or *landing points*

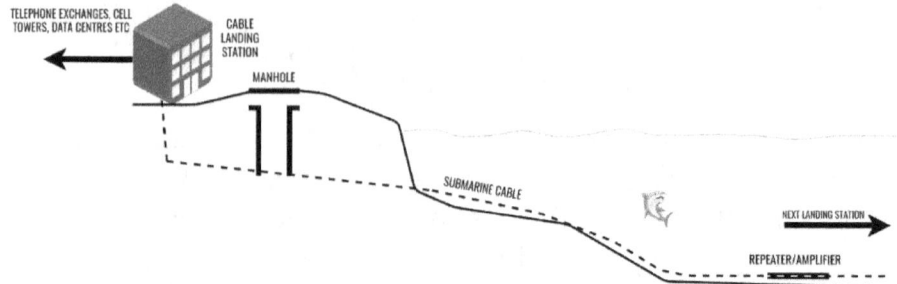

Almost all cable construction is handled by Alcatel Submarine Networks, Subcom, NEC and Huawei Marine and whilst major outages have happened due to earthquakes and other natural events, it would take a lot to knock the Internet out in a physical sense due to the advancement of 'self-healing' fibre optic cables and 'mesh networks' which allow switching to ensure redundancy. Surveillance remains a concern with so many publicly-known passages of submarine cables. Brazil and Europe planned a separate submarine cable network, concerned with U.S. intrusion[70]

In March 2007, pirates stole an 11km stretch of the T-V-H cable (Thailand – Vietnam – Hong Kong) and attempted to sell the salvage[71].

There have even been cases where sharks have had a cheeky little munch on cables.

At the beginning of 2020, it was estimated that approximately 406 submarine cables were in service with over 1.2 million kilometres of submarine cable across the ocean floor. Traditionally, private companies or consortiums have formed by telecom carriers owned cables are were responsible for their rollout and maintenance. In recent years Google, Facebook, Microsoft and Amazon have invested in new cables to deal with the tremendous demand for their data centre traffic.

---

[70] https://www.reuters.com/article/us-eu-brazil-idUSBREA1N0PL20140224 **OR** https://archive.vn/K23yo

[71] http://lirneasia.net/2007/06/vietnams-submarine-cable-lost-and-found/ **OR** https://archive.vn/40vv

UNDER CONSTANT SUPERVISION

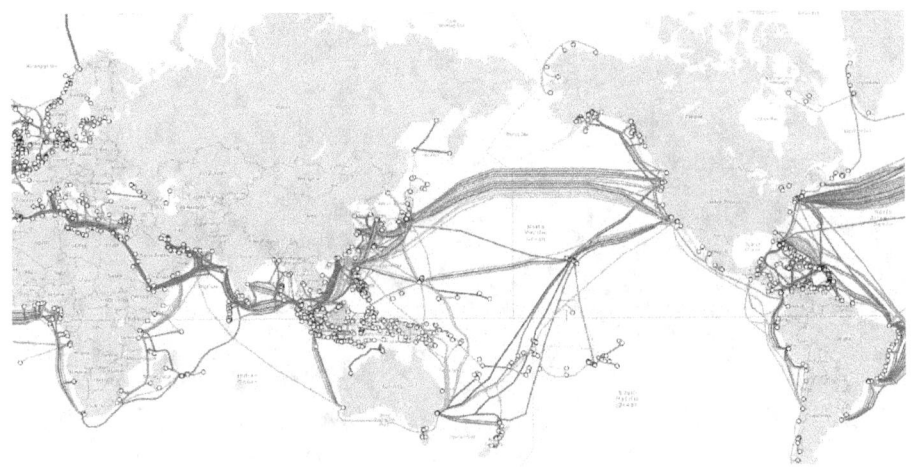

Cables...so...many...cables...
© *TeleGeography*
https://submarinecablemap.com

Due to the complexity of the ocean floor and environmental conditions, Antarctica is the only location not connected by cable. Communications are dealt with by satellite and radio. If you want the best solution to escape *some* spying by elite government networks, pack warm clothes.

Roughly every 100km, cables have repeaters installed which amplify the connections to ensure the speed doesn't degrade and the data remains consistent along its epic journey underwater.
Sometimes these are referred to as 'regeneration spots'
These have been used for *'cable tapping'* in modern-day applications.

ABOVE - NEC Cable Repeaters | BELOW – "Cable Partners" listed in NSA documents

Cable	UK?	REMEDY	GERONTIC	DACRON	Partner LITTLE	PINNAGE	STREET CAR	VITREOUS
Apollo	UK	IRU/LC	DCO	IRU/LC	IRU/LC		IRU/LC	
CANTAT 3	UK	DCO	IRU/LC					
Concerto	UK						DCO	
EIG	UK	DCO	DCO	DCO				
Flag Atlantic 1	UK			IRU/LC	IRU/LC			
Flag EA	UK	IRU/LC	IRU/LC	IRU/LC				
Hibernia	UK				IRU/LC			IRU/LC
Solas	UK		DCO					
SMW-3	UK	DCO	IRU/LC	DCO				
Tangerine	UK				DCO			
TAT-14	UK	DCO	DCO	DCO	DCO			
Tata TGN-Atlantic	UK	IRU/LC						
Tata TGN-Western Europe	UK	IRU/LC						
UK-France 3	UK	DCO	DCO					
UK-Germany 6	UK	DCO	DCO					
UK-Ireland (QX)	UK						DCO	
UK-Netherlands 14	UK	DCO	DCO					
Ulysses	UK			DCO				
Yellow/AC-2	UK	IRU/LC			DCO	DCO		
AAG		DCO						
AC-1		IRU/LC		IRU/LC	IRU/LC	DCO		
Americas II			IRU/LC	DCO	DCO	DCO		
APCN-2		DCO	DCO	DCO				
APCN		IRU/LC	IRU/LC	DCO				
ARCOS					IRU/LC	DCO		
Antillas 1				DCO				
Atlantis II				DCO				
Australia-Japan Cable		IRU/LC	IRU/LC	DCO				
Bahamas 2				DCO				
Carac			DCO					
Cayman-Jamaica FS			DCO					
China-US			IRU/LC		DCO			
Circe N								DCO
Circe S								DCO
Columbus III				DCO				
Denmark-Poland 2		IRU/LC						
Denmark-Russia 1		IRU/LC						
Flag Falcon							IRU/LC	
Flag North Asia Loop			IRU/LC					
Gemini Bermuda			DCO					
Globenet			IRU/LC					
GO-1							IRU/LC	
Guam-Philippines				DCO				
Italy-Malta							IRU/LC	
Japan-US		DCO	DCO	DCO	DCO	IRU/LC		
Kattegat			DCO					
Latvia-Sweden			DCO					
MAC						DCO		
Maya-1		DCO	DCO	DCO		DCO		
PAC						DCO		
Pan American				DCO				
PC-1			IRU/LC	IRU/LC				
PEC						DCO		
Russia-Japan-Korea				DCO				
SAC/LAN						DCO		
SAFE		DCO	DCO	DCO				
SAT-3/WASC		DCO	DCO	DCO				
SMW-4				DCO			IRU/LC	
Southern Cross		IRU/LC	IRU/LC		IRU/LC	IRU/LC		
Sweden-Finland			DCO					
Taino-Carib			DCO					
TPC-5				DCO				
TPE				DCO				

CABLE TAPPING

These cables were frequently 'tapped' by the NSA (and perhaps still are) especially during the Cold War. Submarine cables give intelligence agencies the ultimate ability to pry – or even destroy – communications of the enemy.

Such examples can be traced to the Cold War (1947 – 1991) In the early 1970s, the United States government discovered the presence of an undersea communications cable in the Sea of Okhotsk in the Pacific Ocean.
The joint surveillance operation, known as *Operation Ivy Bells*, was undertaken by the United States Navy, CIA and the NSA.

The Operation successfully discovered a submarine cable connected to a Soviet naval base somewhere on the Kamchatka Peninsula.

A cable tapping "pod" / device laid by the US Submarine

The cables used were copper. Copper wires radiate electromagnetic energy which can transmit small amounts of information that can be safely intercepted by a recording device around the cable.

Just over 120 metres below the surface, a waterproof 'tap' was installed. If Russia ever pulled the cables up for repair, the tap device would remain on the seafloor, undetected.

Divers were deployed monthly to retrieve the recordings and replace the tapes. The submarines used to transport divers – who often didn't have security clearances as to avoid detection – were disguised as diving chambers.

When the tapes were returned to the NSA, they would analyse the recordings. The data was never encrypted and so deciphering was not necessary, perhaps due to the Soviet government being too confident about the security of the cables.

In 1981, America realised a warship had been sitting above the location surveillance imagery revealed a warship had been deployed to the location. When divers were sent to recover the 6-metre 5500kg device, it was nowhere to be seen.

Ronald Pelton served in the United States Air Force where he learned Russian. In the 60s he was a voice intercept processing specialist in Pakistan for 15 months. When the tour ended, he was transferred to the NSA. In 1979, Pelton left his position and filed for personal bankruptcy.

In 1980, Pelton contacted the Soviet Embassy in Washington, D.C. and arranged for a meeting. Little did he know, the FBI had tapped the phone lines and knew of the caller but not were unable to discover his identity at the time of the meeting.

KGB officer Vitaly Yurchenko debriefed Pelton and agreed to pay him for information. That year Pelton flew to Austria and stayed the residence of the Soviet Ambassador and spent eight hours divulging information about America's surveillance programs to KGB officer Anatoly Slavnov. Pelton had no documents and so relied on memory. He returned to Austria in 1983 with more information, despite no longer working in intelligence. He was paid roughly $37,000 for the information – about $95,000 in today's money.

In 1985, Yurchenko defected to the US and recalled the meeting with a red-haired former NSA analyst who had alerted the Soviets to the location of the tap. The FBI dug through NSA personnel files until narrowing their search down to a handful of red-haired males. They identified Pelton's voice and commenced observation, bugging his car and home.

Unable to find anything incriminating, the FBI confronted Pelton directly, playing the bugged recordings from the Soviet embassy five years prior. Pelton was convicted of espionage in 1986 and sentenced to three life terms plus 10 years in prison as well as a $100 fine (around $240 today)

RONALD PELTON
Register Number: 22914-037
Released: 24 Nov 2015

Pelton spent almost 30 years at a medium-security prison in Pennsylvania before being released in November 2015. According to the Bureau of Prisons, he spent the last months of his sentence in a halfway house to aid with his reintegration into society. He was 74 years old when released.

What makes Ronald Pelton's case unique is that unlike nearly every other espionage allegation including those against Edward Snowden, he did not steal documents. His former co-workers told the media that he had an exceptional memory with encyclopaedic expertise of the NSA's intelligence activities. [72]

Vitaly Yurchenko disappeared about a month after Pelton was arrested. He told his CIA guard "I'm going for a walk, if I don't come back, it's not your fault"
The Soviet Embassy a press conference, at which Yurchenko announced he had been kidnapped and drugged by the Americans. The KGB was reported to have covertly interrogated Yurchenko after his return, under the influence of truth serum, to ensure he had not been employed by the CIA as a double agent. It is unsure if he defected to America and regretted it, or defected to gain intelligence and return – the latter of which has been debated as improbable due to conflicts with the Russian image that it was "paradise"
Whatever the truth, Yurchenko was awarded the Order of the Red Star.

---

[72] *"Accused Spy Ronald Pelton Was Preoccupied with Money"* – Washington Post, 7th Dec 1985

Operation Ivy Bells is considered the first time in history underwater submarine cable surveillance has taken place. As a result of the intelligence gathered from the submarine cable, more taps were installed on Soviet lines worldwide, with more advanced nuclear-powered instruments built by *Bell Laboratories* (now *Nokia Bell Labs*) that could store years' worth of data.

The captured device is now on public display at the Great Patriotic War Museum in Moscow, Russia.

Grand Jury Indictment[73]:

JGD:fc

DEC 2 0 1985

IN THE UNITED STATES DISTRICT COURT
FOR THE DISTRICT OF MARYLAND

UNITED STATES OF AMERICA	CRIMINAL NO. HM 85-0621
v.	(Conspiracy to Deliver National Defense Information to a Foreign Government, 18 U.S.C. § 794(c); Delivery of National Defense Information to a Foreign Government, 18 U.S.C. § 794(a); Transmission of Information Concerning the Communication Intelligence Activities of the United States to an Unauthorized Person, 18 U.S.C. § 798(a); Aiding and Abetting, 18 U.S.C § 2)
RONALD WILLIAM PELTON	

****

INDICTMENT

The Grand Jury for the District of Maryland charges that:

A. INTRODUCTION

1. RONALD WILLIAM PELTON was employed by the National Security Agency (NSA) from November 1965 through July 1979.

2. Throughout his employment at NSA, RONALD WILLIAM PELTON possessed a Top Secret security clearance with additional clearances for compartmented information relating to signals intelligence. In the course of that employment, he obtained a wide range of information relating to the national defense of the United States of America.

3. At times relevant to this Indictment, Anatoly Slavnov was an agent, officer and employee of the government of the Union of Soviet Socialist Republics.

[73] Full version available: https://git.io/JvbBc

UNDER CONSTANT SUPERVISION

This section features relevant slides and documents found within the surveillance leaks.

Any redacted documents in this section were redacted prior to release.

Some media outlets chose to redact their files.

Left: published by *Der Spiegel*, Right: published by *The Guardian*.

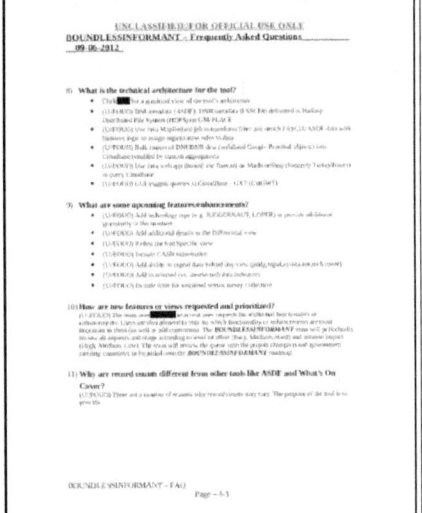

TOP SECRET//UNDER//CONSTANT//SUPERVISION//REL TO READER

The first condition of progress is the removal of censorship.

- George Bernard Shaw
  Playwright and political activist

THE EDWARD SNOWDEN REVELATIONS

On May 20th of 2013, NSA contractor Edward Snowden left his job at a National Security Agency facility in Hawaii. Snowden claimed he required epilepsy treatment on the mainland. He flew to Hong Kong instead of the United States.
In June he revealed thousands of classified NSA documents smuggled from his former employer to journalists Ewen MacAskill, Glenn Greenwald, and Laura Poitras.

Edward Snowden
(Photo: Laura Poitras / Praxis Films)

The documents revealed global surveillance, like that of which had been revealed by Fellwock in the 1970s, had extended its reach into major corporations and that the NSA along with several other intelligence agencies worldwide were using multiple hacking tools to spy on millions of residents around the world. The information would be distributed by a carefully selected group of news outlets.

From his hotel in Hong Kong, Snowden applied for political asylum to 21 countries. Then-Vice President Joe Biden pressured governments to refuse all asylum petitions received by Snowden. On July 1, 2013, Russian President Vladimir Putin stated that he would consider Snowden's application for asylum under the condition he would "stop his work aimed at harming our American partners"

Initially withdrawing his application, based on the conditions, Snowden flew to Moscow's Sheremetyevo Airport. Upon arrival, he learned his U.S. passport had been revoked. He spent nearly 6 weeks in the airport terminal before being granted the political right for asylum and a one-year residence visa on August 1, 2013.

Snowden's disclosure revealed that NSA tools were used to scrape data from unaware users without any authority. One of the tools known as *XKeyscore* allowed analysts to search with no prior through extensive databases containing emails, online chat logs and browser history of individuals anywhere in the world.

> *"A small team of trusted senior reporters examined Snowden's files in a secure fourth-floor room in the Guardian's King's Cross office. The material was kept on four laptops. None had ever been connected to the Internet or any other network. There were numerous other security measures, including round-the-clock guards, multiple passwords, and a ban on electronics."*
>
> *Luke Hardy, The Guardian, January 2014*

Guardian correspondent Luke Harding tells in his book *The Snowden Files: The Inside Story of the World's Most Wanted Man* the lengths the UK government went to contain the information and ensure that the documents – which had already been released – were destroyed securely. Guardian editor Paul Johnson was threatened with the possibility of the Prime Minister shutting down the newspaper. It took several weeks of negotiations, but despite the world now knowing what global surveillance was taking place, the Government Communications Headquarters (GCHQ) ordered the destruction of the computers used.

Two technicians from GCHQ supervised journalists who used power tools including angle-grinders and rotary drills to destroy the internal components. Johnson described the demands as a "purely symbolic act" and claimed that it was the *"most surreal event [that he had] witnessed in British journalism"*

Snowden's story is a complex web of decisions and consequences that can be explored in his 2019 autobiography *Permanent Record.*
As of 2020, he remains in Russia with his long-term girlfriend Lindsay Mills, of whom he revealed are now married. President Vladimir Putin told American film director Oliver Stone – of whom directed the 2016 film, *Snowden*– in *The Putin Interviews* that he believed Snowden was "wrong" to leak the secrets but did not consider him a traitor.

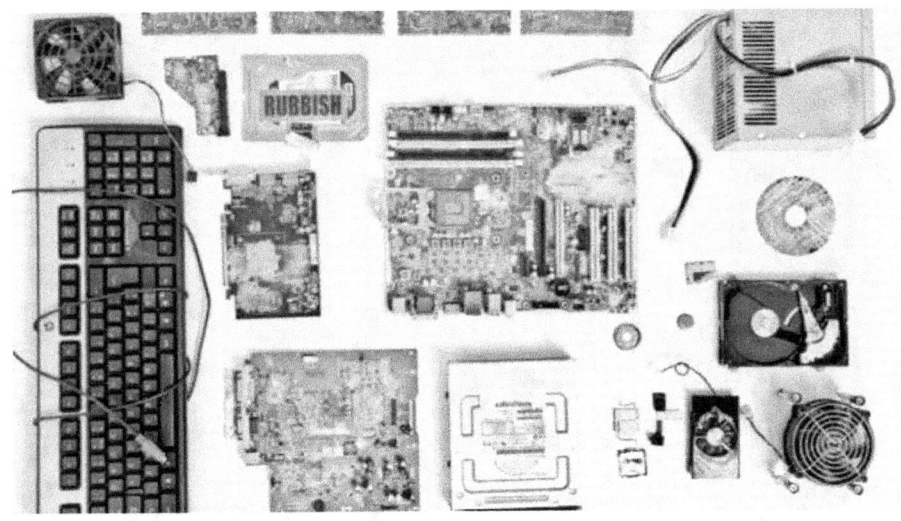

Components destroyed by Guardian staff under watchful eye of GCHQ technicians
© The Guardian

Snowden's documents mostly featured slideshow presentations detailing the methods used by various alliances to spy on the globe for security and to retain information on any potential suspect. In many of the cases, this involved unlawful surveillance. Some slides claim that spy programs had played a major part in capturing 300 terrorists before 2008. The documents do not, however, cite instances of terrorism interference or captures made possible by the surveillance.

The known alliances, subsequent bureaus and **public** surveillance programs are as follows:

FIVE EYES (FVEY)

(Also known under intelligence sharing agreements *UKUSA* and *ECHELON*)

Five eyes include the following five English-speaking countries.

- Australia
    - Australian Secret Intelligence Service (ASIS)
    - Australian Signals Directorate (ASD)
    - Australian Security Intelligence Organisation (ASIO)
    - Australian Geospatial-Intelligence Organisation (AGO)
    - Defence Intelligence Organisation (DIO)
- Canada
    - Canadian Forces Intelligence Command (CFINTCOM)
    - Communications Security Establishment (CSE)
    - Canadian Security Intelligence Service (CSIS)
- New Zealand
    - Director of Defence Intelligence and Security (DDIS)
    - Government Communications Security Bureau (GCSB)
    - New Zealand Security Intelligence Service (NZSIS)
- United Kingdom
    - Defence Intelligence (DI)
    - Government Communications Headquarters (GCSB)

- o British Security Service (MI5)
  - o Secret Intelligent Service (MI6, SIS)
- United States of America
  - o Central Intelligence Agency (CIA)
  - o Defense Intelligence Agency (DIA)
  - o Federal Bureau of Investigation (FBI)
  - o National Geospatial-Intelligence Agency (NGA)
  - o National Security Agency (NSA)

AUSTRALIA

In 2015 Australia implemented the "Data Retention Laws" which is a scheme to track every phone call, text message and email sent by citizens, implemented for protection against organised crime and terrorism. In 2012, Prime Minister Julia Gillard's Labour government devised the idea. Prime Minister Tony Abbott and his Liberal government would introduce the laws into parliament a few years later. Justification once again was placed on protecting the country from terror threats and attacks both locally and abroad. The metadata legally collected includes:

- Emails and their recipients.
- The time and date of the email
- The location and platform from which the email was sent
- The subject line
- Locations and settings of photos and camera models used
- IP addresses and history (allowed, but not mandatory)

Information is stored locally and offshore in various data centres. During the 2020 Corona Virus outbreak, police in South Australia revealed that they had been granted the ability to access metadata of infected Chinese people who had travelled to Adelaide to establish potential locations and the possibility the virus had been spread by those in question.

A bill was raised in 2019 to enact Facial Identification and Verification laws to distinguish the identity of individuals accessing gambling and pornographic websites. Whilst the Home Affairs office claimed the main focus would be to prevent identity crime, the submission read that *"This could assist in age verification, for example by preventing a minor from using their parent's driver licence to circumvent age verification controls."*

Additionally, Western Australia prepared for national biometrics sharing in March of 2020 which would allow driver's licences, photo identification and signatures for 'easier' verification[74]

Australia was ordered to cease intelligence work on East Timor in 2014 by the judicial body of the United Nations known as the *World Court* or *International Court of Justice (ICJ)*. This marked the first time that any of the Five Eyes countries have been commanded to stop infiltration.

UNITED KINGDOM

Like Australia's metadata retention laws, the United Kingdom introduced the Investigatory Powers Act in 2016 which allowed ISP's and telecommunication companies to record browsing history, connections and text messages. The data is permitted to be stored for up to two years and is accessible to any United Kingdom government agency as well as their associates without the need for a warrant. The act itself contains the following obligations:

- UK intelligence agencies and law enforcement can carry out targeted interception of communications, bulk collection of communications data, and bulk interception of communications.

---

[74] https://www.itnews.com.au/news/wa-prepares-for-national-face-matching-database-upload-539863   OR
https://archive.vn/NkjL7

- Communication service providers (CSPs) must retain UK Internet users' connection records which include any websites visited - but not specific pages and history - for one year
- Police, intelligence officers and authorised government agencies are permitted to view Internet connection records, as part of a targeted and filtered investigation, without the need for a warrant.
- Police and intelligence agencies are permitted to carry out targeted equipment interference to any device to access data. Permission is also given for bulk equipment interference for the sake of national security matters related to foreign investigations.
- CSPs are legally obliged to assist with the targeted interception of data and equipment (however, foreign companies are not required to engage in bulk collection of data or communications)

It was also made a criminal offence for the Communication Service Provider or any of its employees to notify anyone that the data had been intercepted or requested.

Safeguards to protect politicians, journalists, lawyers and doctors from the Act were brought in.

THE UNITED STATES, CANADA AND NEW ZEALAND

It should come as no surprise that these countries have similar collection procedures with laws enforced to require ISPs and online businesses to comply with data requests. Despite it being commonplace already, 2017 saw the United States officially grant legal authority for service providers to collect and sell customer data.

All Five Eyes countries have the power to force companies to collect and supply data to authorised agencies.

NINE EYES

Nine Eyes is an alliance that includes all Five Eyes countries, but also adds four non-English speaking countries: Denmark, France, Netherlands and Norway. Whilst no official sources detail the exact rules of these additional nations, it is presumed that the scope of abilities is like those under *Five Eyes*.

SIGINT SENIORS EUROPE (FOURTEEN EYES)

14 Eyes is the *unofficial* name for SIGINT Seniors Europe (SSEUR) and include all countries within 9 Eyes with the addition of Germany, Belgium, Italy, Sweden and Spain. The surveillance agreement is again presumed similar to the previous alliances.

FVEY COLLABORATORS

According to the "NSA Map", collaborators or "third party" spies are involved in partnerships with FVEY countries and share data carried along the SEA-ME-WE-3 and SEA-ME-WE-4 *(South-East Asia – Middle East – Western Europe)* telecommunications cables that runs from Singapore to Southern France. Partners include Israel, Japan, Singapore and South Korea. NATO allies including Denmark and Germany are connected to the sharing scheme.

The partners are remunerated for their collaborations with money or surveillance technology.

An alliance referred to as including "like-minded partners" is called **FIVE EYES PLUS THREE AGAINST CHINA AND RUSSIA** and involves the sharing of threats ascending from China and Russia. The partners are France, Germany and Japan.

FIVE EYES PLUS THREE AGAINST NORTH KOREA involves France, Japan and South Korea sharing information pertaining to military activities carried out by North Korea.

The NSA and GCHQ released documents in 2010 detailing the agreement. To download the documents from The National Archives website, you must first register your information with the department.[75]

---

[75] Download them via the BookRefine repository – 1955 Agreement: https://git.io/JvjrS
1946 Agreement: https://git.io/JvjrH

THE [ALLEGED] ESPIONAGE AND INTERVENTION OF FVEY THROUGHOUT HISTORY

In 1996, acting as a whistleblower, the CIA reported that French company Thomson-Alcatel had been paying bribes to secure a contract with the Government of Brazil to monitor the Amazon rainforest. As a result, major U.S. defence contractor the *Raytheon Company* secured the $1.3 billion contract. Using radars, satellites and aviation censors, the contract was the largest non-military surveillance project of the time.[76]
The company later developed alliances with The Boeing Company.

During the 1990s, the NSA intercepted communications between European aviation and aerospace titans Airbus and the Saudi Arabian national airline. In 1994, Airbus lost a $6 billion contract after the NSA played whistleblower and reported Airbus officials had been bribing Saudi officials to secure the contract. This led to American aerospace manufacturing and defence contractor McDonnell Douglas to gain the contract instead. McDonell Douglas would merge with Boeing just a few years later.

---

[76] https://archive.vn/SzrWC

NOTABLE TARGETS OF FVEY

Nobody is safe from the surveillance, not even political leaders, and celebrities from around the world. Just a few confirmed cases show that:

The NSA intercepted the phone calls of Diana, Princess of Wales up until the moment she died in Paris with Dodi Fayed in 1997. [77] The NSA holds over 1000 pages of classified information which remains top secret due to disclosure being *"expected to cause exceptionally grave damage to the national security"*.
NSA officials have claimed the references to Diana are "incidental" in nature and that she was not herself a target of NSA surveillance. The documents remain top-secret as they allegedly cause security issues over "intelligence gathering"

A BBC report from 2000 claims the Communications Security Establishment spied on two British cabinet ministers in the 1980s at the request of UK PM Margaret Thatcher[78]

Charlie Chaplin was targeted by MI5 and FBI agents to expel the filmmaker from America due to alleged links to communism[79], especially for his statement: *"There is a great deal of good in communism. We can use the good and segregate the bad"* and his arguments against capitalism. Chaplin was one of 300 Hollywood stars placed on an FBI blacklist.

During his protests against the Vietnam War, Beatles star John Lennon was under surveillance by the FBI and MI5 for over twelve months.

---

[77] *The Guardian*, 6 August 1999 and *The Sunday Times*, 27 February 2000
[78] https://archive.vn/VusWp
[79] https://www.theguardian.com/uk/2012/feb/17/mi5-spied-on-charlie-chaplin

UNDER CONSTANT SUPERVISION

In 1962, Nelson Mandela was arrested after details of alleged terrorist activities were discovered by the CIA and MI6 agents were handed over to South African authorities.

Germany's chancellor Angela Merkel was scrutinized by various Special Collection Services agents under the STATEROOM program to be explored.

The Australian Signals Directorate (ASD) placed President of Indonesia Susilo Bambang Yudhoyono and his wife Ani amongst other Indonesian politicians under surveillance and shared the information with the NSA[80]. The leaked slide containing the motto: "Reveal their secrets – protect our own"

Actress and political activist Jane Fonda and her husband Tom Hayden were intercepted by GCHQ who handed the communication data over to the NSA in the 1970s[81].

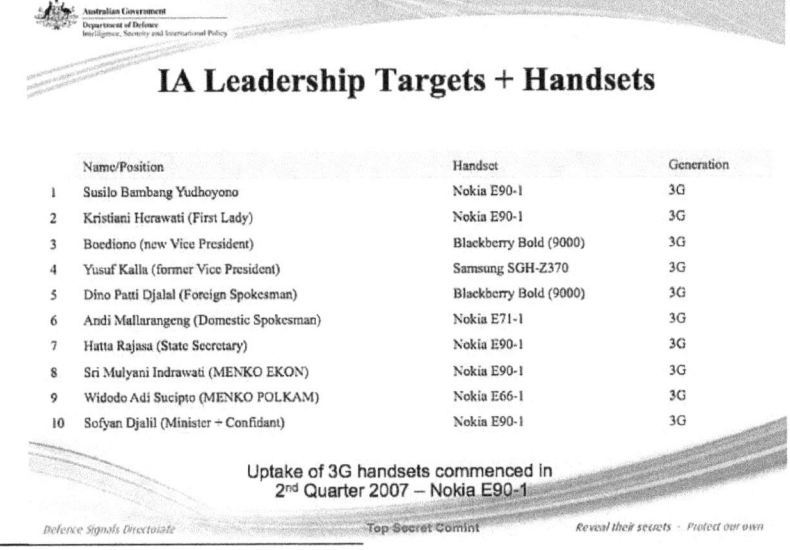

[80] https://www.abc.net.au/news/2013-11-18/australia-spied-on-indonesian-president,-leaked-documents-reveal/5098860 **OR** https://archive.vn/W3pvs

[81] *The Vancouver Sun – August 13, 1982* newspaper clipping at https://git.io/JvhzZ

153

Internet entrepreneur and founder of Megaupload, Kim Dotcom was a victim of surveillance when the GCSB of New Zealand spied on he and his family on behalf of the FBI after the website was taken down by the Department of Justice for alleged copyright infringement facilitation and his New Zealand home was raided by U.S. forces.

American paediatrician Benjamin Spock of whom wrote the guide *The Common Sense Book of Baby and Child Care* was targeted for his anti-Vietnam War stance and his opposition to male circumcision.

Black Panther leader Eldridge Cleaver was also a victim of surveillance.

Al Jazeera, Russian airliner Aeroflot and even financial institutions Mastercard and Visa have been victims of hacking by the NSA during attempts to link information to transactions.

MULTIPLE ACTS OF ABUSE

The U.S. government uses Section 702 to justify all surveillance exposed. Section 702 of the Foreign Intelligence Surveillance Act (FISA) is a bill that allows the collection, use, and dissemination of electronic communications content stored by U.S. Internet service providers (such as Google, Facebook, and Microsoft) or touring across the Internet's "backbone" (essentially, the connections and hardware that provide the web as we know it)
This, in simple terms, allows warrantless surveillance to occur.

Section 215 of the USA Patriot Act gives authorisation for collection of all records from a target *and* anyone who has communicated with that target. This involves the Call Detail Records (CDR) program which gives the government the ability to store information on anyone they suspect of wrongdoing. For example, if the suspect (target) has received a phone call from a company asking for feedback, the records from the *entire* company would be collected.
In 2018 the CDR program collected nearly half a billion records. When caught out for the surveillance, the NSA released a statement claiming it was a mistake and blamed *"technical irregularities"* that had occurred between 2015-2018[82]
A few months later, CDR had another *"technical irregularity"* and claimed they had voluntarily shut the program down. When a government agency has bad press and names like "Call Detail Records" are out there in the media, they shut the programs down and prepare another one as will be clear over the next few pages.

---

[82] https://archive.vn/o5yP9 **OR** https://www.nsa.gov/news-features/press-room/Article/1618691/nsa-reports-data-deletion/

U.S. Director of National Intelligence James Clapper had stated under oath to congress months before the Snowden documents released that the NSA did not collect data.

The transcript reveals the following exchange between U.S. Senator Ron Wyden and James Clapper:

SENATOR RON WYDEN: *"This is for you, Director Clapper, again on the surveillance front. And I hope we can do this in just a yes or no answer because I know Senator Feinstein wants to move on. Last summer, the NSA director was at a conference, and he was asked a question about the NSA surveillance of Americans. He replied, and I quote here, 'The story that we have millions or hundreds of millions of dossiers on people is completely false.'*

"The reason I'm asking the question is, having served on the committee now for a dozen years, I don't really know what a dossier is in this context. So, what I wanted to see is if you could give me a yes or no answer to the question, does the NSA collect any type of data at all on millions or hundreds of millions of Americans?"

DIRECTOR JAMES CLAPPER: *"No, sir."*
SENATOR RON WYDEN: *"It does not?"*
DIRECTOR JAMES CLAPPER: *"Not wittingly"*

Responding to the allegations of false testimony after Snowden's leaks, Clapper stated he had misunderstood Senator Wyden's question and that he answered what he thought was the *"least untruthful manner"*
He later issued an apology[83].

---

[83]https://www.dni.gov/files/documents/2013-06-21%20DNI%20Ltr%20to%20Sen.%20Feinstein.pdf **OR** https://www.webcitation.org/6I9BnJX1H

Despite demands for Clapper to resign, he maintained his "forgetfulness" was to blame. White House National Security Council spokesperson Caitlin Hayden released a statement that President Barack Obama had *"full faith in Director Clapper's leadership of the intelligence community. The Director has explained his answers to Senator Wyden and made clear that he did not intend to mislead the Congress."*
Clapper remained director and resigned at the end of President Obama's term at the beginning of 2017.

This event wasn't the first time Clapper had been called out for his unsubstantiated claims. In 2003 when he was head of the National Geospatial-Intelligence Agency, he explained the reason America could not prove weapons of mass destruction were in Iraq was due to *"personal assessment"* that the weapons were *"unquestionably"* shipped out of Iraq to Syria and others before America invaded.

Section 215 has a long history of abuse since September 11, 2001, and to fully understand why the NSA and affiliated agencies were given powers and justifications to commit mass surveillance, one needs to investigate the War on terror.
Since the 1980s, the U.S. has been in dispute with the Middle East, within weeks of the 9/11 attacks, this dispute had flared up to what is considered the *main phase* of the war.

Multiple factors make up the various acts that permitted mass surveillance to take place. A few of these Acts and abilities are:

FISA – Foreign Intelligence Surveillance Act
United States federal law that establishes procedures for physical and electronic surveillance and collection of "foreign intelligence information" between "foreign powers" and "agents of foreign powers" suspected of espionage or terrorism

SECTION 215 of FISA –
"Access to records and other items under the Foreign Intelligence Surveillance Act"

FISC – Foreign Intelligence Surveillance Court
Sometimes referred to as the FISA Court, the federal court that oversees requests for surveillance warrants often made by the NSA and FBI.

USA PATRIOT Act –
Act signed into law by President George W. Bush in October 2001. PATRIOT stands for *Uniting and Strengthening America by Providing Appropriate Tools Required to Intercept and Obstruct Terrorism* and is listed as: *"An Act to deter and punish terrorist acts in the United States and across the globe, to enhance law enforcement investigatory tools, and for other purposes."*

National Security Letters –
The PATRIOT Act gives the FBI the ability to issue National Security Letters without a court order. These letters demand a variety of records including phone records, bank account information and Internet activity.

KEY EVENTS IN THE WAR ON TERROR AND LOCAL INTELLIGENCE GATHERING:

11 September 2001:
A series of coordinated terrorist attacks take place by Islamic group al-Qaeda on Tuesday, September 11, 2001. Four passenger airlines are hijacked by nineteen al-Qaeda-affiliated terrorists. Two planes are crashed into the North and South towers of the World Trade Center complex in Manhattan, New York. One plane is crashed into the headquarters of the U.S. Department of Defense – the Pentagon – and another fails to make it to Washington, D.C. and crashes into a field in Pennsylvania.

13 September 2001:
Bush states apprehending bin Laden is his main concern saying: *"The most important thing is for us to find Osama bin Laden. It is our number one priority and we will not rest until we find him"*

20 September 2001:
George W. Bush demands the Taliban government of Afghanistan hand over Osama bin Laden and al-Qaeda leaders operating in the country or face vengeance. (The phrase "War on Terror" is used officially during Bush's address)

21 September 2001:
Taliban ambassador to Pakistan, Abdul Salam Zaeef, announces refusal to comply with Bush's demands and asks the United Nations to investigate the attacks saying *"If they want to show their might, we are ready and we will never surrender before might and force"*
The Taliban then demands evidence bin Laden was responsible for or linked to, the attacks.

7 October 2001:
British and U.S. forces conduct airstrike campaigns over enemy targets. This is the official beginning of the main phase of War on Terror with the invasion leading to al-Qaeda retreating to the mountains of Afghanistan – Tora Bora. This date marks the *War in Afghanistan* with the invasion taking place under the codename *Operation Enduring Freedom.*

26 October 2001:
Congress passes the PATRIOT Act to allow the search and electronic surveillance of federal agencies while investigating terror suspects.

November 2001:
Department of Justice Office of Legal Counsel concludes that FISA *"cannot restrict President"*
Soldiers begin distribution of leaflets in Afghanistan offering a $25 million reward for bin Laden's capture. This is later raised to $27 million with donations from the *Airline Pilots Association* and *Air Transport Association.*

6-17 December 2001:
U.S. forces and allies commence the *Battle of Tora Bora* claiming al-Qaeda are headquartered in caves with Bin Laden. 200 al-Qaeda and Taliban fighters are killed, but it is suspected that bin Laden has escaped. On the 13th the Pentagon releases a video purportedly showing bin Laden discussing the attacks with dinner guests in Afghanistan.

January 2002:
Guantanamo Bay detention camp is opened.

16 October 2002:
The Iraq Resolution is passed by U.S. Congress, sanctioning military action against Iraq.

November 2002:
Saddam Hussein invites United Nations weapons inspectors into the country after the United States alleges Iraq's weapon's declaration leaves materials unaccounted for.

8 November 2002:
Saddam Hussein is accused of having Weapons of Mass Destruction. The United Nations Security Council adopts *Resolution 1441* which offers Hussein's regime a *"final opportunity to comply with its disbarment obligations"*

25 November 2002:
The United States Department of Homeland Security is created.

January 2003:
United Nations weapons inspectors report no indication that Iraq possesses nuclear weapons or an active program.

5 February 2003:
Secretary of State, Colin Powell, addresses a session of the United Nations Security Council stating Saddam Hussein is working to obtain key components to produce nuclear weapons.

11 March 2004:
The PATRIOT Act is reauthorised by Bush. The Madrid train bombings in Spain kill 193 people and leave over 2,000 people injured. It is the deadliest European attack since the 1988 bombing of Pan Am Flight 103 over Lockerbie in Scotland. The U.S. later revealed to have blocked access to al-Qaeda cell responsible[84].

19/20 March 2003:
Invasion of Iraq begins which sees the U.S., UK, Australia and Poland carry out combat operations. Bush addresses America from the Oval Office: *"The people of the United States and our friends and allies will not live at the mercy of an outlaw regime that threatens the peace with weapons of mass murder."*

13 December 2003:
Operation Red Dawn leads to capture of Saddam Hussein who is found hiding in a 'spider hole' near a farmhouse in Iraq.

30 June 2004:
U.S. forces hand over Saddam Hussein to the temporary Iraqi government to stand trial for crimes against humanity.

---

[84] *"Spain furious as US blocks access to Madrid bombing 'chief.*
The Times. London, UK. February 2007 states "The al-Qaeda leader who created, trained and directed the terrorist cell that carried out the Madrid train bombings has been held in a CIA "ghost prison" for more than a year.

9 July 2004:
The United States Senate Select Committee on Intelligence releases The Senate Report on Iraqi WMD intelligence, concluding that the Bush Administration's statements about Iraqi WMD were misleading and unsupported by intelligence information.

7 July 2005:
London bombings take place targeting commuters during peak transport times killing 52 people and injuring more than 700. Deadliest British attack since Lockerbie. Britain's first Islamist suicide attack.

1 October 2005:
Suicide bombings are carried out in Kuta, Bali in Indonesia known as the *2005 Bali Bombings*.
15 Indonesians, 4 Australians and 1 Japanese are killed with over 100 injured.

December 2005:
The New York Times reveals details about the STELLARWIND program.

2006:
The FBI issues National Security Letters for information the FISC twice refused to issue Section 215 orders for due to the First Amendment.

March 2006:
Section 215 is amended to permit the collection of all phone records of all customers on a potential basis.

September 2006:
FBI fails to establish "minimisation procedures" as required by Congress. Definition:

> *50 U.S.C. 1806 (A): Information acquired from an electronic surveillance conducted pursuant to this subchapter concerning any United States person may be used and disclosed by Federal officers and employees without the consent of the United States person only in accordance with the minimization procedures required by this subchapter. No otherwise privileged communication obtained in accordance with, or in violation of, the provisions of this subchapter shall lose its privileged character. No information acquired from an electronic surveillance pursuant to this subchapter may be used or disclosed by Federal officers or employees except for lawful purposes.*

October 2006:
Al-Qaeda announces the creation of the Islamic State of Iraq (ISI)

5 November 2006:
Saddam Hussein is found guilty of crimes against humanity sentenced to death by hanging.

30 December 2006:
Saddam Hussein is hanged at Camp Justice in Baghdad, Iraq

11 September 2008:
A division of the Joint Special Operations Command shuts down multiple jihadist websites.

20 January 2009:
Barack Obama is elected as the 44th President of the United States

July 2009:
Boko Haram Insurgency begins, starting an armed rebellion against the Nigerian government.

August 2009:
Obama administration ceases using the term "War on Terror" and claims the U.S. is "at war with al-Qaeda"

Between 2006 and 2009:
Roughly 3,000 domestic phone identifiers are wrongfully designated as suspicious.
NSA Tools "routinely" analyse data that is not approved by FISC, therefore violating orders. In March 2009 FISC Judge Reggie Walton states: *"The record before the Court strongly suggests that from the inception of this program, the NSA's data accessing technologies were never adequately designed to comply with the governing minimisation procedures"*

February 2010:
Congress reauthorises section 215 without modification.

17 December 2010:
Anti-government protests, uprisings and rebellions spread across the Arab world and sees social media dominated to spread the message. This is the Arab Spring.

March 2011:
The NSA informs FISC of a large amount of illegitimately collected credit card numbers.

15 March 2011:
The Arab Spring protests eventually evolve into the Syrian Civil War after demands to remove President Bashar al-Assad are suppressed.

13 May 2011:
The FBI tells members of Congress that Section 215 has "not been abused"

26 May 2011:
Congress reauthorises section 215.

18 December 2011:
U.S. military forces are withdrawn from Iraq, leading to the end of the Iraq war.

Between 2012 and 2014:
"Systemic errors" allow unauthorised FBI personnel to access records and overcollection of email subjects. The mass collection of records take place beyond authorised timescale.

February 2012:
The NSA realises it has kept more than 3000 call data files beyond the time allowed under the law.

March 2013:
DNI Clapper tells Senate that the U.S. government is not collecting the information of millions of Americans.

April 2013:
Islamic State of Iraq changes its name to the Islamic State of Iraq and the Levant (ISIL)

20 May 2013:
NSA contractor Edward Snowden leaves Hawaii Cryptologic Center and flies to Hong Kong with thousands of digital files relating to U.S. surveillance.

June 2013:
The first part of Edward Snowden's disclosure is distributed through *The Guardian* and *The Washington Post;* beginning with an article regarding the bulk collection of telephone data.

July 2013:
The FBI finally adopts the minimisation procedures ordered by Congress seven years earlier.

November 2013:
The NSA unlawfully collects mass amounts of cellular base station location data.

February 2015:
Al-Qaeda formally disassociates itself with ISIL.

May 2015:
The U.S. Court of Appeals deems Section 215 use was "unprecedented and unwarranted"

2 June 2015:
Barack Obama signs the USA FREEDOM Act *(Uniting and Strengthening America by Fulfilling Rights and Ensuring Effective Discipline Over Monitoring)* into power. The act imposes limits on bulk collection of metadata on U.S. citizens but restores authorisation for wiretaps and tracking 'lone wolf terrorists'

Between June 2015 and May 2018:
Unlawful collection of call data records results in deletion of records collected before May 23, 2018.

October 2018
Unlawful collection of call data records. This leads the NSA to shut down the program.

March 2019:
NSA fails to delete the call data that was wrongfully collected.

August 2019:
Director of National Intelligence tells Congress that Section 215 and its related authorities *"have no history of abuse after more than 18 years"*

March 2020:
PATRIOT Act reauthorised[85].

```
TOP SECRET//UNDER//CONSTANT//SUPERVISION//REL TO READER


There will be no going back to the era
before September the 11th, 2001 - to
false comfort in a dangerous world.

 - George W. Bush
```

---

[85] http://clerk.house.gov/evs/2020/roll098.xml **OR** https://archive.vn/QjQw2

GLOBAL REACTIONS TO GLOBAL SURVEILLANCE

The European Council (European Union) released a signed statement by all 28 EU leaders criticising the surveillance, whilst claiming the *"intelligence gathering is a vital element in the fight against terrorism.*
Germany attempted to create an agreement against spying but claimed that they had "given up hope" of such a deal being made.[86]
Countries like Italy, Spain and France confirmed that data allegedly collected by the NSA was collected by their intelligence agencies, then shared to the NSA.

William Hague, Foreign Minister of Britain claimed confirmed that the GCHQ was collaborating and had conducted surveillance with the NSA but backed the measures as *"indispensable"*
The director of GCHQ argued that the large U.S. tech companies *"may dislike it, [but] they have become the command and control networks of choice for terrorists and criminals"*

Australian Prime Minister Tony Abbott defended the NSA and called Snowden a *"traitor"* who had *"betrayed his country"* Foreign Minister Julie Bishop said: *"Snowden claims his actions were driven by a desire for transparency, but in fact they strike at the heart of the collaboration between those nations in world affairs that stand at the forefront of protecting human freedom."*

---

[86] https://www.thelocal.de/20140114/germany-gives-up-hope-of-no-spy-deal-with-nsa-usa **OR** https://archive.is/gL7rV

Whilst these are just a few global reactions, it shows the anger was directed at the leaker and not the content itself, which echoes previous anger over WikiLeaks and Julian Assange. Icelandic legislator Birgitta Jónsdóttir who had assisted WikiLeaks in the release of U.S. secrets in 2010 said that the UN Secretary-General Ban Ki-moon *"seemed entirely unconcerned about the invasion of privacy by governments around the world, and only concerned about how whistleblowers are misusing the system"* after expressing his opinion Snowden had abused his rights and created problems that would be greater than any benefit provided by public disclosure.

U.S. non-profit Information Technology and Innovation Foundation, ITIF, reported the leaks severely cost tech companies Microsoft and IBM over $1 billion and predicted cloud computing would be adversely affected by the revelations that had cost many users their trust.

The Wikimedia Foundation, the company behind the online encyclopedia Wikipedia, launched legal action against the NSA[87] but their case was dismissed

Many NSA documents feature the security classification:
```
TOP SECRET//COMINT//REL TO USA,AUS,CAN,GBR,NZL
```

This translates to:
```
CLASSIFICATION LEVEL//COMPARTMENT// DISTRIBUTION
```

Meaning, for example, the slide shown is top secret, the control system is Special Intelligence and relates to

---

[87] https://blog.wikimedia.org/2015/03/10/wikimedia-v-nsa/

In yesterday's ruling, the Court largely accepted the government's contentions. In particular, it held that the Foundation had not presented sufficient evidence that the NSA was monitoring Wikimedia communications, but that even if we were able to present sufficient evidence, the state secrets privilege would prevent the matter from proceeding. The Court found that further litigation on the standing issue would require the government to disclose classified details of how Upstream surveillance operates, and it refused to conduct a closed-door review of the evidence. We respectfully disagree; we believe that the government's public disclosures about the program offer more than enough evidence to show that the NSA is using Upstream to surveil the communications of Wikimedia users and Foundation staff.
- *Senior legal counsel members from Wikipedia Foundation statement on dismissal of the case in December 2019*

TOP SECRET//UNDER//CONSTANT//SUPERVISION//REL TO READER

The way things are supposed to work is that we're supposed to know virtually everything about what they [the government] do: that's why they're called public servants. They're supposed to know virtually nothing about what we do: that's why we're called private individuals.

- Glenn Greenwald

SURVEILLANCE IN NUMBERS

The exact sizes are unknown, but the following estimates have been calculated by the documents collected by the NSA analyst Perry Fellwock, NSA employees William Binney and Thomas Andrews Drake, GCHQ employee Katharine Gun, AT&T employee Mark Klein, journalist Michael Hastings, Julian Assange and Bradley – later Chelsea – Manning, NSA employee Russ Tice and British Cabinet Minister Clare Short. Edward Snowden's exhaustive leaks are also included.

Approximately **20,000 files** relating to Australian intelligence.
Approximately **60,000 British intelligence files**
1.8 million United States intelligence files (including Pentagon claims that Snowden committed the biggest theft of secrets in U.S. history, downloading around 1.7 million files) However, Snowden claims this widely attributed number is fabricated and is closer to **50,000-200,000** files.

The numbers above or based on documents that detail surveillance by major governments. Just under a million documents regarding war and confidential US Embassy cables were leaked by Manning in 2010.

Whilst there are plenty of files, some are of little use:

Classification: TOP SECRET//COMINT//ORCON//NOFORN//X1

10. Nowicki, Marvin, E., Ph.D., "Letters to the Editor: Tragic 'Gross Error' In a 1967 Attack," The Wall Street Journal, 16 May 2000.

Classification: TOP SECRET//COMINT//ORCON//NOFORN//X1

THE SPY PROGRAMS

Documented throughout various slides and letters, the NSA surveillance systems show the reach that the NSA and its alliances have across the globe. Some of the leaks proved what was otherwise alleged or known, whilst some systems became public for the first time. Edward Snowden claims these programs demonstrate *"the hypocrisy of the US government when it claims that it does not target civilian infrastructure, unlike its adversaries"*

A few important programs or systems are described, many of which are entwined with one another:

BLARNEY: A codename for the NSA communications surveillance program. It began in 1978 and was extended significantly after 9/11.

BOUNDLESSINFORMANT: A data analysis and visualisation tool used by the NSA with laws introduced by President George W. Bush and renewed by President Obama in 2012. By March 2013, Boundless Informant had captured 14 billion reports from Iran, 6.3 Billion from India and 2.8 billion from the U.S.

BULLRUN: A highly classified U.S. NSA program to preserve its ability to eavesdrop on encrypted communications by influencing and weakening the standards available and by gaining access to master encryption keys, or to gain access to the data BEFORE it was encrypted either by court-enforced order, an agreement with a business such as a telecommunications provider or government, or by hacking.

DCSNet: Digital Collection System Network is an FBI "point-and-click" system that can gain instant wiretaps on most devices in the U.S. Known software developed for it was **Carnivore** and **Digital Storm**.

DISHFIRE: a covert global surveillance collection system by GCHQ and NSA collecting hundreds of millions of text-based data such as geolocation, digital business cards, financial transactions, missed calls and travel information. The analytical tool known as **PREFER** was used to process messages to extract information.

ECHELON: A Signals Intelligence collection and analysis alliance that is operated across the *FVEY* states.

FAIRVIEW: a secret program operated by the NSA. American telecommunications company AT&T cooperated with the NSA to collect phone, Internet, and email data of foreign countries' citizens at major cable landing stations and switching stations within the United States. AT&T is described as highly cooperative with one document hailing AT&T's "extreme willingness to help"
The program started in 1985, a year after Bell Communications, of whom assisted in the Cold War surveillance, split into several companies including Bell Atlantic.

FASCIA: NSA database storing trillions of records, including Location Area Codes (LACs), Cell Tower IDs (CeLLIDs), Visitor Location Registers (VLRs), International Mobile Station Equipment Identity (IMEIs) and MSISDNs (Mobile Subscriber Integrated Services Digital Network-Numbers). A total of 27 Terabytes of location data were stored within seven months.

FRENCHELON: A nickname given to the SIGINT system used by France. Interception is done on submarine cables across DGSE (Directorate-General for External Security)[88] headquarters including the large station in Domme near Périgord and several smaller stations in Alsace, Agde and Nice. Overseas territories such as New Caledonia and Réunion also gather data in respective bases and stations.

MUSCULAR: GCHQ and NSA joint operation that connected into communication links of data centres from Google and Yahoo

XKeyscore: A system used by the United States National Security Agency for searching and analysing Internet data about foreign nationals.

Lustre: a codename for a secret treaty between France (DGSE) and FVEY which exchanged collected data. Over 70 million records were handed over to the NSA by DGSE between December 2012 and January 2013.

MYSTIC: Revealed in 2014, MYSTIC was a secret program that collected the metadata and content of phone calls from Afghanistan, the Bahamas, the Philippines, Kenya and Mexico. The NSA documents claim that the unauthorised surveillance of the Bahamas led to the arrest of narcotics traffickers and that this intelligence would be related, which never happened, causing the Bahamas to take legal action.

---

[88] Direction Générale de la sécurité extérieure

Project 6: Operated by the CIA and German intelligence agencies to combat terrorism. The project includes an extensive database of photos, license plate numbers, Internet search history and telephone metadata of those believed to be related to Muslim extremism.

RAMPART-A: The codename for a signals intelligence partnership program led by the NSA and including 37 partner countries, of which 17 were European Union member states. The partnership is run to *"gain access to high-capacity international fiber-optic cables that transit at major congestion points around the world"*

PRISM: A covert surveillance program operated by the NSA which can target customers of participating corporations in the United States and overseas.
Microsoft, Facebook, Apple and Google were the "commercial partners" of whom denied any knowledge of the programs.

STATEROOM: A secret SIGINT program that involved the interception of international radio, telecommunications and Internet networks. Evolved from the Special Collection Service (SCS)

STELLARWIND: A warrantless surveillance program introduced under George W. Bush's Principle Surveillance Program. It was approved by Bush after the 9/11 attacks and was the foundation to expanded versions by Bush and eventually Obama.

STORMBREW: a surveillance program that the NSA used to collect phone numbers, emails, IP addresses of people and organisations in which the NSA were interested in. The surveillance was carried out entirely in the United States. The partner was revealed as Verizon Communications Inc, formerly known as Bell Atlantic Corporation.

TAO/ANT: Office of Tailored Access Operations (later renamed Computer Network Operations) is the cyber-warfare intelligence-gathering division of the NSA. Active since at least 1998, the division is expected to have at least 1,000 military and civilian hackers, analysts as well as hardware and software designers. According to the Snowden documents, TAO has software templates allowing workers to easily break into common hardware such as routers and switches on the consumer market. The ANT catalogue lists the technology available and operational to the FVEY alliance. TAO developed a set of cyberattacking software called QUANTUM and FOXACID which sends back exploits.

Tempora: Tempora uses intercepts on the fibre-optic cables that serve as the backbone of the Internet to gain access to large amounts of Internet users' personal data, without any individual suspicion or targeting. The intercepts are placed in the United Kingdom and overseas, with the knowledge of companies owning either the cables or landing stations. Commercial partners listed with their codenames in brackets were British Telecoms (Remedy), Interoute (Streetcar), Level 3 (Little), Global Crossing (Pinnage), Verizon Business (Dacron), Viatel (Vitreous) and Vodafone Cable (Gerontic)

The NSA was also getting data directly from communications companies that were not revealed in the 2013 leaks. These code-names include:

Artifice
Lithium
Serenade
SteelKnight
X

SteelKnight is described as an NSA *partner* facility.

The reason for their anonymity is because they were protected as EXCEPTIONALLY CONTROLLED INFORMATION in the leaks which prevents wide circulation to those even with the necessary security clearance. Many of the 2013 leaks were comprised of slides – most of which are redacted or look rather amateur. There is also the possibility that the Snowden hysteria in the media led to more leaks by NSA staff posing as Snowden to protect their own identities.

UNDER CONSTANT SUPERVISION

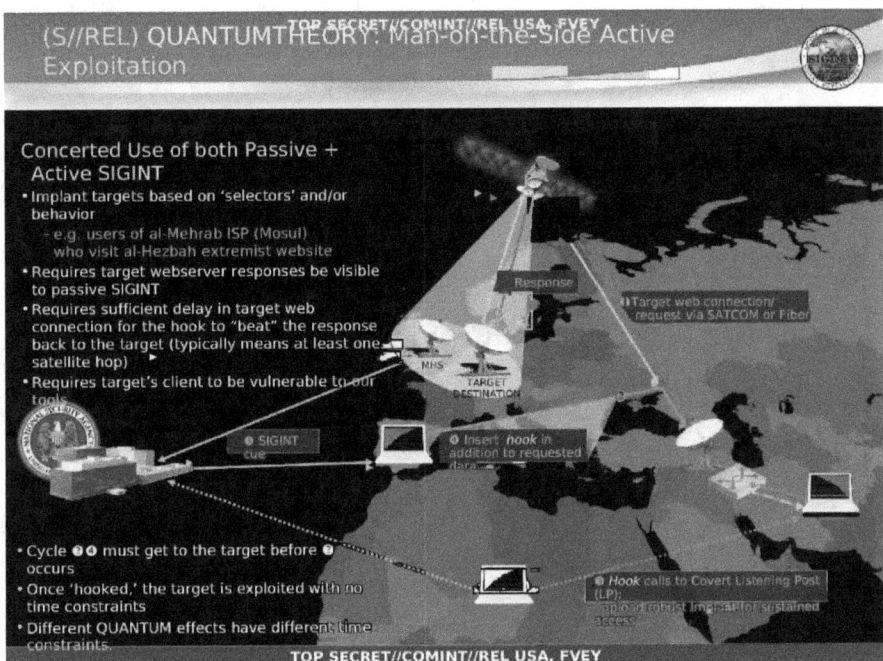

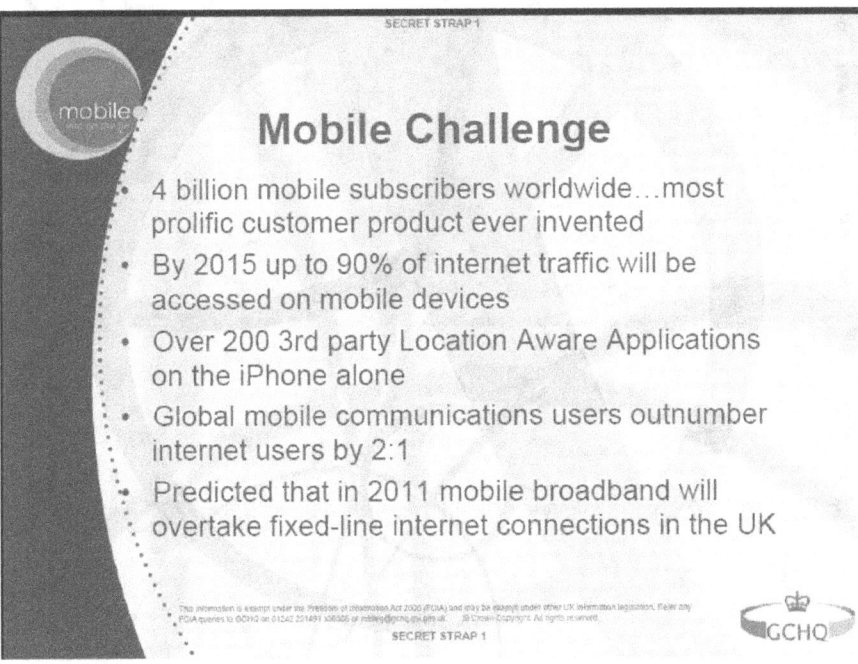

A warning displayed on document *Congressional Budget Justification:*

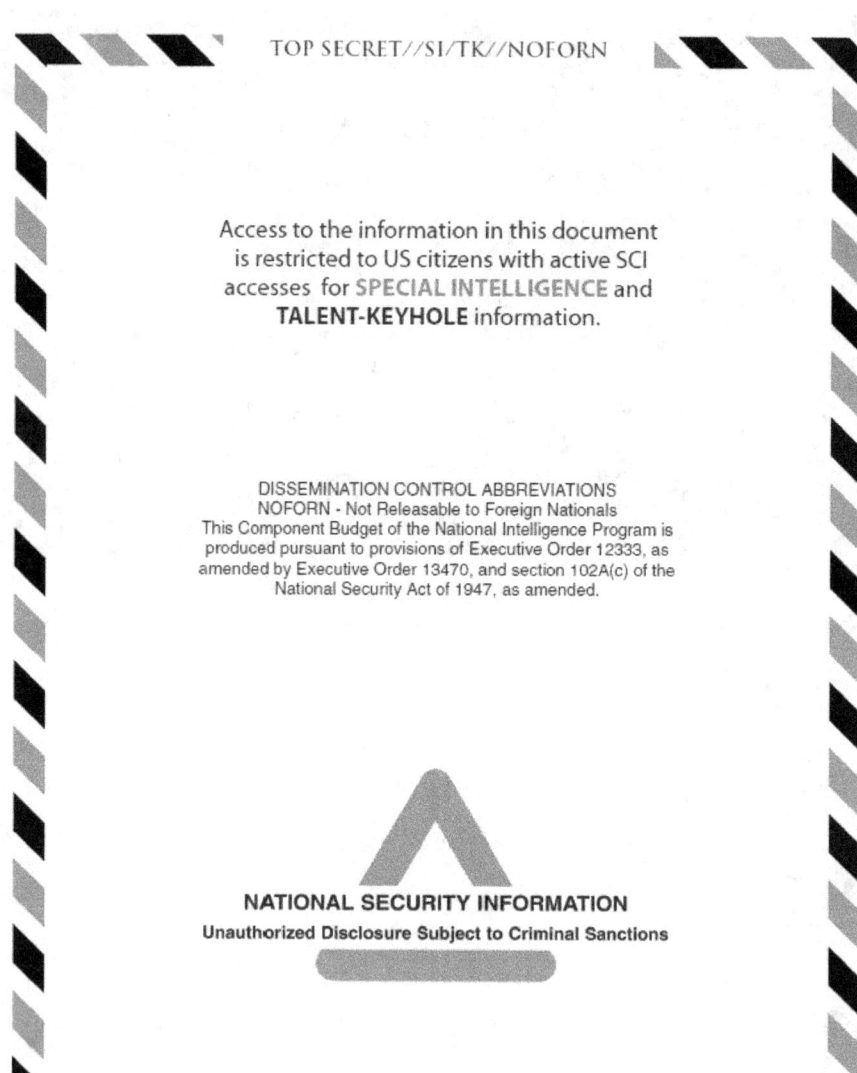

ECHELON

ECHELON is a grid of surveillance stations operated by Five Eyes countries either collaboratively or individually. Although not entirely an officially acknowledged surveillance program – with both the United States and the United Kingdom reputably evasive when questioned about its existence – ECHELON was revealed by the European Parliament in 2001 as a cryptonym or codename used by Five Eyes.

The investigation, which began in June 2000, was set up by a Committee of the European Parliament as the *Temporary Committee on the ECHELON Interception System* which concluded that the ECHELON surveillance system "almost certainly" existed. The committee found that they had no power to request the European Union to avoid or request that surveillance be halted. The report gives considerations and suggestions to the European Union to negotiate a Code of Conduct. It also called on the USA to:

> "sign the Additional Protocol to the International Covenant on Civil and Political Rights, so that complaints by individuals concerning breaches of the Covenant by the USA can be submitted to the Human Rights Committee set up under the Covenant; calls on the relevant American NGOs, in particular the ACLU (American Civil Liberties Union) and the EPIC (Electronic Privacy Information Center), to exert pressure on the US Administration to that end"

The report states that in 1997 and 1999, the Science and Technology Options Assessment (STOA) – another committee of members of the European Parliament – brought the surveillance system to public light but failed to reveal the purpose of the global spying network.

The investigation also specifies the following:

> *Satellite receiver stations and spy satellites in particular are alleged to give it the ability to intercept any telephone, fax, Internet or e-mail message sent by any individual and thus to inspect its contents. The second unusual feature of ECHELON is said to be that the system operates worldwide on the basis of cooperation proportionate to their capabilities among several states (the UK, the United States, Canada, Australia and New Zealand), giving it an added value in comparison to national systems: the states participating in ECHELON (UKUSA states) can place their interception systems at each other's disposal, share the cost and make joint use of the resulting information.*

The final 2001 report was approved by 367 votes. 159 votes were against. 39 abstained. simply raises the question *"Are EU citizens adequately protected against intelligence services?"* as well as if European businesses are wrongly being spied on.
The report led to little, if any, action and failed to gather the attention of the mainstream media in Europe and the world. Many powerful political parties staunchly opposed the report whilst Britain and the Netherlands declined to co-operate or contribute any information that could be used to explain ECHELON's purpose and necessity. [89]

---

[89] *European Parliament resolution on the existence of a global system for the interception of private and commercial communications (ECHELON interception system) (2001/2098(INI))*

Page 54 of the 194-page report lists the following ground stations as suspected of intercepting or having intercepted transmissions from telecommunication satellites. Since the report, many of the stations have been closed. However, many new and previously listed intercept stations and their codenames were revealed in Edward Snowden's 2013 document release. Some of the stations may no longer be operational, with satellite data showing little maintenance on certain cites. The table on the next pages includes many of the stations believed to be facilitating interception, with some exact locations of stations unknown. The 2001 report states that the RAF Menwith Hill located in Harrogate, United Kingdom is the largest operating ECHELON facility known. The codename SHAMROCK was used before 1975. In the late 80s the name used was Project P415

Despite revelations by multiple documents leaked since Pellwock's revelations in the 1970s and investigations carried out by governmental and independent bodies, ECHELON has never been formally acknowledged as existing by many agencies like the NSA and GCHQ. Former New Zealand PM Keith Locke, however, commented Waihopai Valley Listening Post is part of ECHELON.

In 2015, a document from the NSA was released as part of the Snowden revelations showed an internal newsletter titled "The Northwest Passage" using the words ECHELON and stating the program was part of an umbrella program with the codename FROSTING. The document details two divisions:

> FROSTING's two sub-programs were TRANSIENT, for all efforts against Soviet satellite targets, and ECHELON, for the collection and processing of INTELSAT communications. Two years later, approval was given for FROSTING's West Coast project (JACKKNIFE)

POTENTIAL ECHELON LOCATIONS:

The next page features a chart of locations and names of ECHELON locations present and former.

There have, however, been a few stations that cannot be confirmed as linked to ECHELON or used for surveillance – such as stations that may be used for space research or television satellites – and therefore are listed here:

LOCATION	COUNTRY	PRIMARY AGENCY
Osan Air Base	South Korea	US
Karramursel	Turkey	US
?	Malta	UK
Rota	Spain	US
Silvermine, Cape Town	South Africa	US
Elmendorf Air Force Base Alaska	US	US
Chicksands, Bedfordshire	UK	UK
Feltwell, Norfolk	UK	?
Masset, British Columbia	Canada	?
Alert, Ellesmere Island, Nunavut	Canada	?
Bremerhaven	Germany	UK
West Cape, Exmouth Gulf	Australia	US

KNOWN ECHELON SURVEILLANCE LOCATIONS

Many of these locations were used beyond the scope of the ECHELON network.

Country	Location	Facility / Station	Codename	Coordinates (DMS)
Australia	Geraldton, Western Australia	Australian Defence Satellite Communications Station	STELLAR	28° 41' 42" S 114° 50' 32" E
Australia	Shoal Bay, Northern Territory	Shoal Bay Receiving Station	SHOAL BAY	12°21'32"S 130°58'56"E
Australia	Pine Gap, Alice Springs, NT	Joint Defence Facility Pine Gap	RAINFALL	23°48'11.02"S 133°44'34.13"E
Brazil	Brasília, Federal District	U.S. Embassy of Brasília		23°37'45.85"S 46°41'50.97"W
Canada	Newfoundland	CFB Gander		48° 56' 13"N 54° 34' 5"W
Canada	Ontario	CFS Leitrim		45° 20' 11.38"N 75° 35' 15.01"W
Hong Kong	Chung Hom Kok	(GCHQ) Chung Hom Kok		22°12'46.86"N 114°11'57.14"E
Hong Kong	Siu Sai Wan	RAF Little Sai Wan (later GCHQ)[90]		22°15'42.06"N 114°15'14.27"E
Cyprus	British Sovereign Base Area of Dhekelia	Ayios Nikolaos Station	SOUNDER	35° 5'35.60"N 33°53'16.32"E
Germany	Bad Aibling, Munich	Bad Aibling Station (BAS)	GARLICK	47° 52' 46"N 11° 59' 4"E
Germany	Teufelsberg	Field Station Berlin		52°29'52.44"N 13°14'26.02"E
India	New Delhi	U.S. Embassy New Delhi		28°37'38.38"N 77°13'25.03"E
Japan	Misawa, Tōhoku region	Misawa Air Base	LADYLOVE	40° 42' 19"N 141° 22' 19"E
Kenya	Nairobi	British High Commission	SCAPEL	1°17'44.72"S 36°49'2.96"E
New Zealand	Waihopai, Blenheim	GCSB Waihopai	IRONSAND	41° 34' 33.6" S 173° 44' 20.4" E
New Zealand	Palmerston North	GCSB Tangimoana		40° 18' 53.9" S 175° 14' 59.44"E
Oman	Muscat	British Embassy	SNICK	23°36'28.00"N 58°26'20.10"E

---

[90] *"Mandarin Blue: RAF Chinese Linguists - 1951 to 1962 - and the Cold War"* by Keith Scott, Geoffrey Russell and Reginal Hunt [ISBN 9780956023506]

Thailand	Khon Kaen, Bangkok	U.S. Embassy	LEMONWOOD	16°25'43.41"N 102°49'49.34"E
United Kingdom	Harrogate, Yorkshire	Royal Air Force (RAF) Menwith Hill	MOONPENNY	54°00'31.3"N 1°41'22.2"W
United Kingdom (British Overseas Territory)	Diego Garcia	Diego Garcia Telecommunications Station / GEODSS - Ground-based Electro-Optical Deep Space Surveillance (US)		7°16'38.52"S 72°22'7.93"E
United Kingdom	Bude, Cornwall	GCHQ Composite Signals Organisation Station Morwenstow / GCHQ Bude	CARBOY	50°53'10"N 4°33'13"W
United Kingdom (British Overseas Territory)	Gibraltar	Devils Tower Camp		36° 8'56.15"N 5°20'33.37"W
United Kingdom	Alnwick, Northumberland	RAF Boulmer		55° 25' 19" N, 1° 36' 12" W
United Kingdom	Angus, Scotland	RAF Edzell		56° 48' 44" N, 2° 36' 17" W
United States	Sugar Grove, West Virginia	Sugar Grove Listening Station	TIMBERLINE	8° 30' 53.99" N 79° 17' 3.16" W
United States	Yakima, Washington	Yakima Training Center (YTC)	JACKKNIFE	46°45'55.88"N 120°11'12.58"W
United States	Toa Baja, Puerto Rico	Sábana Seca Base	CORALINE	18°27'15.92"N 66°13'35.93"W
United States	Grovetown, Georgia	Fort Gordon		33° 24' 48" N 82° 8' 7" W
United States	Guam	Naval Computer and Telecommunication Station		13°24'52.08"N 144°39'52.45"E
United States	Bexan County, Texas	Lackland Air Force Base		29° 23' 16.8" N 98° 37' 14.52" W
United States	Oahu, Hawaii	Kunia Regional SIGINT Operations Center		21° 28' 32.99" N 158° 3' 4.16" W
United States	Aurora, Colorado	Buckley Air Force Base		39° 42' 6" N 104° 45' 6" W

Shaded entries indicate no visible usage according to current satellite imagery.
Australian locations are operated by the Australian Signals Directorate.
Kenya and Oman are operated by UK GCHQ
Cyprus operated by GCHQ and NSA and is within UK-controlled territory
New Zealand by GCSB

UNDER CONSTANT SUPERVISION

Germany Operated by BND and NSA
Japan Operated by NSA and United States Air Force
Menwith Hill, UK operated by NSA and GCHQ
All others operated by NSA (Thailand: NSA and CIA)
The Hong Kong station was decommissioned with equipment shipped to Australia
Brazil and India Locations also used for Special Collection Service (SCS)

In 2004 Bad Aibling Station, Germany was dismantled and relocated to the Darmstadt district in Hesse, Germany. The coordinates given in the table are of the relocated station. Despite the NSA claiming that the station was decommissioned, it still appears active. It is unknown if FVEY are operating it.

Widemouth Bay in Cornwall has several cable landing points including Apollo North, TAT-8 and TAT-14 and Yellow AC2. These landing points are 5km along the coastline from the Bude GCHQ Composite Signals Organisation Station. A 2010 WikiLeaks document states TAT-14 is included in a U.S. Government list of critical infrastructure susceptible to terrorist attacks. An estimated 25% of Internet traffic travels through these landing points. Documents show 200 cables coming into Cornwall were tapped by GCHQ.
Apollo and Yellow AC2 are listed in the NSA documents as "partner cables".

5km south of Crooklets Beach is a submarine cable landing point that carries financial trading data from New York. More locations are explored further into the section.

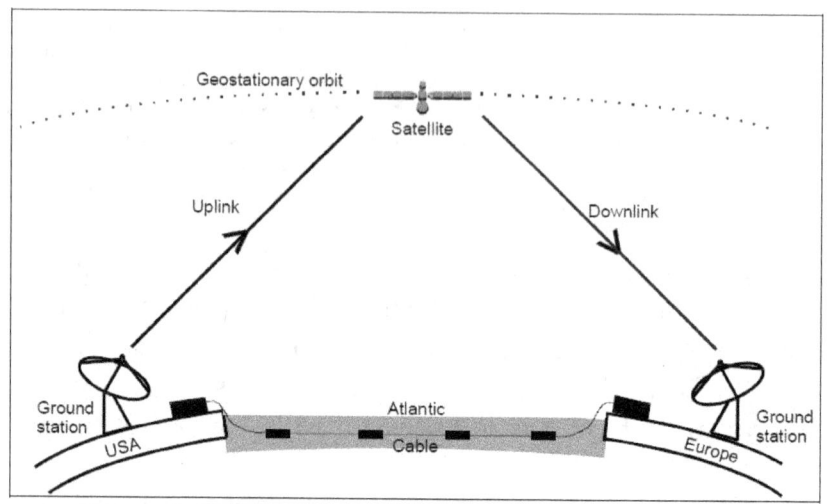

Diagram of satellite link operation featured in the European Parliament report

Second generation of INTELSAT satellites providing global coverage

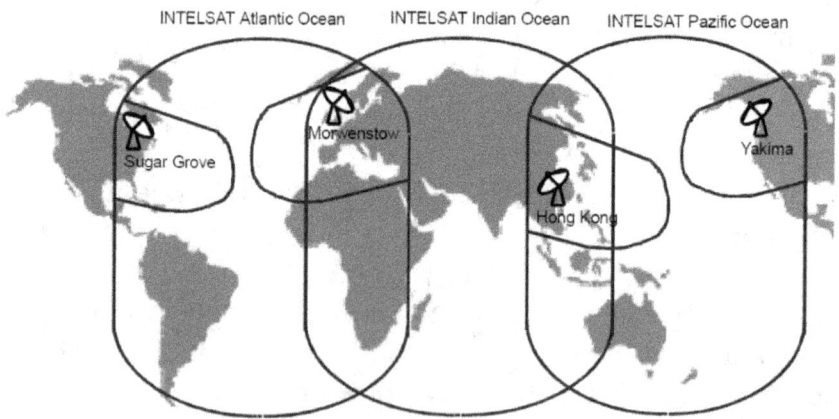

UNDER CONSTANT SUPERVISION

Diego Garcia, an island of British Indian Ocean Territory has long been alleged a location of spying. According to Wikileaks cablegate documents, Diego Garcia was used to store US weaponry to avoid UK parliamentary supervision.
© 2020 DigitalGlobe

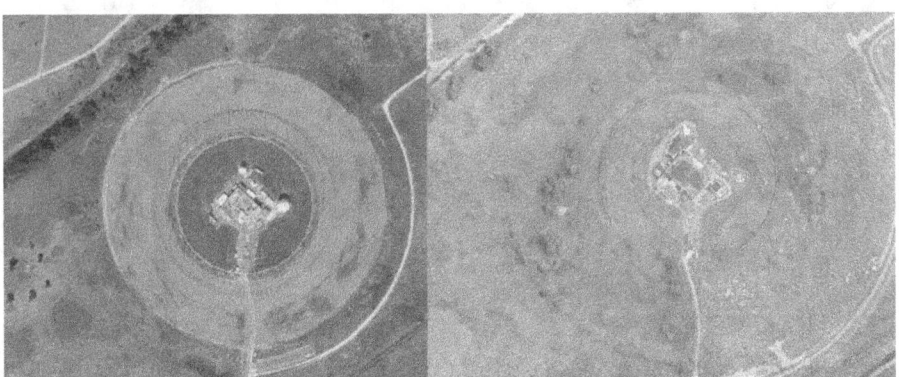

Left: Puerto Rico base in 1994 Right: Remnants in 2019 (Image:Landsat/U.S. Geological Survey)

NASA Satellite Image of RAF Menwith Hill

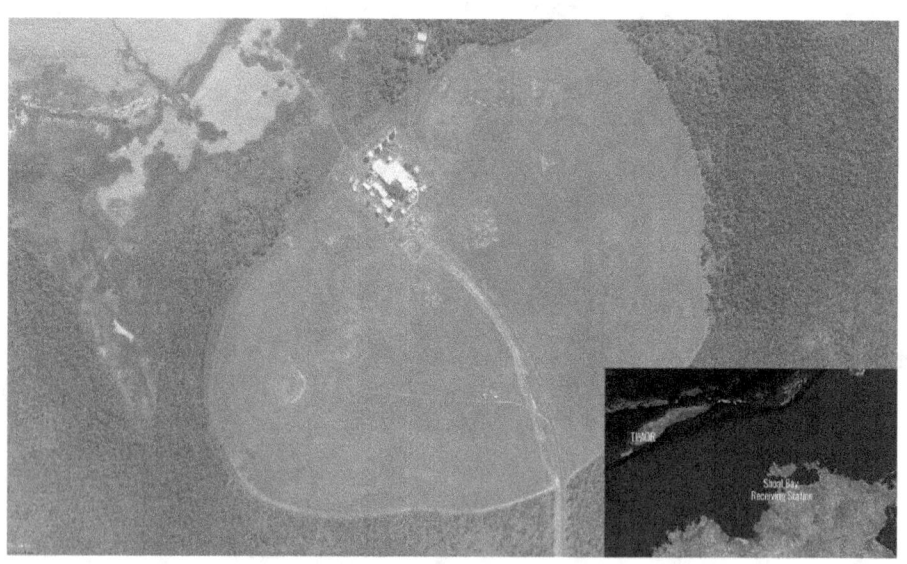

Satellite image of Shoal Bay Receiving Station, Australia
© 2020 Maxar Technologies

Further reports suggested the possibility of communications satellites being within perfect range of stations able to intercept any communications. Some of these satellites have since been moved to a graveyard orbit (an orbit used to dispose of old satellites to decrease the chance of collisions)

Satellites	Interception Stations
INTELSAT 604 (60°E), 602 (62°E), 804 (64°E), 704 (66°E) EXPRESS 6A (80°E) INMARSAT Indian Ocean area	Geraldton, Australia Pine Gap, Australia Morwenstow, England Menwith Hill, England
INTELSAT APR1 (83°), APR-2 (110,5°)	Geraldton, Australia Pine Gap, Australia Misawa, Japan
INTELSAT 802 (174°), 702 (176°), 701 (180°) GORIZONT 41 (130°E), 42 (142°E), LM-1 (75°E) INMARSAT Pacific area	Waihopai, New Zealand Geraldton, Australia Pine Gap, Australia Misawa, Japan Yakima, USA - only Intelsat and Inmarsat
INTELSAT 805 (304,5°), 706 (307°), 709 (310°) 601 (325,5°), 801 (328°), 511(330,5°), 605 (332,5°), 603 (335,5°), 705 (342°) EXPRESS 2 (14°W), 3A (11°W) INMARSAT Atlantic area	Sugar Grove, USA Sábana Seca, Puerto Rico Morwenstow, England Menwith Hill, England
INTELSAT 707 (359°)	Morwenstow, England Menwith Hill, England

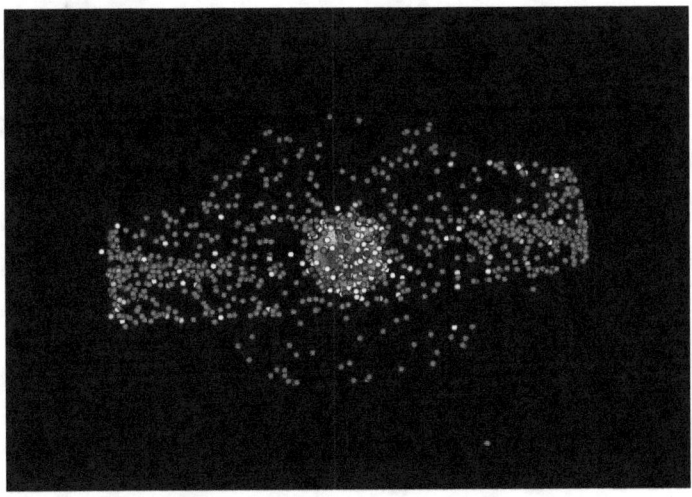

Active satellites surrounding the Earth as of 2020 (Source: ESRI)

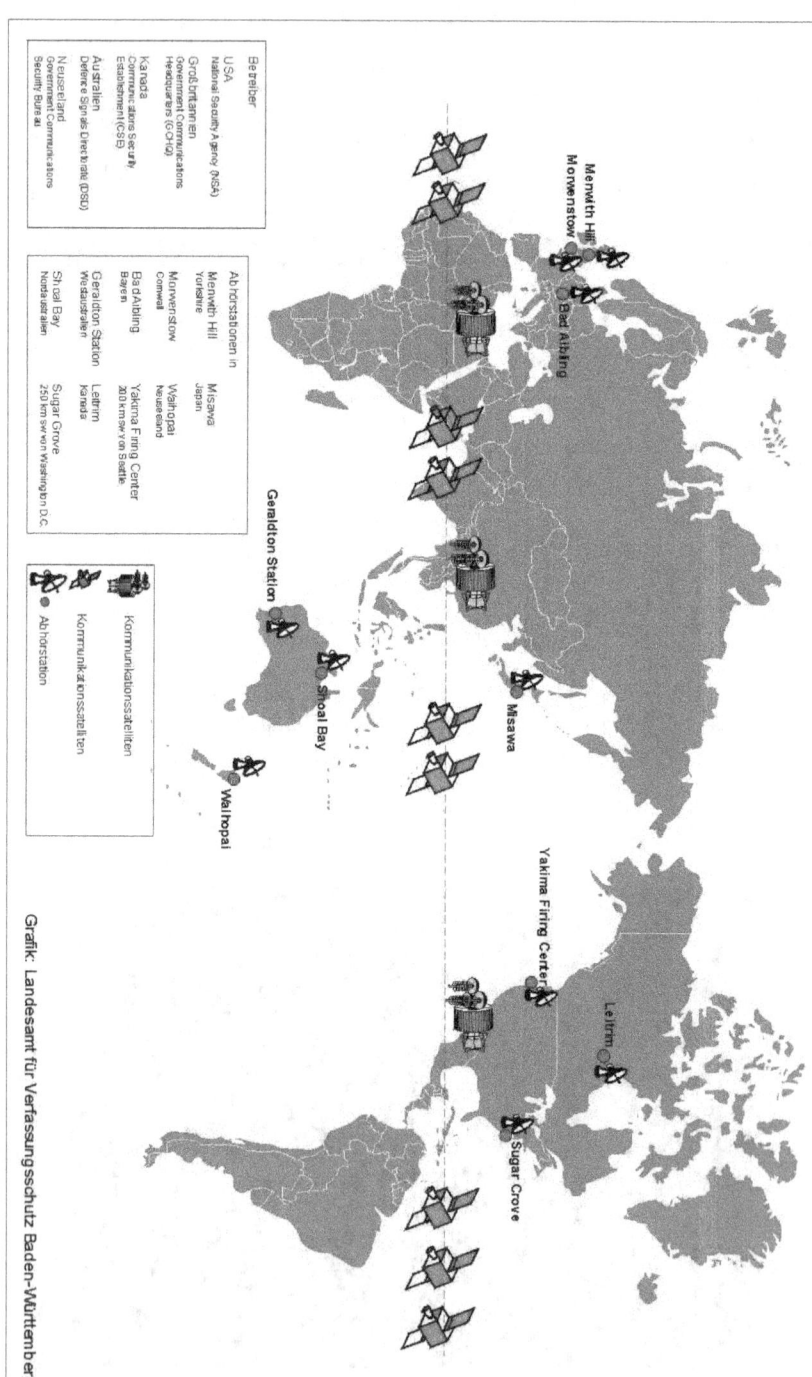

A 1998 diagram from a German report showing the interception of satellites

SPECIAL COLLECTION SERVICE / STATEROOM

Operating out of the FVEY/ ECHELON is the Special Collection Service (SCS) that operates a deeper network of surveillance. Originating in 1978 during the Cold War

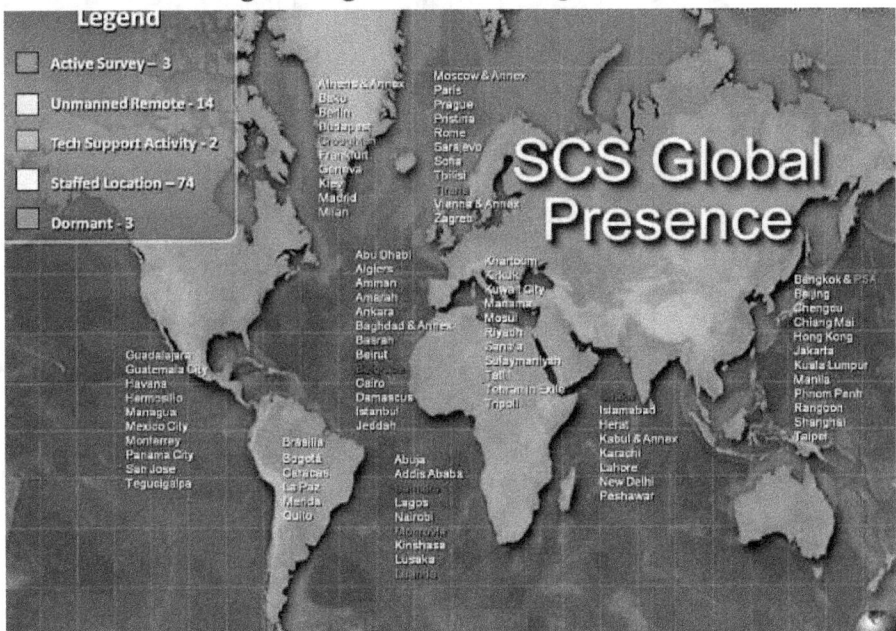

between the U.S. and Soviet Union, SCS evolved into STATEROOM as revealed in 2013 leaks. The NSA partners with the CIA for SIGINT collection.

Many of the specific locations are strict secrets, with employees directly related to the program given limited information. Most of the intelligence is collected through embassies, consulates, and high commissions, and judging by some of the cities, military installations.

CONFIRMED LOCATIONS OF EAVESDROPPING SPOTS ARE:

COUNTRY OPERATING	LOCATION OF SIGINT
United States	Athens (Greece)
	Bangkok (Thailand)
	Berlin (Germany)
	Brasília (Brazil)
	Budapest (Hungary)
	Frankfurt (Germany)
	Geneva (Switzerland)
	Lagos (Nigeria)
	Milan (Italy)
	New Delhi (India)
	Paris (France)
	Prague (Czech Republic)
	Vienna (Austria)
	Zagreb (Croatia)
	Baku (Azerbaijan)
	Kiev (Ukraine)
	Madrid (Spain)
	Moscow (Russia)
	Pristina (Kosovo)
	Rome (Italy)
	Sarajevo (Bosnia and Herzegovina)
	Tbilisi (Georgia)
	Tirana (Albania)
Australia	Bangkok, (Thailand)
	Beijing (China)
	Dili (East Timor)
	Hanoi (East Timor)
	Jakarta (Indonesia)
	Kuala Lumpur (Malaysia)
	Port Moresby (Papua New Guinea)
United Kingdom	Berlin (Germany)
New Zealand	Honiara (Solomon Islands) codenamed **CAPRICA**

Canada are involved, but confirmed locations are not available.

Information from the UK Berlin listening post is relayed to RAF Croughton, Northamptonshire and transmitted to the NSA and CIA facility in Maryland, United States.

Unconfirmed or partially available information either due to redaction or lack of information – some of which are likely the ECHELON locations:

COUNTRY	CITY
Afghanistan	Herat
Afghanistan	Kabul
Africa	Nairobi
Africa	Lukasa
Africa	Luanda
Algeria	Algiers
Austria	Vienna
Azerbaijan	Baku
Bahrain	Manama
Bangladesh	Dhaka
Bolivia	Nuestra Señora de La Paz
Bulgaria	Sofia
Cambodia	Phnom Penh
Cameroon	Tello
China	Shanghai
China	Chengdu
China / Hong Kong	Hong Kong
China / Taiwan	Taipei
Colombia	Bogotá
Costa Rica	San Jose
Croatia	Zagreb
Cuba	Havana

Democratic Republic of the Congo	Kinshasa
Ecuador	Quito
Egypt	Cairo
Ethiopia	Addis Ababa
Guatemala	Guatemala City
Haiti	Port-au-Prince
Honduras	Tegucigalpa
Iran	Tehran
Iraq	Baghdad
Iraq	Basra
Iraq	Amarah
Iraq	Kirkuk
Iraq	Sulaymaniyah
Iraq	Mosul
Jordan	Amman
Kuwait	Kuwait City
Lebanon	Beirut
Liberia	Monrovia
Libya	Tripoli
Mali	Bamako
Mexico	Hermosillo
Mexico	Monterrey
Mexico	Guadalajara
Mexico	Mexico City
Myanmar	Yangon /Rangoon
Nicaragua	Managua
Nigeria	Abuja
North Macedonia	Skopje
Pakistan	Karachi
Pakistan	Islamabad
Pakistan	Lahore
Pakistan	Peshawar
Panama	Panama City

Philippines	Manila
Republic of Albania	Tirana
Republic of Kosovo	Pristina
Republic of Tajikistan	Dushanbe
Republic of Uzbekistan	Tashkent
Saudi Arabia	Riyadh
Saudi Arabia	Jeddah
Serbia	Belgrade
South America (Venezuela or Mexico)	Merida
Sudan	Khartoum
Syria	Damascus
Thailand	Chiang Mai
Turkey	Ankara
United Arab Emirates	Abu Dhabi
Venezuela	Caracas
Yemen	Sana'a

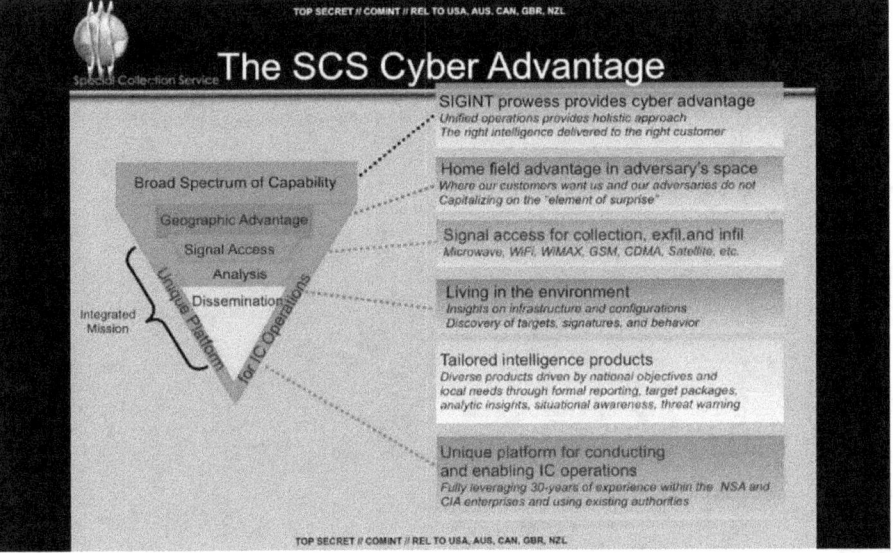

(S//SI//REL) This guide provides classification of facts concerning covert SIGINT collection from Diplomatic facilities overseas (STATEROOM sites).

Information	Classification Markings*	Reason**	Remarks	Declas/ Exempt**
1. GENERAL INFORMATION				
1.a (U) Coverterms or ECI names, such as STATEROOM, standing alone.	UNCLASSIFIED		(U//FOUO) Association of the coverterm STATEROOM with intelligence or SIGINT is U//FOUO. However, additional details could result in the need for classification.	
1.b (S//REL) The terms "Special Collection Service" (SCS) or Communications Systems Support Group (CSSG), when not associated with NSA, CIA, or an intelligence mission.	UNCLASSIFIED		(U) Any association with an intelligence agency or mission is SECRET.	
1.c (U) SCS program and budget data (e.g., line item details).	SECRET	1.5 (c)		X1
7. GLOSSARY				
(S//SI//REL) STATEROOM sites	STATEROOM sites are covert SIGINT collection sites located in diplomatic facilities abroad. SIGINT agencies hosting such sites include SCS (at U.S. Diplomatic facilities), Government Communications headquarters or GCHQ (at British diplomatic facilities), Communication Security Establishments or CSE (at Canadian diplomatic facilities), and Defense Signals Directorate or DSD (at Australian diplomatic facilities). These sites are small in size and in number of personnel staffing them. They are covert, and their true mission is not known by the majority of the diplomatic staff at the facility where they are assigned.			
(C//REL) Concealed collection system	Collection equipment whose location on a building is concealed so as not to reveal a SIGINT activity. For example, antennas are sometimes hidden in false architectural features or roof maintenance sheds.			
(S//SI//REL) Mock site	A typical SCS site set up at SCS HQS primarily for demonstration purposes, but which is incidentally used for processing SIGINT collected overseas and forwarded back via the SCS wide area network.			
(U) Diplomatic facilities or premises	Embassies or Consulates.			

PRISM

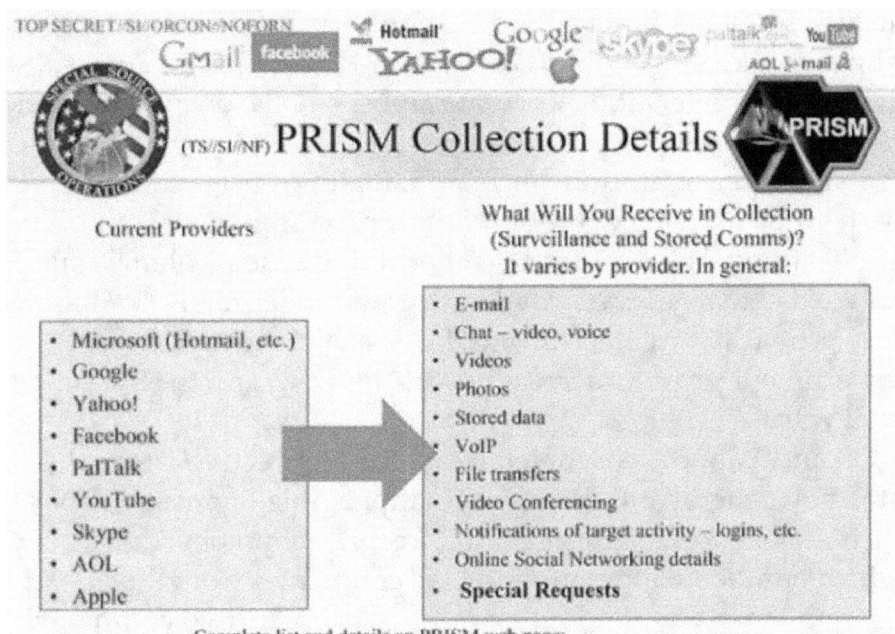

PRISM collected and stored Internet communications based on demands made to Internet companies such as Google under the previously mentioned *Section 702* of the *FISA Amendments Act of 2008*. Companies would be required to provide any data that matched court-approved terms. The NSA documents suggest PRISM is "the number one source of raw intelligence" and that over 91% of the data collected by the NSA was through the PRISM program.

PRISM tapped into the central servers of nine U.S. Internet companies: Microsoft, Yahoo, Google, Facebook, Paltalk, AOL, Skype, YouTube, Apple.

Several of these companies have denied knowingly giving access to the NSA. Apple spokesman Steve Dowling claimed he had never heard of the program and that government agencies had no direct access without court orders.

Through these providers, the NSA and FBI collected audio and video conversations, photographs, emails, documents and connection logs.

Paltalk has been around since 1998. It allows users to chat with video and voice through desktop and mobile applications. The documents suggest that videos, phone calls and text chats were recorded and stored indefinitely. Paltalk was primarily targeted during the Arab Spring (anti-government protests across the Middle East) and the Syrian civil war.

AOL and Yahoo were forced to accept a "directive" from the attorney general and director of national intelligence to expose their servers to the FBI's Data Intercept Technology Unit, which handled cooperation to U.S. companies from the NSA. The two companies were given legal immunity for their compliance.

The use of the "Unified Targeting Tool" (UTT) is mentioned as part of the PRISM program

UNDER CONSTANT SUPERVISION

RAMPART

The documents show the aim to *"gain access to high-capacity international fiber-optic cables that transit at major congestion points around the world"* and that the program had *"access to over 3 terabits per second of data streaming world-wide and encompasses all communication technologies such as voice, fax, telex, modem, email Internet chat, virtual private network (VPN), voice over IP (VoIP), and voice call records"*

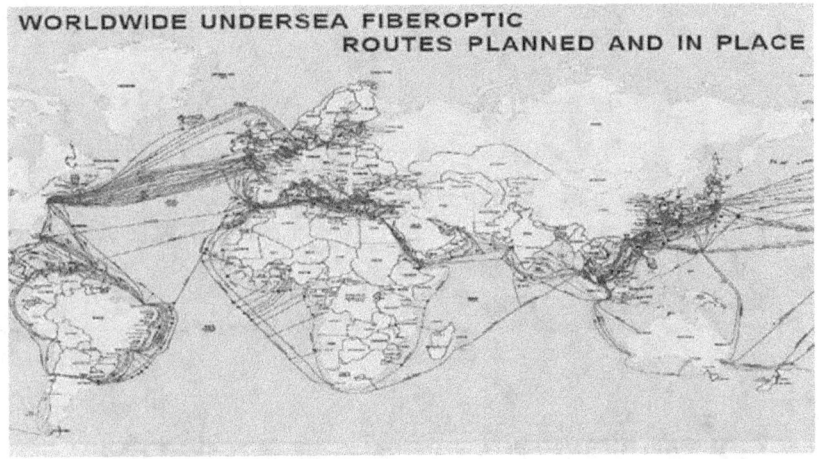

RAMPART A

(TS//SI//NF) Unconventional special access program leveraging Third Party partnerships:

- High-capacity international fiber transiting major congestion points around the world
- Foreign Partners provide access to cables and host U.S. equipment
- U.S. provides equipment for transport, processing and analysis
- No U.S. collection by Partner and No Host Country collection by U.S. – there ARE exceptions!
- Shared tasking and collection

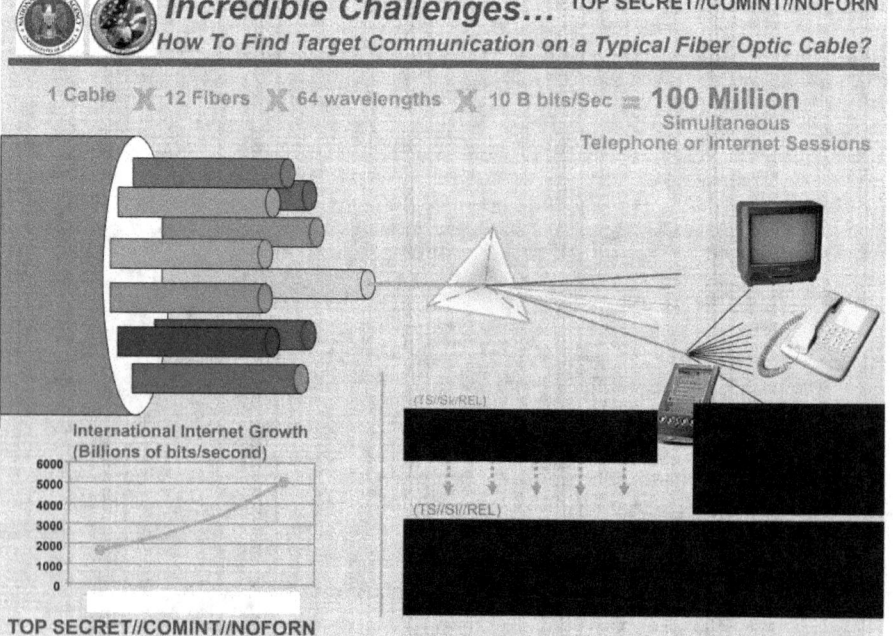

Incredible Challenges...
How To Find Target Communication on a Typical Fiber Optic Cable?

1 Cable × 12 Fibers × 64 wavelengths × 10 B bits/Sec = **100 Million** Simultaneous Telephone or Internet Sessions

International Internet Growth (Billions of bits/second)

STELLARWIND

Stellarwind was the codename for what is now known as part of a program that was approved by President Bush after 9/11.

Whistleblower Mark Klein, who worked as an AT&T technician, revealed details of cooperation with the NSA. He claimed to have built hardware at a facility known as Room 641A that the NSA was using to monitor, store and process telecommunications.

*The location as seen in 2002
(Image Landsat © U.S. Geological Survey)*

Data is believed to be stored and archived at an NSA facility in Utah as well as in secured rooms at both AT&T and Verizon. The Utah Data Center (UDC) has a classified purpose but was completed in May 2019, costing $1.5 billion[91] The data centre supposedly can store exabytes of information. An exabyte being a million terabytes.

---

[91] MILCOM EOM Aug Report 17 Sep 2014

Image: Landsat / Copernicus

Stellarwind was used to obtain suspicious activity reports known as SARS that relate to large transactions submitted by financial institutions under anti-money laundering law. On top of this, the program captured emails, telephone conversations and Internet activity. UDC is located at Camp Williams near Bluffdale and is one of the largest data centres in the world.

Room 641A is located inside the SBC Communications building at 611 Folsom Street in San Francisco (coordinates 37°47'07"N 122°23'48"W)

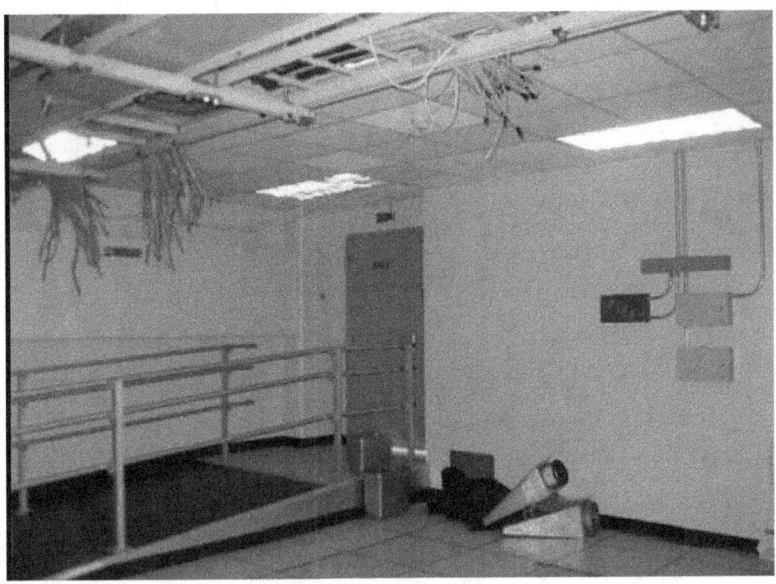

Room 641A as witnessed in 2004 (Photos: Mark Klein)

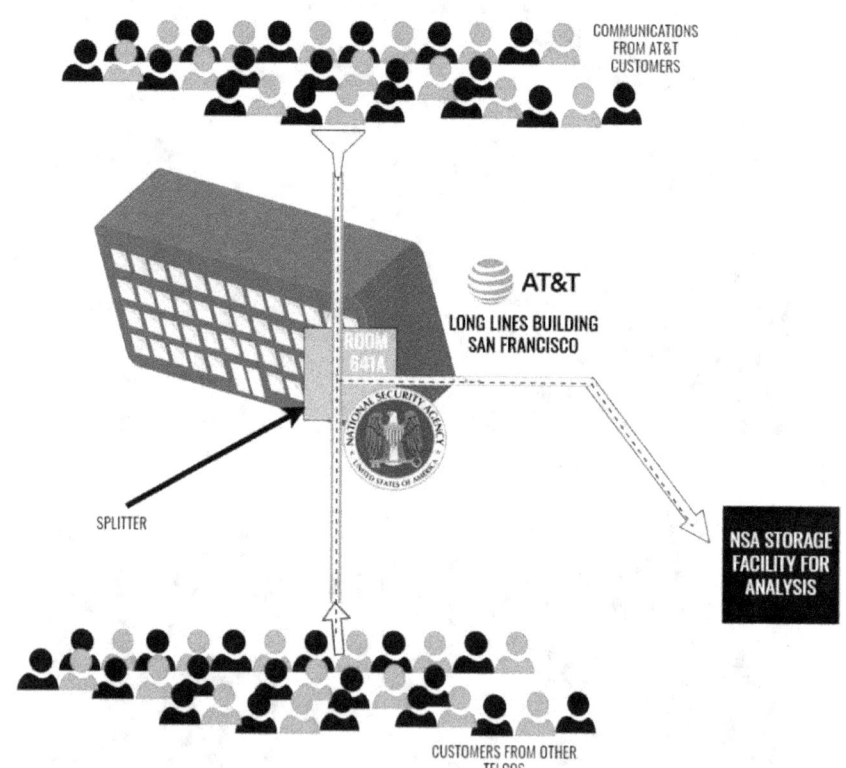

TEMPORA

The operation codenamed Tempora is the GCHQ's answer to the mass collection of data. Using fibre-optic cables, the GCHQ managed to scoop up hordes of information without deliberation. Whilst intelligence experts claim the data collected was only ever done lawfully and led to advances in identifying and blocking serious crimes, Snowden disputed that, calling the GCHQ "worse than the US"
The documents list Britain's technical abilities to tap into cables carrying global communication as "special source exploitation".

According to The Guardian, who broke the story, it is believed over 850,000 private contractors with top-secret clearance had access to the databases.
Numerous "intercept partners" were used to achieve the mass collection with some documents suggesting these partners were paid to comply.
The NSA's intercept station at Menwith Hill in North Yorkshire was vital for the Tempora program. The very same station linked to ECHELON years before.
The GCHQ tapped the SEA-ME-WE 3 optical submarine cable overseen by Singtel; a telecommunications company owned by the Government of Singapore. The cable landing points range from Germany to Australia
A document quotes Lieutenant General Keith Alexander, the head of the NSA who visited Menwith Hill in June 2008, asking *"Why can't we collect all the signals all the time? Sounds like a good summer project for Menwith."*
Well, as one document puts it:
"Sniff it all, collect it all, know it all, process it all and exploit it all."

TOP SECRET//UNDER//CONSTANT//SUPERVISION//REL TO READER

Surveillance is the business model of the Internet.

- Bruce Schneier
    Cryptographer and Computer security/privacy specialist

TAO AND THE ANT CATALOGUE

TAO – Tailored Access Operations – used "implants" to target web browsers and hardware like computer routers. The NSA ANT – Advanced Network Technology – catalogue features multiple available technologies that other NSA affiliates could purchase.

The British GCHQ collaborated to create MUSCULAR to attack Google services. This would tie-in with XKeyscore, an analytic database that would detail machines that were exploitable and worthy of attack. One method of finding vulnerable machines was by intercepting Windows Error Reporting, which would then be logged into the XKeyscore database.

One of the slides by the NSA even jokes about how the error reports sent from Windows XP were being used to send data to SIGINT:

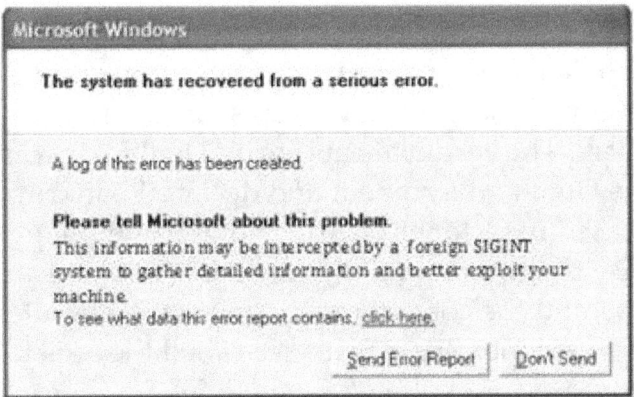

An attack suite called QUANTUM would utilise a compromised router that duplicates Internet traffic to send the data to both the NSA and the user accessing. Through affiliations with U.S. telecom companies, the NSA placed secret servers with the QUANTUM codename at key locations. The servers would impersonate a visited website, thereby tricking the target's browser to visit a FOXACID server. The FOXACID server would then install spyware. These methods are often referred to as "man-in-the-middle" (MITM) attacks or "man-on-the-side" attacks. A leaked diagram reveals how the attack was carried out, showing the NSA to effectively impersonate Google to trick users. Two years before the leaks, Google along with Microsoft and Firefox developers Mozilla had reported MITM attacks against Google users, primarily affecting Iran.[92] Using fraudulent google security certificates, browsers would redirect users. The certificate authority DigiNotar was taken over by the Dutch government and declared bankrupt. A report released in October of 2012 shows a complete compromise of the companies' systems. Whilst it is unknown who was behind the compromise, American computer security professional Bruce Schneier called the attack "the work of the NSA, or exploited by the NSA"

> **DEFINITION:**
> Secure Sockets Layer (SSL) is a standard security technology for establishing an encrypted link between a server and a client—typically a web server (website) and a browser, or a mail server and a mail client (e.g., Outlook). SSL allows sensitive information such as credit card numbers, social security numbers, and login credentials to be transmitted securely.
> - DigiCert

---

[92] https://security.googleblog.com/2011/08/update-on-attempted-man-in-middle.html **OR** https://archive.vn/WgiK2

UNDER CONSTANT SUPERVISION

Roel Schouwenberg, a security researcher at Kaspersky Labs, warned: *"with some 500 authorities out there globally it's hard to believe DigiNotar is the only compromised CA out there."*[93] Rogue SSL certificates were issued to Facebook, Yahoo, Microsoft, Skype, Twitter and the website of the Tor project as well as intelligence agencies such as Mossad, the CIA and MI6.

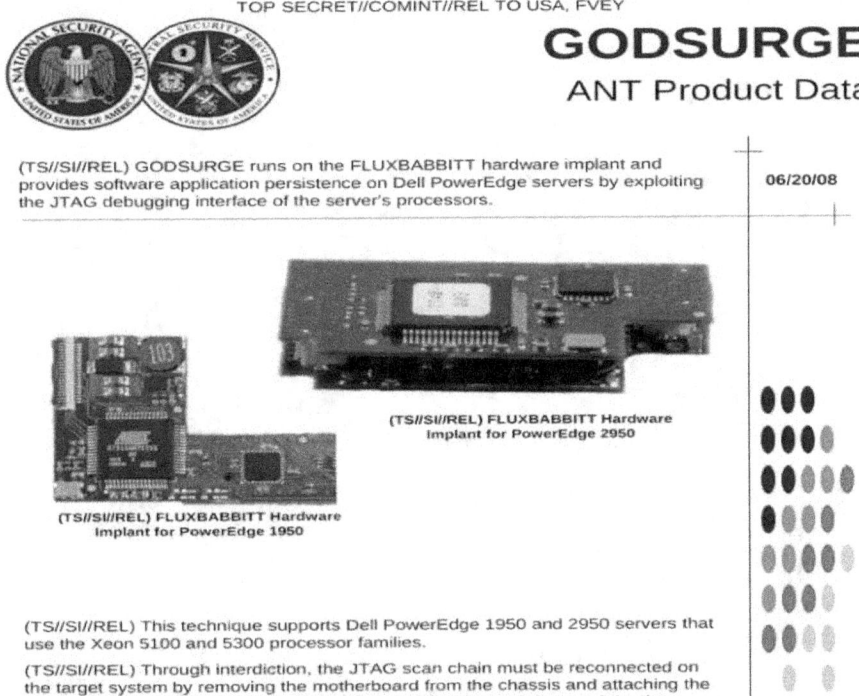

For $500, you could have easy access to the popular Dell PowerEdge servers

---

[93] https://securelist.com/why-diginotar-may-turn-out-more-important-than-stuxnet/30826/ **OR** https://archive.is/frEmp

The fibre submarine communications cable SEA-ME-WE 4 (*South East Asia–Middle East–Western Europe*) is a known target by the TAO. The cable carries data between Singapore, Malaysia, Thailand, United Arab Emirates, Saudi Arabia, Egypt, Italy and France to name just a few. This is the 'Internet Backbone' between South East Asia, the Indian Subcontinent and the Middle East and Europe.

SEA-ME-WE 4 cable with 'landing station' points (source: PriMetrica, Inc.)

The anonymous Internet access tool Tor was targeted by TAO to determine user activity and connect it with the mass amounts of hidden users.

OPEC (Organization of the Petroleum Exporting Countries) was also a target of TOA's surveillance, which subsequently aligns with the SEA-ME-WE 4 cable taps.

The operations group would also intercept laptops purchased online and divert them to secret warehouses where spyware would be installed, before sending them to the intended customers.

UNDER CONSTANT SUPERVISION

The Ant Catalogue was released by news magazine *Der Spiegel* who described the document as reading like a mail-order catalogue *"which other NSA employees can order technologies from the ANT division for tapping their targets' data."*

The catalogue features spying tools for cell phone networks, mobile phones, routers, servers, firewalls, computers, monitors, keyboards, USB, Wireless LAN and even room surveillance. Software is typically listed as free-of-charge to US and FVEY alliances, with some hardware costing as much as $250,000

The ANT catalogue also revealed software by major companies have either been used to spy on people without the company knowing, or the company has complacently allowed such surveillance. One development offers the ability to intercept Apple devices:

(TS//SI//REL) DROPOUTJEEP is a software implant for the Apple iPhone that utilizes modular mission applications to provide specific SIGINT functionality. This functionality includes the ability to remotely push/pull files from the device, SMS retrieval, contact list retrieval, voicemail, geolocation, hot mic, camera capture, cell tower location, etc. Command, control, and data exfiltration can occur over SMS messaging or a GPRS data connection. All communications with the implant will be covert and encrypted.

(TS//SI//REL) The initial release of DROPOUTJEEP will focus on installing the implant via close access methods. A remote installation capability will be pursued for a future release.

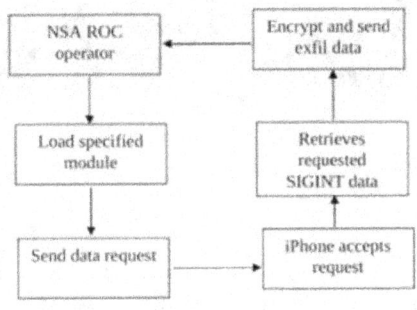

(U//FOUO) DROPOUTJEEP - Operational Schematic

A 2012 TAO budget document asserts that American telecom companies like AT&T, Verizon and Sprint "*insert vulnerabilities into commercial encryption systems, IT systems, networks and endpoint communications devices used by targets*"
U.S. companies Cisco and Dell released statements denying the insertion of back doors (a secret method of circumventing authentication or encryption) in their products. The NSA backdoors are supposedly planted in hard drives manufactured by Western Digital and Seagate in sectors of the disk drive inaccessible to the user.

"Cisco does not work with any government to modify our equipment, nor to implement any so-called security 'back doors' in our products"

---- Cisco responding to claims of supporting or knowing about the intelligence solutions used on their technology.

"[Dell] respects and complies with the laws of all countries in which it operates."

UNDER CONSTANT SUPERVISION

One product, COTTONMOUTH-I (CM-I), is a USB hardware implant that gives the ability to load exploit software allowing peripherals such as keyboards to collect and transmit data. Sold in blocks of 50, costing roughly $20 each, the small tool is comparable to physical keyloggers which can be inserted between the keyboard and USB port making unsuspecting users hand over passwords and any keystrokes entered. Hardware keyloggers are usually undetectable by security software and involve having to re-access the computer to remove the device and retrieve the information logged on the internal memory. With the CM-I, this appears to solve that problem. If the NSA were intercepted laptops, it is also plausible they had installed CM-I units on intercepted keyboards.

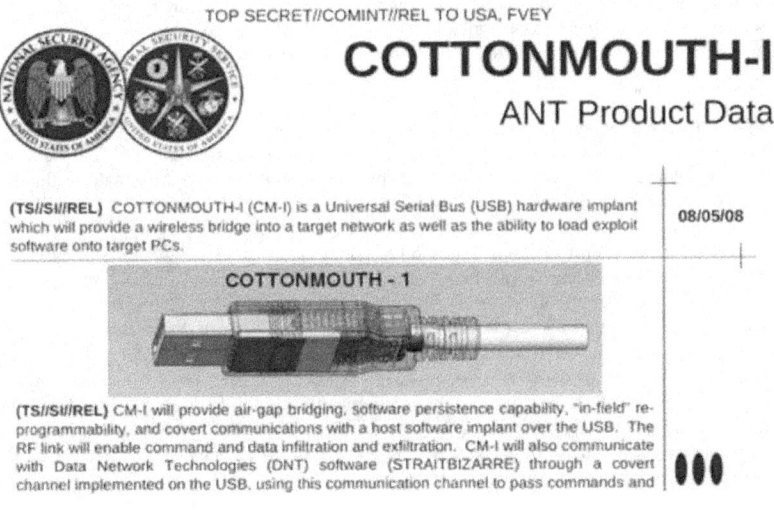

Director of National Intelligence James Clapper released a statement[94] after the leaks titled *"Why the Intelligence Community Seeks to Understand Online Communication Tools & Technologies"* once again reiterating that global surveillance was in the name of security.

> **October 4, 2013**
>
> Recently published news articles discuss the Intelligence Community's interest in tools used to facilitate anonymous online communication. The articles accurately point out that the Intelligence Community seeks to understand how these tools work and the kind of information being concealed.
>
> However, the articles fail to make clear that the Intelligence Community's interest in online anonymity services and other online communication and networking tools is based on the undeniable fact that these are the tools our adversaries use to communicate and coordinate attacks against the United States and our allies.
>
> The articles fail to mention that the Intelligence Community is only interested in communication related to valid foreign intelligence and counterintelligence purposes and that we operate within a strict legal framework that prohibits accessing information related to the innocent online activities of US citizens.
>
> Within our lawful mission to collect foreign intelligence to protect the United States, we use every intelligence tool available to understand the intent of our foreign adversaries so that we can disrupt their plans and prevent them from bringing harm to innocent Americans.
>
> In the modern telecommunications era, our adversaries have the ability to hide their messages and discussions among those of innocent people around the world. They use the very same social networking sites, encryption tools and other security features that protect our daily online activities.
>
> Americans depend on the Intelligence Community to know who and what the threats are, and where they come from. They want us to provide policy makers with the information necessary to keep our nation safe, and they rightfully want us to do this without compromising respect for the civil liberties and privacy of our citizens.
>
> Many of the recent articles based on leaked classified documents have painted an inaccurate and misleading picture of the Intelligence Community. The reality is that the men and women at the National Security Agency and across the Intelligence Community are abiding by the law, respecting the rights of citizens and doing everything they can to help keep our nation safe.
>
> James R. Clapper
> Director of National Intelligence

---

[94] https://icontherecord.tumblr.com/post/63103784923/dni-statement-why-the-intelligence-community

UNDER CONSTANT SUPERVISION

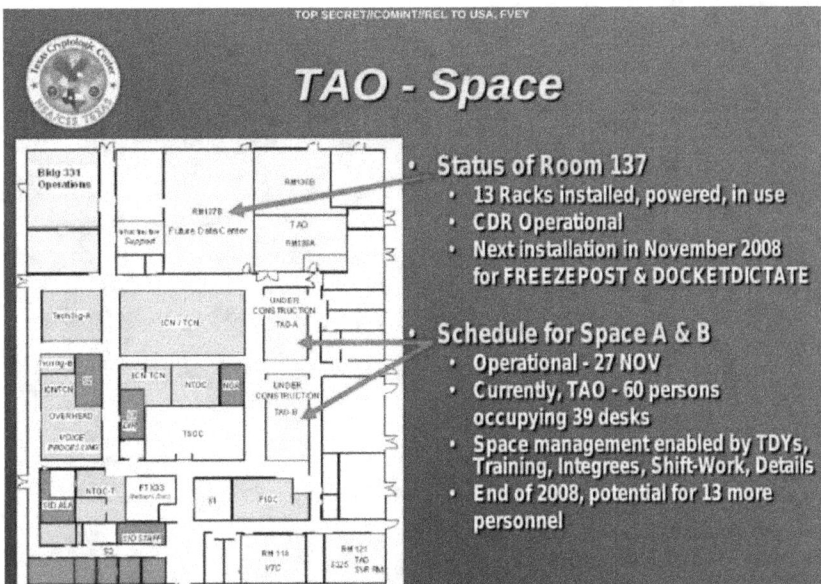

(TS//SI//NF) Such operations involving **supply-chain interdiction** are some of the most productive operations in TAO, because they pre-position access points into hard target networks around the world.

(TS//SI//NF) Left: Intercepted packages are opened carefully; Right: A "load station" implants a beacon

(TS//SI//NF) In one recent case, after several months a beacon implanted through supply-chain interdiction called back to the NSA covert infrastructure. This call back provided us access to further exploit the device and survey the network.

TOP SECRET//COMINT//REL TO USA, FVEY

(Report generated on: 4/11/2013 3:31:05PM)

NewCrossProgram		Active ECP Count:	1
CrossProgram-1-13	New	ECP Lead:	[NAME REDACTED]
Title of Change:	Update Software on all Cisco ONS Nodes		
Submitter:	[NAME REDACTED]	Approval Priority:	C-Routine
Site(s):	APPLE1 : CLEVERDEVICE : HOMEMAKER : DOGHUT : QUARTERPOUNDER : QUEENSLAND : SCALLION : SPORTCOAT : SUBSTRATUM : TITAN POINTE : SUBSTRATUM : BIRCHWOOD : MAYTAG : EAGLE : EDEN :	Project(s):	No Project(s) Entered
System(s):	Comms/Network : Comms/Network : Comms/Network : Comms/Network :	SubSystem(s):	No Subsystem(s) Entered
Description of Change:	Udate software on all Cisco Optical Network Switches.		

Reason for Change: All of our Cisco ONS SONET multiplexers are experiencing a software bug that causes them to intermittently drop out.

Mission Impact: The mission impact is unknown. While the existing bug doesn't appear to affect traffic, applying the new software update could. Unfortunately, there is now way to be sure. We can't simulate the bug in our lab and so it's impossible to predict exactly what will happen when we apply the software update. We propose to update one of the nodes in NBP-320 first to determine if the update goes smoothly.

Recently we tried to reset the standby manager card in the HOIMEMAKER node. When that failed, we attempted to physically reseat it. Since it was the standby card, we did not expect that would cause any problems. However, upon reseating the card, the entire ONS crashed and we lost all traffic through the box. It took more than an hour to recover from this failure.

The worst case scenario is that we have to blow away the entire configuration and start from scratch. Prior to starting our upgrade, we will save the configuration so that if we have to configure the box from scratch, we can simply upload the saved configuration. We estimate that we will be down for no more than an hour for each node in the system.

Additional Info: 3/26/2013 8:16:13 AM [NAME REDACTED]
We have tested the upgrade in our lab and it works well. However, we can't repeat the bug in our lab, so we don't know if we will encounter problems when we attempt to upgrade a node that is affected by the bug.

Last CCB Entry: 04/10/13 16:08:11 [NAME REDACTED]
09 Apr Blarney CCB - Blarney ECP board approved
ECP lead: [NAME REDACTED]

Programs Affected: Blarney Fairview Oakstar Stormbrew

No Related Work Tasks

XKEYSCORE

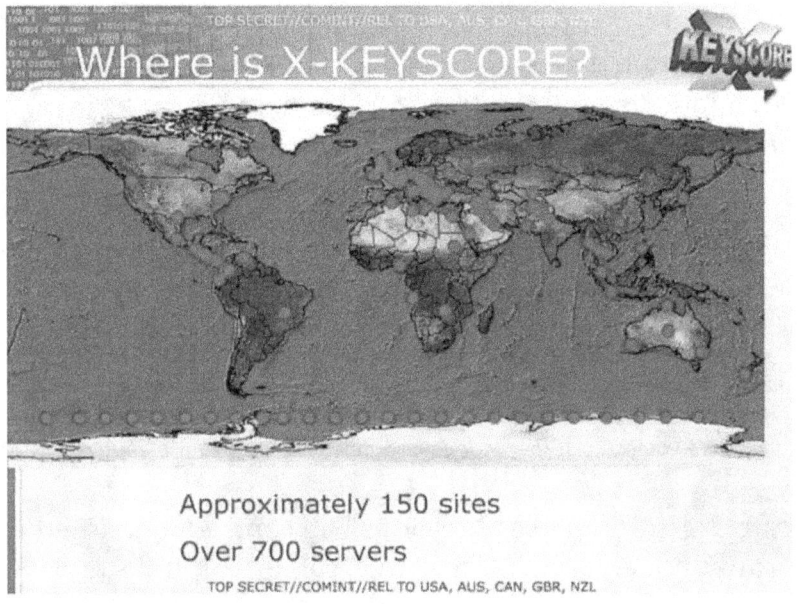

XKeyscore or XKS was used to search and analyse continuously collected Internet data. With no authorisation required, the NSA program lets analysts sift through comprehensive databases of emails, online messages and browsing history. Snowden explained that with XKS he could *"wiretap anyone, from you or your accountant, to a federal judge or even the president, if I had [your] personal email"* a claim that was fervently denied by Intelligence Committee chairman Mike Rogers who said *"He's lying. It's impossible for him to do what he was saying he could do."*
FISA requires a warrant for using the technology to target **U.S. Persons** but not if they have been in touch with a **foreign target.** This simple loophole made everything possible with XKS.

In 2014 Snowden was asked by a German broadcaster what could be done using the retrieval system, to which he responded[95]:

> "You could read anyone's email in the world; anybody you've got an email address for. Any website: You can watch traffic to and from it. Any computer that an individual sits at: You can watch it. Any laptop that you're tracking: you can follow it as it moves from place to place throughout the world. It's a one-stop-shop for access to the NSA's information. ... I can track your real name, I can track associations with your friends and I can build what's called a fingerprint, which is network activity unique to you, which means anywhere you go in the world, anywhere you try to sort of hide your online presence, your identity."

Australia's Pine Gap uses Missions 7600 and 8300 to intercept data from phone, radio, microwave, satellite uplinks and transmissions from civilians and the military.

Phone and email communication are also collected using the spy program[96]. As we've learned already, Pine Gap is the perfect location for programs like XKeyscore to operate. Central in the middle of Australia, Pine Gap looks north and west to cover Africa, the Middle East, Russia, China and East Asia. Menwith Hill covers the western hemisphere which includes the Middle East and Africa but also covers a distance of Europe and the Atlantic.

According to the documents, "The Mission 8300 system has four satellites in near-geosynchronous earth orbits"

---

[95] https://archive.vn/syX5X

[96] SECRET//COMINT/TALENT KEYHOLE//REL TO USA, AUS, and GBR//25X1 and TOP SECRET//SI//REL TO USA, FVEY *Top-Secret: NSA Intelligence Relationship with Australia*

A 2008 document claims the NSA received so much data, they had to clear it due to the lack of storage space. The document reads:

> "At some sites, the amount of data we receive per day (20+ terabytes) can only be stored for as little as 24 hours"

The data is stored across multiple data centres where processing may also occur.

Pine Gap stores the data as do three Australian Signals Directorate facilities: The Shoal Bay Receiving Station near Darwin, the Australian Defence Satellite Communications Facility at Geraldton (also known as Kojarena) and the naval communications station HMAS Harman outside Canberra. New Zealand's GCSB facility at Waihopai also had connections.

The program and XKS system have been secretly shared with Germany, Sweden and Japan.

"Slowing down the Internet"

- XKS goal is to store the full-take content for 3-5 days, effectively "slowing down the Internet" so that analysts can go back and recover sessions that otherwise would have been dropped by the front end

- Meta-data is saved off longer, with the goal of 30 days retention

- A lot of analysis can be done through meta-data only (MARINA is meta-data only)

Data Sources

- FORNSAT (downlink)
- Overhead (uplink)
- Special Source
- Tailored Access
- F6
- FISA (limited)
- 3rd party

MUSCULAR

MUSCULAR is the name of a surveillance program operated by GCHQ and the NSA. GCHQ is listed as the primary operator. The two agencies have secretly broken into the main communications links that connect data centres of Yahoo and Google.

The slide below reveals access to Google's data centres. Google responded to the program by announcing encryption protocols for all traffic, as did Yahoo and Microsoft.

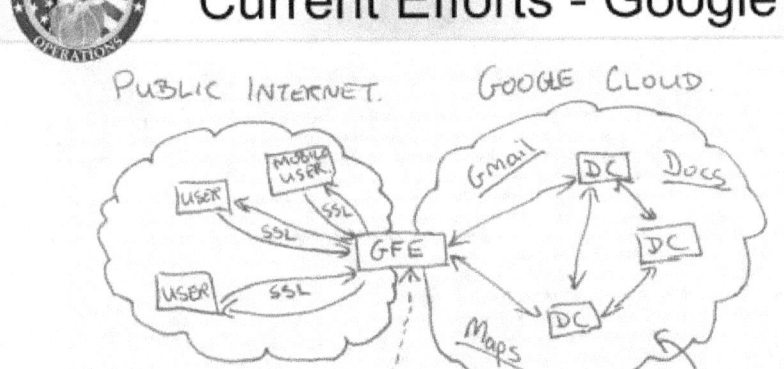

Based on analysis of Narchive email data by ▓▓▓▓ and ▓▓▓▓, we were able to indentify statistics for the original communications date for Narchive email messages collected:

< 30 days	1118	11%
> 30 days, < 90 days	1758	17%
> 90 days < 180 days	1302	13%
> 180 days, < 1 year	2592	26%
> 1years, < 5 years	3084	31%
> 5years	154	>1%

Numerous target offices have complained about this collection "diluting" their workflow. One argument for keeping it is that it provides a retrospective look at target activity – this argument is hampered by a) the unreliable and non-understood nature of when the transfer occurs for an account, and b) that FISA restrospective collection would retrieve the exact same data "on demand".

SSO Optimization believes that while this is "valid" collection of content, the sheer volume and the age – coupled with the unpredictable nature of Narchive activity – makes collecting older data a less desirable use of valuable resources. 59% of Narchive email collected was originally sent and received more than 180 days after collection. This represents about 8.9 GB a day of "less desirable" collection – long term allocation that could be easily filled with more timely, useful FI from this lucrative SSO site. As always with our optimization, the data would still be available at the site store for SIGDEV. This would not impact metadata extraction.

Past DO volume reduction efforts:
Webmail OAB- Leap day 2012: the original defeat only targeted gmail, yahoo, and hotmail webmail protocol
FB buddylist sampling since last year

Today: FB OAB defeat/atxks/facebook/ownerless_addressbook : this is a JSON addressbook

Speaker's Notes

From Feb 28 2013: Proposed/imminent latest DO/Volume reduction: Narchive

BLUF: Requested S2 concurrence at S2 TLC on 25 Feb with partial throttling of content from Yahoo, Narchive email traffic which contains data older than 6 months from MUSCULAR. Numerous S2 analysts have complained of its existence, and the relatively small intelligence value it contains does not justify the sheer volume of collection at MUSCULAR (1/4th of the total daily collect).

Background: Since July of 2012, Yahoo has been transferring entire email accounts using the Narchive data format (a proprietary format for which NSA had to develop custom demultiplexers). To date, we are unsure why these accounts are being transferred – movement of individuals, backup of data from overseas servers to US servers, or some other reason. There is no way currently to predict if an account will be transferred via Yahoo Narchive.

Currently, Narchive traffic is collected and forwarded to NSA for memorialization in any quantity only from DS-200B. On any given day, Narchive traffic represents 25% (15GB) of DS-200B's daily PINWALE content allocation (60GB currently). DS-200B is scheduled to be upgraded in the summer of 2013; it is likely that memorialized Narchive traffic, if still present in the environment, will grow proportionally (i.e. double now, to 30 GB/day).

Narchive traffic is mailbox formatted email, meaning unlike Yahoo webmail, any attachments present would be collected as part of the message. This is a distinct advantage. However, it has not been determined what causes an Narchive transfer of an account, so these messages are rarely collected "live".

UNDER CONSTANT SUPERVISION

INTELLIPEDIA

SIDtoday is the name of an internal newsletter for the Signals Intelligence Directorate.

In the November 2006 issue, an article details a wiki site for analysts throughout the intelligence community: Intellipedia. Intellipedia features information with limits based on an intelligence workers clearance level. The article claims the wiki had "only about 20 registered users" which is a small number compared to the claims there were over 200 CIA users. It's noted that the CIA offered staff a six-day vacation to study Intellipedia and other cooperation tools. A Freedom of Information Act request confirms the existence of Intellipedia up to at least 2014 with 255,402 top-secret cleared users and over 110,000 pages. Three wikis are running on separate networks:

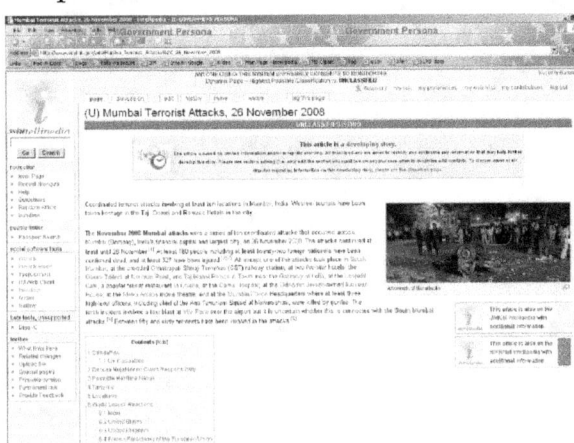

JWICS – Top Secret
SIPRNET – Secret
DNI-U – Sensitive But Unclassified (SBU or FOUO – *For Official Use Only*)

JWICS was allegedly one of the networks accessed by Chelsea – then known as Bradley – Manning who leaked classified material in 2010, including the WikiLeaks' video showing an airstrike killing civilians and reporters released as *Collateral Murder*.

According to SIDtoday, Intellipedia was launched in conjunction with an instant-messaging system for discussion between agencies and a blog for *"sharing your knowledge and point of view with others"*

MFR

INTELLIPEDIA Searches

Some, if not most, of these requests call for a search the three wikis that comprise Intellipedia:

      JWICS

      SIPRNET

      DNI-U

All ODNI deletions (b)(3)(b)(6)

    It appears we get the TS JWICS feeds on Intelink and DNI-U is, of course, our system. I checked with ▇▇▇ via Sametime and asked her if we should not refer the requester to DoD for the SIPRNET aspect of these requests. ▇▇▇ advised that since SIPRNET is not an ODNI system we are not required to search it. She further advised that we respond without referring the requester to DoD. Simply search the systems we are required to search (DNI systems).

    In view of this, since JWICS is a DIA system, we need not search JWICS separately either. A search of Intelink and DNI-U should be sufficient for ODNI searches.

▇▇▇

10Feb11

NSA LOCATIONS

The locations in which the NSA asserts its dominance are far from secretive. These extend past the Utah Data Center covered previously and the multitude of locations around the world that are often advertised as space research satellite stations and defence hubs. You may notice a few of these locations are listed in the ECHELON locations list.

NSA HEADQUARTERS: FORT MEADE, MARYLAND

Image: Landsat/Copernicus

Location: 39° 6'35.49"N / 76°46'14.42"W

The NSA Headquarters is located near Baltimore and is one of the largest employers in the United States, employing over 20,000. It's the largest employer of mathematicians according to the NSA.

The HQ is also believed to house one of the world's most powerful supercomputers and have the largest single group of supercomputers – this, however, is unconfirmed by the NSA themselves or any leaks.

Photo: NSA

The NSA facility maxed out the electricity grid several times between 2000 and 2006 with the electricity provider providing 75 megawatts in 2007 and claiming they were unable to sell any more power.

It is not known if solar power is utilised to reduce power consumption.

The NSA HQ has its own fire department, police service and post office.

NSA AEROSPACE DATA FACILITY: AURORA, COLORADO

Image: Landsat/Copernicus

Location: 39°43'3.84"N / 104°46'37.38"W

There is believed to be around 900 employees at the Buckley Air Force Base known as Aerospace Data Facility. The NSA gathers intelligence collected from geostationary satellites as well as signals from other spacecraft and overseas listening stations.

NSA TEXAS CRYPTOLOGIC CENTER: SAN ANTONIO

Image: Landsat/Copernicus

Location: 29°26'50.36"N / 98°38'26.28"W

Home to the TAO. The Texas Cryptology Center (TCC) has an independent power grid. TCC conducts signals intelligence at the location and began leasing a nearby computer chip fabrication plant previously owned by Sony. A data storage complex was built in 2010. The total number of employees is classified. Microsoft's San Antonio data centre is located not far from the TCC and it's been theorised that the NSA waited for Microsoft to open before constructing their centre.

NSA SUGAR GROVE RESEARCH STATION: WEST VIRGINIA

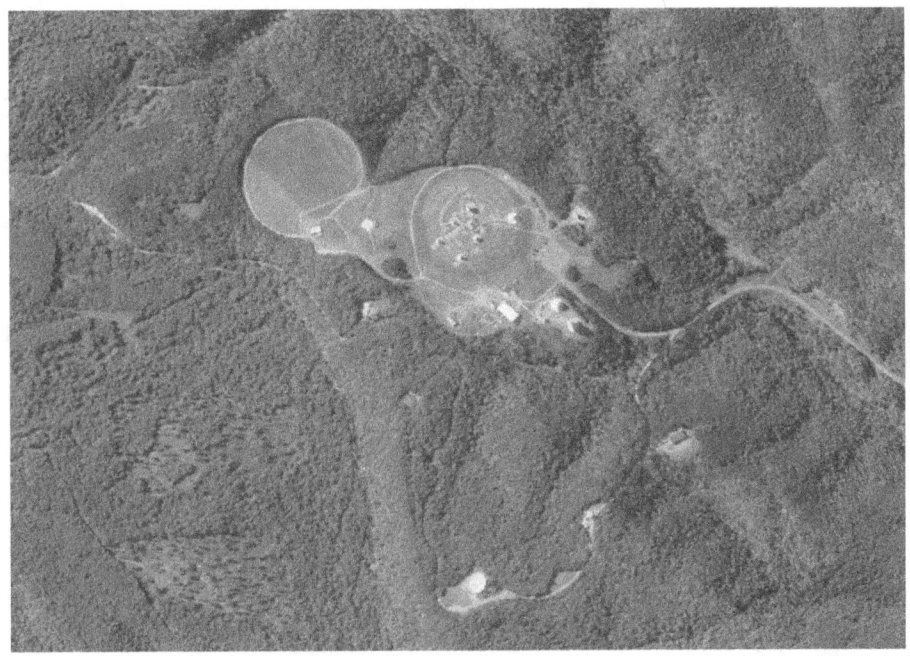

Image: Landsat/Copernicus

Location: 38°30'53.87"N / 79°16'47.97"W

Codenamed Timberline in many leaked documents, the NSA Sugar Grove Research Station in Sugar Grove, West Virginia is allegedly one of three so-called "SIGINT Activity Designators" and is marked as one of the major stations of ECHELON. In 2005, a New York Times article stated the site intercepted all international signals entering the Eastern United States. Whilst the main base has supposedly been sold after several failed bids[97], the South NSA listening station is still operational.

---

[97] https://web.archive.org/web/20130502003808/http://cryptome.org/dodi/2013/opnav-5400-2215.pdf

NSA GEORGIA CRYPTOLOGIC OPERATIONS CENTER: AUGUSTA

Image: Landsat/Copernicus

Location: 33°24'44.05"N / 82°10'6.58"W

Houses roughly 4000 employees specialising in cryptology and linguistics. The location occupies 160 acres and is spread over three levels and 22 "caves"
According to the NSA, the location is used to *"conduct continuous security operations on selected targets in support of national and warfighter intelligence requirements"*

NSA OAK RIDGE / MULTIPROGRAM COMPUTATIONAL DATA CENTER: TENNESSEE

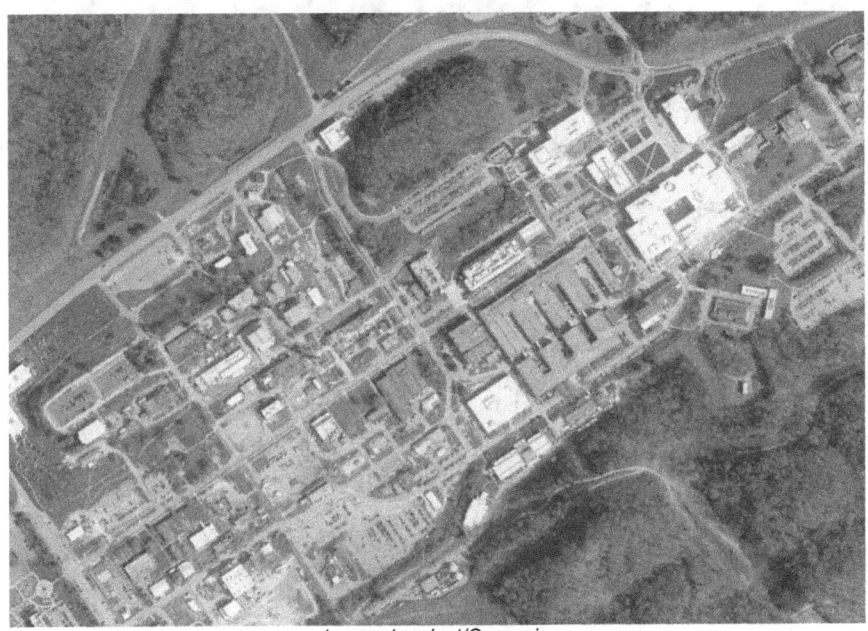

Image: Landsat/Copernicus

Location: 35°55'51.01"N / 84°18'44.11"W

Located within the Oak Ridge National Laboratory Campus. Scientists and computer engineers with top security clearance build supercomputer and work on cryptanalytic projects as well as a multitude of undisclosed projects. The facility known as *Multiprogram Computational Data Center* is an Internet surveillance lab which allegedly works alongside the Utah Data Center (UDC)
Oak Ridge previously housed *Jaguar*, a supercomputer with over 220,000 AMD processors built by Hewlett Packard subsidiary *Cray Inc.*
Jaguar was upgraded to *Titan* which was decommissioned in 2019 to make way for a larger project.

NSA CRYPTOLOGIC CENTER: HAWAII

Image: Landsat/Copernicus

Location: 21°31'22.51"N / 158° 0'43.05"W

Located between Kunia Camp and Wheeler Army Airfield in Oahu, Hawaii. The NSA Central Security Service's Regional Security Operations Center is used to gather and analyse intelligence from U.S. interest areas such as the Middle East and Southeast Asia. It is constructed on 70 acres. The Hawaii Cryptologic Center (HCC) was where Edward Snowden worked before departing with the global surveillance documents.

The facility was opened in 2012 to replace the Kunia Regional SIGINT Operations Center (KRSOC) which was located on the same plot. KRSOC was built as an underground bay in response to the 1941 Pearl Harbor attack.

OTHER LOCATIONS:

Roaring Creek Earth Station in Pennsylvania is operated by AT&T and used by the NSA to capture and monitor satellite telecom.
Location:
40° 53' 34.8" N
76° 26' 24" W

Salt Creek Earth Station located near California was formerly licensed to AT&T. It is also used by the NSA for the same reasons as *Roaring Creek*.
Location:
38°56'18.60"N
122° 8'52.96"W

Friendship Annex (or FANX/FANEX) in Maryland is a cyber espionage station and is the location where new employees are subject to polygraph tests.
Location:
39°12'4.19"N
76°41'2.39"W

Multiple "3rd *Party Partners*" of the NSA such as Thailand are used as NSA collectors. The US Embassy in Bangkok is used as a joint NSA-CIA Special Collections Service unit (SCS). A facility in the Thai city of Khon Kaen codenamed INDRA and LEMONWOOD is believed to be used as a Foreign Satellite Interception site (FORNSAT).

INDRA is used to relay data back to the Hawaii base.

GCHQ SURVEILLANCE AND SIGNAL TRACKING LOCATIONS

These locations also include those found in the ECHELON locations list.

CAT HILL, ASCENSION ISLAND

© 2020 Maxar Technologies

Location: 7°57'8.68"S / 14°24'25.73"W

Cat Hill is a settlement on Ascension Island which forms part of the British Overseas Territories. The location is a joint NSA-GCHQ Composite Signals Organisation. Ascension Island is located in the Southern Atlantic Ocean with data from the 2016 census showing a population of 806 people. The mid-Atlantic position of the island is utilised for communications. The European Space Agency has a tracking station on the island. The RAF base is used by the U.S. Space Force to track rocket launches from Cape Canaveral in Florida.

AYIOS NIKOLAOS STATION:

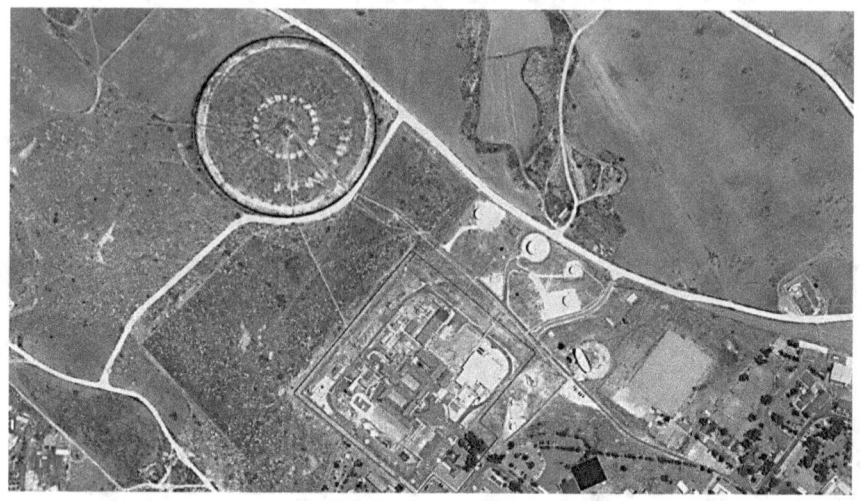

© 2020 Maxar Technologies

Location: 35° 5'35.60"N / 33°53'16.32"E

The *Ayios Nikolaos Station* is a satellite ground station and eavesdropping centre in the British Overseas Territory on the island of Cyprus.
It is now used as an intelligence-gathering station and has been since ECHELON.

GCHQ BUDE / GCHQ CSO MORWENSTOW:

© 2020 Maxar Technologies

Location: 35° 5'35.60"N / 33°53'16.32"E

GCHQ Composite Signals Organisation Station Morwenstow abbreviated to GCHQ CSO Morwenstow or simply referred to as GCHQ Bude is a UK Government satellite ground station and eavesdropping centre located on the north Cornwall coast. It is located on part of the site of former WWII airfield RAF Cleave which was almost entirely transformed. The site has been used for satellite inception since at least 1960. The NSA funds most of the project, even spending nearly $200 million on redevelopment, and pays for all technology utilised. Intelligence is shared between the NSA and GCHQ. The location was initially operated under FVEY, gathering data for the ECHELON network. Many of the activities remain classified.

The location presents an opportunity for mass submarine cable surveillance at nearby landing points with TAT-3 travelling from Cornwall to New Jersey, United States owned by GPO (later BT) and AT&T. When TAT-14 was launched, the GCHQ and NSA gained more cable landing points including Denmark, Germany, Netherlands and France. Submarine cables Apollo, CANTAT-1, TAT-8, AC-2, EIG and GLO-1 make landfall 10km south from the location. Financial trading data is carried from New York through cables south of GCHQ Bude. GCHQ is located roughly 100km from Goonhilly Downs where Goonhilly Satellite Earth Station, previously one of the largest satellite stations in the world, was

Goonhilly Earth Station satellites and site antennas
(Photo: GES Ltd)

established. Bude was able to intercept the Intelsat communication satellites in the mid-1960s. The Satellite Earth Station also links into Transatlantic communications cables including SEA-ME-WE 3 *(South-East Asia – Middle East – Western Europe)*, which was intercepted by GCHQ.

RAF DIGBY

Photo: NSA Document

Location: 53°5'50.42"N / 0°25'57.11"W

RAF Digby may look like a small location with minimal obvious satellite features, but it is, in fact, one of the biggest players for targeting, Sudanese, Lebanese and Palestinian communications. One NSA employee wrote in the March 2005 issue of SIDtoday that RAF Digby *"does not attract the kind of press attention lavished on RAF Menwith Hill to the north — and long may that continue"*

According to NSA documents, the location has also been used as a surveillance hub for General Atomics MQ-1 Predator and MQ-9 Reaper drones and collecting near real-time location data from GSM mobile phone networks.

GCHQ CHELTENHAM

© 2020 Maxar Technologies

Location: 51°53'55.94"N / 2° 7'19.44"W

Although not exactly a spying station or eavesdropping location, the main headquarters are worth including due to many GCHQ personnel operating from the Cheltenham location and analysing data collected from the multitude of stations under their control or partnership.

AT&T: INTERNET SURVEILLANCE PROVIDER

As we have established, the NSA's biggest resource is AT&T. In-fact, AT&T is seen as VIP's in one document saying *"This is a partnership, not a contractual relationship"*

What makes AT&T so special is the list of submarine cables and data hubs owned and operated by the major company. The company features a blog on their website written by a member of a specialised team of cable engineers who maintain nearly 440,000 miles of cable[98]. Access to cables like these is priceless for spies looking to capture the information travelling. With Google now becoming one of the major holders in cables, it will take a lot of trust to ensure the NSA don't have access to tap in.

The legal declaration[99] signed by former AT&T worker Mark Klein state that millions of customers were intercepted using a "splitter" which diverted all information into the secretive room (641A) described before. According to Klein, the telecom company outfitted the room with biometric fingerprint and retinal scanners. Over 1.1 billion domestic phone call records were handed over to the NSA. In an interview with PBS[100], Klein described the splitter with a simple correlation:

> The analogy I can give you, which most people are familiar with is, say you get cable TV in your living room and then want to watch all the channels you get in the living room, you want to get all those same channels in your bedroom. So, they install on the cable what they call a splitter, which splits off all the signals, duplicates of the same signals which go to the bedroom. ...

---

[98] https://about.att.com/innovationblog/undersea_cables **OR** https://archive.vn/dHb99

[99] https://www.eff.org/files/filenode/att/mark_klein_unredacted_decl-including_exhibits.pdf

[100] https://www.pbs.org/wgbh/pages/frontline/homefront/interviews/klein.html **OR** https://archive.vn/HPJ9A

> What the splitter does is make a duplicate copy of all the signals going across the fibre-optic cables. ... We're talking about billions and billions of bits of data going across every second, right? And it's going into the router, and it's coming back from the routers in that office. So, what they do with the splitter is they intercept that data stream and make copies of all the data, and those copies go down on the cable to the secret room. ...

Klein also claimed that there was an issue with the splitter, to which a technician replied: *"Oh, yeah, we're having the same problem with the splitters going into other offices"* before listing Seattle, San Diego, Los Angeles and San Jose as having similar issues.

When asked about the 9/11 attacks and why the government agencies didn't relay information or respond to prevent further attacks, Klein replied:

I think if they needed anything, they had it already on the books. There's lots of -- maybe too much -- leeway for surveillance as it is. And they had lots of information that 9/11 was going to happen. But for some strange reason, they didn't act.

> So, I think you're asking this government -- which is full of prevarications and misleading statements and not very truthful and also a large component of simply incompetence -- handing them the keys to everybody's private information. I don't trust them with that. I think they're far more interested in just aggrandizing power for power's sake, and they're just using it as an excuse -- the so-called war on terror, which is their excuse for everything they do. Everything is aggrandizing power secretly, with no oversight. And I'm against that. It's dangerous.

UNDER CONSTANT SUPERVISION

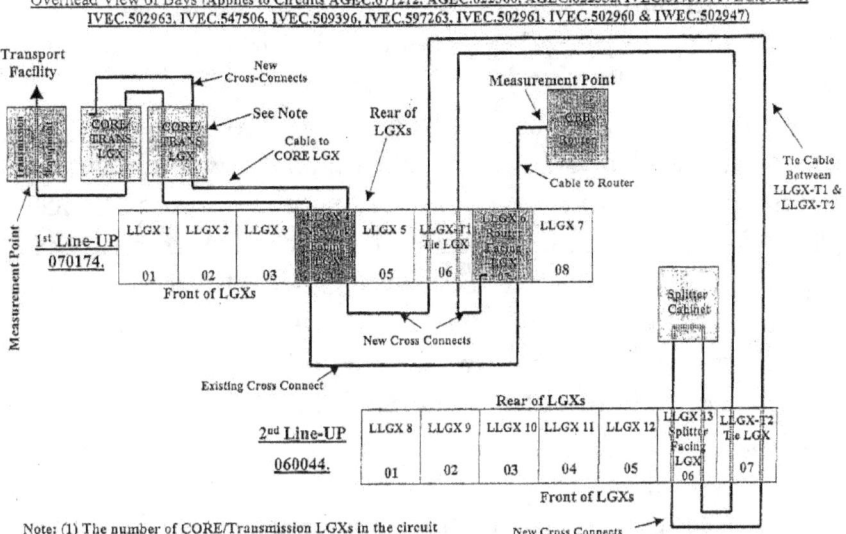

Diagrams detailing the AT&T wiretapping systems that allowed the NSA to monitor communications warrantlessly.
Source: EFF Legal Cases (Hepting v. AT&T lawsuit)

SIDE NOTE:
Eric Schmidt was an intern at AT&T Bell Laboratories.
From 2001 to 2011 he served as CEO of Google before becoming chair of the US Department of Defense's Defense Innovation Advisory Board. He is also a member of the Bilderberg Group, a lucrative annual meeting spearheaded by elite leaders and industry experts of which has encouraged multiple conspiracy theories over the past six decades.

Despite multiple accusations and leaks pointing to AT&T Inc. as the United States' key provider, this didn't hurt the company in any way. AT&T's reported 2019 revenue exceeded $180 billion.

In 2016 the company announced a deal to buy Time Warner. A year later they were officially revealed as the world's largest telecom company and largest provider of telephone services. With Time-Warner under their belt, there's no stopping the company who now owns HBO, TBS, CNN, DC Entertainment, Warner Bros., New Line Cinema to name just a few. Before the Time-Warner deal, AT&T already owned Yellowpages.com and the AT&T satellite fleet, a constellation of direct broadcast satellites.

In 2010 grey hat hacking group, *Goatse Security*, a division of the Internet trolling organisation *Gay Nigger Association of America (yes, really)*, who goes by the slogan "Gaping Holes Exposed" about their discovery of security flaws, successfully unveiled a vulnerability within the AT&T website.

At the time, the company were the only provider of 3G for Apple's iPad in the U.S.

Goatse Security proved that AT&T was retrieving the integrated circuit card identifier (ICCID) from SIM cards and linking them to email addresses provided during sign-up and that the information was easily exposed. The email address leaks of 114,000 users including military and government personnel were revealed to the media before notifying AT&T. The FBI raided one of the hackers in 2011 who stated, *"we tried to be the good guys"* defending their exposition of poor security in major websites. A year later, the group were acknowledged by the Microsoft Security Response Center for privately disclosing vulnerabilities in Microsoft's online services.

AT&T purchased Spanish cyberattack security start-up AlienVault in 2018, which speculatively could be used to prevent further threats against their systems.

UNDER CONSTANT SUPERVISION

AT&T landed a multi-billion-dollar contract with the NSA to outsource their IT systems.

An NSA document refers to a mass surveillance hub codenamed TITANPOINTE with rooftop equipment pertaining to the SKIDROWE Intelligence System. The windowless AT&T Long Lines Building in Manhattan likely is the location discussed.

Photo: Keyur Khamar

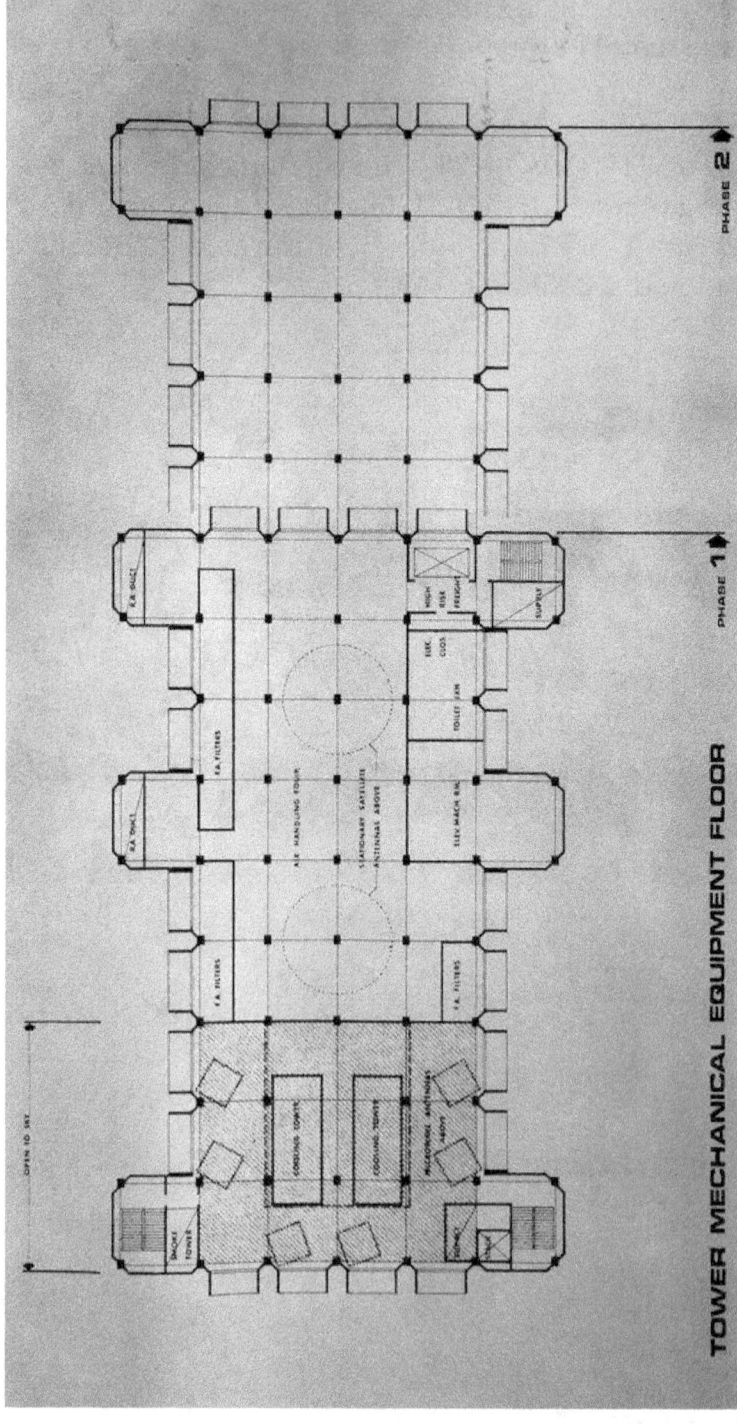

TOWER MECHANICAL EQUIPMENT FLOOR

COMMUNICATION, INTERFERENCE AND‹ SACRED GEOMETRY?

One final mention of note is an Australian base in Western Australia called *Naval Communication Station Harold E. Holt*. The incredibly powerful station is used for radio transmissions to U.S. and Royal Australian Navy submarines. It is the most powerful transmission station in the Southern Hemisphere, using more than a megawatt of power. There are thirteen radio towers, one of which is almost 400 metres tall. The town of Exmouth was built specifically to house employees of the mega-facility. The Space Surveillance Telescope (SST) was transferred to the location from New Mexico after DARPA handed over operations.
The next few paragraphs are a little speculative.

In 2008, a Qantas flight – QF72 – had to make an emergency landing near Exmouth after the plane dropped nearly 200m, injuring most of the passengers and crew members. The Australian Transport Safety Bureau (ATSB) claimed the fault was due to an error within the air data computer system. People were quick to jump at the idea that the nearby signals from the station had interfered with the aircraft's navigation system. The ATSB's final report stated this was "extremely unlikely" and concluded the incident had occurred due to a faulty design in the flight control software. The plane suffered

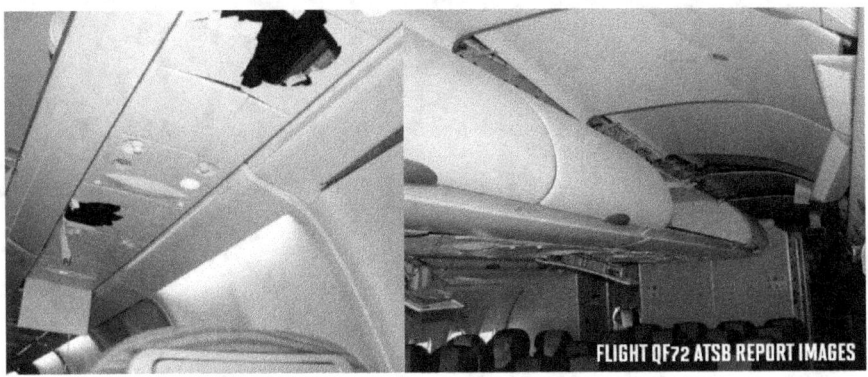

FLIGHT QF72 ATSB REPORT IMAGES

 internal damage due to passengers being thrown from their seats and luggage falling out of the overhead lockers. Two months later, it happened again to another flight – although also an A330-300 – passing near the facility. The Australian and International Pilots Association demanded commercial aircraft be barred from the area until better research was done. The manager of the station emphasised it was "highly, highly unlikely" that interference was the cause.

Speculation aside, the location remains an interesting communication station due to the layout of the giant towers which can be compared to a *Metatron's cube,* a sacred shape of Judaic teaching that's said to *"represent the journey of energy throughout the universe, and of balance within the universe."*
The shape may look like a pentagram, but it's more science than sinister as the design aids in the use of the antennae.

© CNES/AIRBUS   21°48'54.07"S / 114° 9'56.56"E

UNDER CONSTANT SUPERVISION

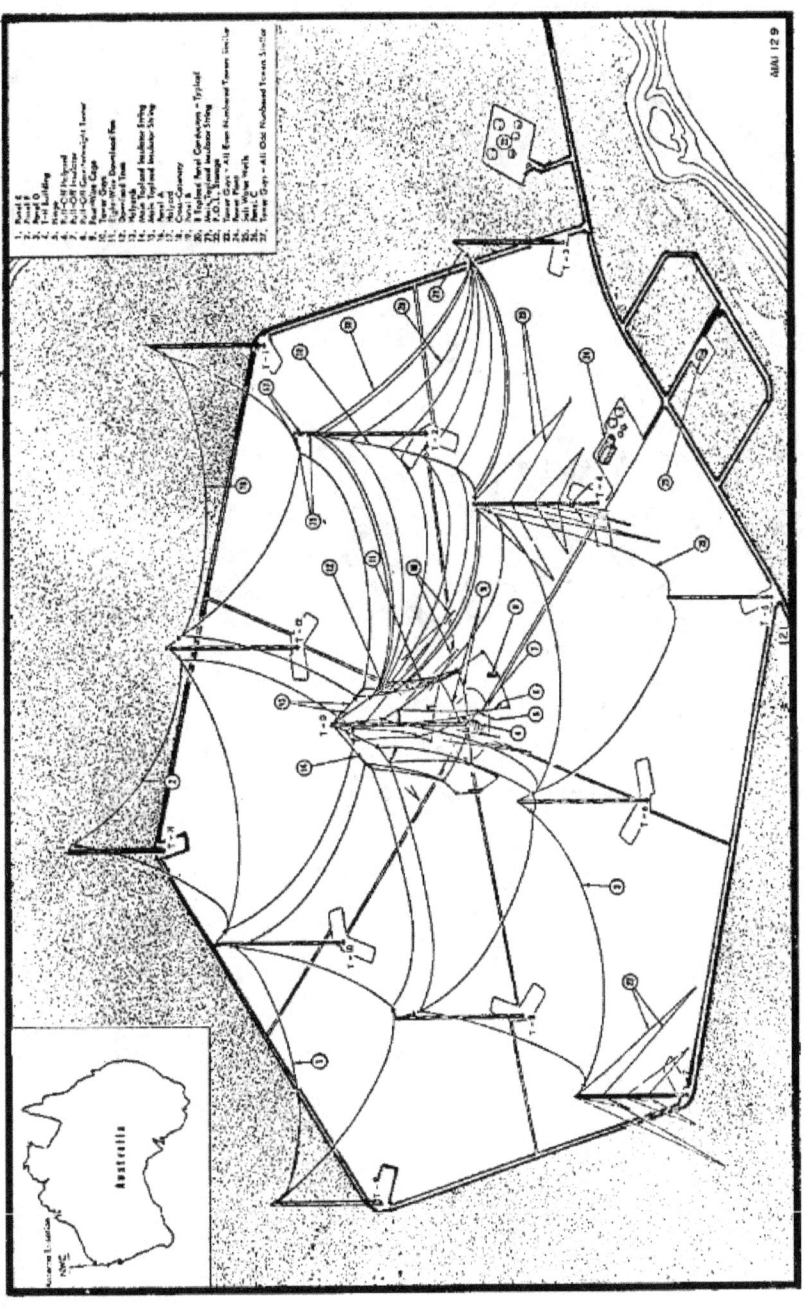

Figure 3-14. Australia, Antenna Location

11km from Harold E. Holt is another array (Image: CNES/Airbus 2020)

The building of the space surveillance system was carried out from 2013 by a local building company who were contracted by Raytheon[101], America's military contractor of choice.

---

[101] https://exmouthbuilder.com.au/commercial **OR** https://archive.vn/3sEKg

WITH UFED, IT'S EASY TO DOWNLOAD EVERYTHING

Several utilities are available to law enforcement agencies, many of which are manufactured by non-governmental organisations and sold along with training to countries electing to keep a closer eye on their citizens.

Cellebrite, are a company founded in Israel that manufacture devices used for data extraction, transfer and analysis – essentially hacking devices. Cellebrite operates in the US and Germany and produces software and hardware that is used for forensics and security by intelligence agencies and military divisions. The company's most popular offering is the Universal Forensic Extraction Device or UFED.

UFED's are portable computers that can export the entire contents of a mobile device bypassing passwords, fingerprints, facial recognition and other security features within seconds. Cellebrite boasts to be the first in the industry to have achieved physical extraction and deciphering of Blackberry, Android and Apple mobile devices as well as GPS units. UFED devices come with a selection of cables and adapters that connect to multiple device outlets[102] Should officers or UFED owners be unable to physically gain access to a device, the UFED can list all Bluetooth-enabled devices in its vicinity and give the user the ability to decrypt the device and download all data. Cellebrite's most popular product the UFED Ultimate can even translate content on-demand using its proprietary software. The website lists purpose-built kiosks[103] marketed toward border control checkpoints by enabling *"frontline teams to quickly extract and act on mobile data at specific locations"*

UFED's are frighteningly easy to use.
1. Your device is attached the UFED
2. The user selects the make and model of the phone on the UFED display
3. The data is 'cracked' if protected, and the user can select to download logs, media or the entire image of the phone
4. The data is now stored on the computer, USB drive or internal storage of the UFED
5. That's it!

The tools are marketed for criminal investigation and preventing terrorist attacks with training and various software suites available for almost any situation. The company lists every device, chipset and software platform they have cracked with multiple security features on your mobile device becoming useless almost immediately after release[104]

---

[102] https://www.cellebrite.com/en/ufed-ultimate/
[103] https://www.cellebrite.com/en/platforms/
[104] https://www.cellebrite.com/en/about/innovation-timeline/

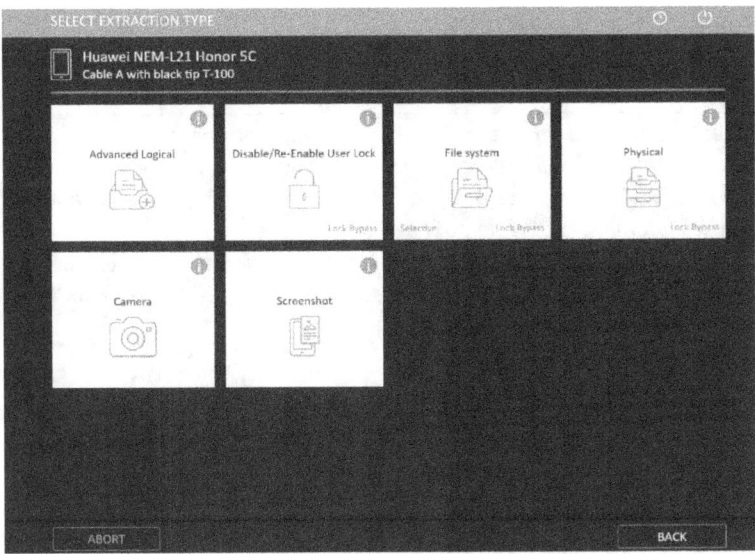

Any item that hasn't been securely deleted (if the deletion was quick, it wasn't securely deleted) can be retrieved easily and almost immediately by the UFED. Cellebrite lists devices that can export data from a SIM card. Some devices even feature a camera for evidence collection.

The UFED Cloud Analyzer is a software set that *"allows you to extract, preserve and analyze public- and private-domain, social-media data, instant messaging, file storage, web pages and other cloud-based content using a forensically sound process."*
Appropriate legal authority assumed, the company also gives its elite clients the ability to *"Move beyond the examination of physical devices to tap into new evidence sources hiding in social media and private, cloud-based data archives"*

According to Cellebrite's datasheet on the cloud software:

> Cloud-based sources and the web represent virtual goldmines of potential evidence for investigations. However, acquiring information from private cloud service providers, which requires a warrant, can be lengthy process for time-sensitive cases. Manually scouring public data from social media is a cumbersome and time-consuming process. Not to mention that analyzing such large volumes of disparate data presents a complex, labour-intensive challenge in and of itself.

The "key benefits" section lists numerous drool-worthy features that any enforcement worker or hacker would love to see in action:

> Fulfill requests for cloud-based private data
> Gather private user data in accordance with due process from more than 40 of the most popular social media and cloud-storage
> sources, including Gmail, Dropbox, Facebook, Google Drive, Instagram, WhatsApp, Amazon, iCloud and more. Use login credentials provided by the subject, or tokens extracted from digital devices to gain access to time-sensitive evidence.

Already, the documents either give an example of the companies involved in giving easy access to law enforcement agencies, or they simply list which popular services have been proven to crack without passwords.

The **Track online behaviour** section continues to list Google and Apple as examples:

> Gain insights into the subject's intentions, interests and relationships by analyzing posts, likes, events and connections. View text searches conducted with Chrome on iOS devices backed-up on iCloud. Extract extensive details from Google web history including private location information from a suspect or victim, so investigators can track time-stamped movements minute by minute

And you're not safe from information voluntarily uploaded, with a web scraping feature included:

> Easily access, view and incorporate publicly available data into your investigations, such as location information, profiles, images, files and social communications from popular apps, including **Facebook, Twitter and Instagram.** Simplify the collection and review of digital evidence from HTML-based web pages to generate new leads or access not yet supported cloud-based apps.

UFED technology has been abused in the United States in multiple cases. In Atlanta, the Federal Court deemed the access to a mobile phone unnecessary in a 2013 case. The Supreme Court of the United States document[105] states *"even though the search incident to arrest exception does not apply to cell phones, other case-specific exceptions may still justify a warrantless search of a particular phone... The police generally may not, without a warrant, search digital information on a cell phone seized from an individual who has been arrested."*

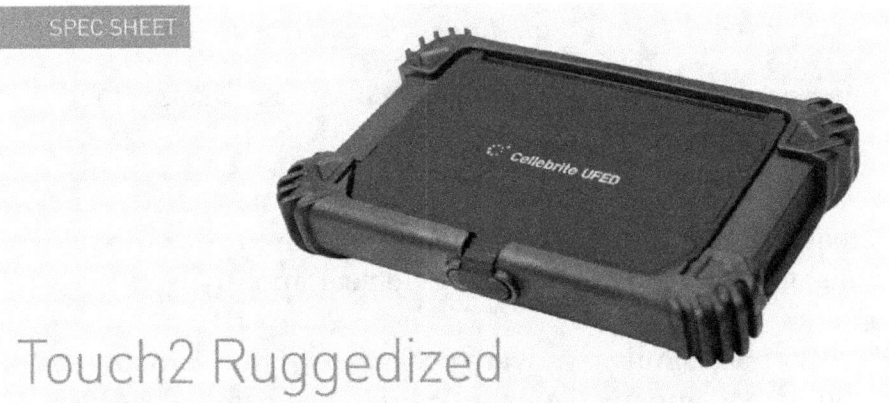

Does this look like a device that can download data almost instantly, complete with screen (hidden under cover) SIM card reader and internal cameras?

---

[105] https://github.com/BookRefine/references/blob/master/supervision/13-132_8l9c.pdf

As seems to be the pattern in data tools that are intended to be held under lock and key, nearly 1 Terabyte of confidential data was downloaded from Cellebrite's external servers in 2017. The data included files from seized mobile devices including logs from the UFED devices themselves. Cellebrite has a publicly known contract with U.S. Immigration and Customs Enforcement but the data leak revealed Cellebrite also provided its products to the United Arab Emirates, Turkey and Russia for undisclosed purposes.

Despite the few sentences found across the Cellebrite website stating the technology should only be used for lawful purposes, the products End User Licence Agreement (EULA) does not specify the software should not be used against journalists, charity workers or for human rights abuse. This is rather strange, with most companies like Apple adding unnecessary additions to their EULA in-place preventing people from using their software while working on nuclear weapons.[106]

> You also agree that you will not use these products for any purposes prohibited by United States law, including, without limitation, the development, design, manufacture, or production of nuclear, missile, or chemical or biological weapons.

A real bummer if you were hoping to listen to your iPod whilst getting ready to begin the nuclear apocalypse!

FinFisher is a similar software package by UK/German technology company *Gamma Group*. The business has been strongly criticised by human rights organisations for selling the intrusion software to repeat offenders like Bahrain, Egypt,

---

[106] https://www.apple.com/legal/Internet-services/itunes/us/terms.html or https://archive.vn/E7iFm

Turkmenistan and Oman. Reporters Without Borders described the company as *digital era mercenaries*. According to research by multiple non-governmental organisations, the software has been sold to essentially every country within the EYES agreements. RSF lists at least 20 countries **known** to have obtained the software[107] with countries Australia, Estonia, Indonesia, Qatar, the UAE and the United States and more all actively running the software for undefined purposes. Gamma Group has also been involved in data breaches causing data to be shared online. Swedish company MSAB offer similar technology, even having a suite for drones. American corporation **Berla** offers a suite of hardware and software for vehicle data retrieval. The company claims the forensic tools are for law enforcement agencies and "select private industry organisations "

---

[107] https://web.archive.org/web/20130316130016/http://surveillance.rsf.org/en/gamma-international/

TOP SECRET//UNDER//CONSTANT//SUPERVISION//REL TO READER

If you trust the government is going to do
the right thing, I think you're alone in
that respect

- Pete Ashdown
    XMission founder - an ISP with a policy of refusing
    government agency requests without authority

Despite being ousted and shamed by multiple documents, world governments will continue their insistence that without their spy programs, we will be susceptible to attacks. As technology becomes more connected, many unsuspecting citizens are likely to 'invite' governments and corporations into their homes.

Elon Musk's company SpaceX were the biggest company to generate hype in 2015 when they revealed the intention to launch a constellation of Low Earth Orbit satellites (LEO) that would provide Internet access to the world. 5 years later, SpaceX began to launch their prototype network, releasing a constellation of 242 satellites in January of 2020. They intended to have at least 12,000 satellites in orbit with the eventual goal of 30,000. SpaceX announced their intention to provide underserved areas of Earth as well as to sell Internet services to fund their plans to colonise Mars. Should man ever attempt to reside on another planet, an unfailing communication system would be crucial.

A 'train' of Starlink satellites visible in the night sky

At the time of the announcement, several others revealed their plans to add to the LEO network above us.

Amazon announced *Project Kuiper* which would provide Internet broadband through partnerships with other companies. Amazon had previously announced the AWS Ground Station unit which comprises of 12 satellite ground stations which would transmit data to and from satellites in orbit.

Submarine cables will always be the fastest, most convenient way of transferring data but with satellites connecting to more remote locations; we may see wireless surveillance increase. We already live in a world where small drones are used to provide high definition imagery to those in control whether it be government or everyday user.

Global Internet access has been a philanthropic pledge by organisations and corporations for many years with initiatives like **Internet.org by Facebook** combining Facebook with Samsung, Ericsson, MediaTek, Opera Software, Nokia and Qualcomm. The *Free Basics* service offered many parts of Africa, the Middle East and India with a small selection of websites including *Facebook*, *Wikipedia*, *Dictionary* as well as HIV and Aids research group *HIV360*. The platform works by partnering with governments, non-profit organisations and mobile operators to entice people to 'bring people online' using bandwidth-optimised websites.
In India, the service was highly controversial with many Indian startups pulling out citing net neutrality concerns. The Telecom Regulatory Authority of India, or TRAI, decided to bar telecom providers from charging differential rates for data services and thus, Internet.org was not eligible to operate in the country. India's regulations are deemed to be the strongest *commercial* net neutrality rules in the world, ensuring free and open Internet for nearly half a billion people. However, in

terms of internet shutdowns, India led the world with over 130 reported incidents in 2018 and over 106 in 2019[108].

In the past, Facebook and Google had developed autonomous high-flying drones intended to 'beam' Internet to remote locations across the Earth. When both Google and Facebook abandoned their projects, they began to focus their efforts on satellite software and hardware. With claims they would provide Internet access to developing nations, are their intentions to provide a free service that collects data to be sold to advertising networks?
If you can't bring the people to you, you need to travel to the people.

With 5G technology succeeding 4G LTE mobile networks, developments have been focused on connection speeds that far excel the 4G network infrastructure. In the United States, officials and politicians within the federal government raised concerns that Chinese technology giants Huawei Technologies may manufacturer equipment such as 5G cells and towers to allow the Chinese government and Chinese People's Liberation Army (PLA) to spy on residents and government agencies.

Huawei's founder Ren Zhengfei was an engineer in the PLA during the 80s. Zhengfei's connections to the Communist Party of China have earned Huawei major government contracts.

American communications hardware manufacturer 3Com formed a project with Huawei called H3C allowing 3Com to sell rebranded Huawei products in 2003.

---

[108] https://internetshutdowns.in/

In August 2006, the CEO of 3Com and H3C resigned seven months after taking the position citing concerns over dubious business morals and possible cyber risks.
In 2007, American investment firm Bain Capital's attempts to acquire 3Com fell-through due to equity financing sourced from Huawei. The U.S. government opposed the deal concerned over cybersecurity threats and surveillance on military-grade technologies.

Chief Financial Officer Meng Wanzhou (also known as Cathy Meng) – the daughter of Ren Zhengfei – was arrested in 2018 over allegations the company swindled financial institutions in breach of U.S. sanctions against Iran. Huawei was accused of selling technology to Iran despite the law prohibiting the sale of technology and resale of US-made technology. Meng assured Huawei's banking partners that the company was complying with US sanctions and convinced the banks to proceed with business affairs.

The T-Mobile robotic arm "Tappy" – an Epson-built SCARA assembly arm – was built to simulate user activity. As you can guess by its name, Tappy uses a robotic finger to tap a screen. Huawei spent months trying to get the American company to share how the robot worked despite confidentiality agreements. After almost a year of pestering, T-Mobile threatened to ban Huawei employees from their laboratory if they didn't stop asking questions about the robotic arm. Huawei decided to kidnap Tappy instead.
According to the indictment, a Huawei employee entered the T-Mobile test centre, put Tappy in their bag and walked out. After taking multiple photos and potentially reverse engineering the robot, the employee returned it to T-Mobile claiming they had *accidentally* taken it home.
The indictment details *"some of the photographs depicted the precise width of certain parts of the robot arm by showing a measuring device next to the parts"*

Huawei was ordered to pay almost $5 million in damages after it was deemed the company had committed industrial espionage in the U.S. and breached the conditions of the contract.

Huawei opposed the lawsuit stating *"T-Mobile's statement of the alleged trade secret is an insufficient, generic statement that captures virtually every component of its robot"*

T-Mobile shrugged off the dispute as the Epson arm was modified specifically to feign human finger input. Robotic espionage aside, the prosecutors even alleged that Huawei was giving employees incentives for stealing technology:

> "Under the policy, Huawei established a formal schedule for rewarding employees for stealing information from competitors based on the confidential value of the information obtained."
> [The policy] "emphasized that no employees would be punished for taking actions in accordance with the policy."

Outraged ensued with the Chinese ambassador to Canada, Lu Shaye, accusing Canada of *"white supremacy"* [109]
On the 13th of February 2020, Federal prosecutors formally indicted Huawei and Wanzhou with thirteen counts of bank and wire fraud, obstruction of justice and misappropriating trade secrets[110].

Chairman Guo Ping equally tackled the concerns stating that the company would not provide backdoors in its equipment, calling out the U.S. for double standards: *"if the NSA wants to modify routers or switches to eavesdrop, a Chinese company will be unlikely to co-operate"*

---

[109] https://www.theguardian.com/world/2019/jan/09/china-ambassador-canada-white-supremacy-huawei **OR** https://archive.vn/OogoN

[110] https://arstechnica.com/tech-policy/2019/01/us-indicts-huawei-for-stealing-t-mobile-robot-selling-us-tech-to-iran/ **OR** https://archive.vn/PUkYu

A ban on government purchases of Huawei and ZTE equipment was enacted in a 2018 defence funding bill. The *John S. McCain National Defense Authorization Act for Fiscal Year 2019* also lists Dahua Technology, Hikvision and Hytera overs security and surveillance concerns.[111]

The Australian federal government banned Huawei and Chinese multinational telecommunications manufacturer ZTE from participating in proposals worth billions of dollars after ASIO deemed the company untrustworthy due to alleged links to the Chinese government.

ZTE was criticised for selling eavesdropping equipment to the government-controlled Telecommunication Company of Iran.[112]

The Intelligence and Security Committee in Britain expressed similar concerns in a report released in 2013 that questioned the potential that Huawei could be prying on government and business interests on behalf of China[113].

China's Internet laws require technology corporations to provide network data to the government. Ren Zhengfei defended Huawei saying he would not allow Chinese governments to access any data *"Even if we were required by Chinese law, we would firmly reject that"*[114]
Moreover, he stated his membership in the Communist Party of China was irrelevant. Legal scholar at the Chinese Academy of Social Science's law institute wrote an article in *Wired* claiming the Chinese law does not *"compel the installation of backdoors or other spyware"*[115] which was later

---

[111] https://www.govtrack.us/congress/bills/115/hr5515/details

[112] https://www.reuters.com/article/us-iran-telecoms/special-report-chinese-firm-helps-iran-spy-on-citizens-idUSBRE82L0B820120322

[113] ISC Report: Foreign Investment in the Critical National Infrastructure June 2013

[114] https://www.cnbc.com/2019/03/05/huawei-would-have-to-give-data-to-china-government-if-asked-experts.html

[115] https://www.wired.com/story/law-expert-chinese-government-cant-force-huawei-make-backdoors/

disputed by Chinese and U.S. lawyers who also made note the Academy was government-backed.

Australia, Canada, New Zealand and the U.S. have deemed the use of Huawei equipment as a risk to security, making the United Kingdom the only Five Eyes country to allow the company to roll out 5G.

Japan convinced carriers to exclude Huawei or ZTE in their networks.
Vietnam avoided the use of Huawei in the development of their 5G network[116]

Germany stated that strict requirements would be enforced to prevent concerns. Previously, concerns against Huawei were raised by cybersecurity company *G Data* who accused Huawei and several other Chinese companies of shipping smartphones with malware-infected versions of preinstalled applications.[117]

China has been established as the major supplier of technology, among many other things, to the world – with surveillance tech one of the most dominant markets. One of the reasons China could potentially control and abuse the surveillance industry is through their mass-production of semi-conductors aimed at machine learning (artificial intelligence).
The Western world relies on China for its manufacturing of cheap computer components with Foxconn factories in Taiwan and Shenzhen outputting millions of devices with nearly half of electronics devices manufactured by the giant.

---

[116] https://www.bangkokpost.com/tech/1715339/vietnam-quietly-avoids-huawei-in-building-5g-network **OR** https://archive.vn/vNFQq

[117] https://www.pcworld.com/article/2978120/bought-a-brand-new-phone-it-could-still-have-malware.html

UNDER CONSTANT SUPERVISION

```
TOP SECRET//UNDER//CONSTANT//SUPERVISION//REL TO READER
```

"Before you become too entranced with gorgeous gadgets and mesmerizing video displays, let me remind you that information is not knowledge, knowledge is not wisdom, and wisdom is not foresight. Each grows out of the other, and we need them all."

— Arthur C. Clarke
Science fiction writer

THEY'RE WATCHING YOU

As suggested, the 9/11 attacks came at a time where the internet was already kicking off. At a time where our Internet dependency was beginning with the Dot-com boom, government-sponsored surveillance wasn't always so hidden.

Video Surveillance or closed-circuit television (CCTV) have been a fantastic development for security and general monitoring. As with all technology, however, it has been used against the people of the world. Mechanical CCTV was created by Russian inventor Léon Theremin (of whom invented the Theremin itself – a strange-sounding instrument that bases its sound on hand gestures) in 1927. His invention eventually inspired the production of monitoring systems by Siemens AG for Nazi Germany. These surveillance systems required constant monitoring due to the lack of a storage medium. Fast forward to the 1970s and video surveillance became normal thanks to VCR technology.

Side note: Theremin invented the first covert listening device, known as The Thing or the Great Seal Bug, which was concealed inside a wooden plaque of the Great Seal of the United States and gifted to America for spying. When a British radio inventor accidentally heard conversations on a radio channel, the U.S. was alerted and the FBI hired British scientist Peter Wright – whom later became an MI5 counterintelligence officer – to examine the device leading to the development of multiple 'bugs' used by the FVEY alliance.

Surveillance cameras don't necessarily equal safety. 2019 research conducted by *Comparitech*[118] shows that the cities with the most surveillance don't necessarily have low crime rates.

---

[118] https://www.comparitech.com/vpn-privacy/the-worlds-most-surveilled-cities/ **OR** https://archive.vn/Yapcf

Country	City	Number of cameras	CCTV Cameras per 1000 people	Crime index
China	Chongqing	2,579,890	168.03	33.18
China	Shenzhen	1,929,600	159.09	42.91
China	Shanghai	2,985,984	113.46	40.87
China	Tianjin	1,244,160	92.87	29.15
China	Ji'nan	540,463	73.82	15.93
United Kingdom	London	627,707	68.4	52.24
China	Wuhan	500,000	60.49	21.18
China	Guangzhou	684,000	52.75	47.43
China	Beijing	800,000	39.93	42.31
United States	Atlanta	7,800	15.56	62.86
Singapore	Singapore	86,000	15.25	28.36
UAE	Abu Dhabi	20,000	13.77	10.92
United States	Chicago	35,000	13.06	64.12
China	Urumqi	43,394	12.4	36.76
Australia	Sydney	60,000	12.35	36.02
Iraq	Baghdad	120,000	12.3	63.92
UAE	Dubai	35,000	12.14	16.69
Russia	Moscow	146,000	11.7	40.69
Germany	Manila	39,765	11.18	40.3
India	New Delhi	179,000	9.62	58.77
China	Nanchang	50,400	9.22	8.09
Pakistan	Islamabad	9,950	9.09	29.3
Poland	Warsaw	13,935	7.85	30.9
Austria	Vienna	14,141	7.38	23.28

In 1949, Mao Zedong – *Chairman Mao* – established the Communist Party of China and along with it, surveillance. By observing each other closely, the Chinese people would essentially blow the whistle on each other if they suspected misconduct or conversation that went against the Maoist narrative.

China has a long-standing history of surveillance within the medical system. This *disease surveillance* system includes a National Disease Reporting System that covers the entirety of China and the Nationwide Disease Surveillance Points that is comprised of random sampling across 145 reporting sites.

Multiple health issues monitored by these systems have decreased and control has been taken to stop the spread of viruses such as COVID-19 – or, at least according to China.

Number 7 on the chart is the Chinese city of Wuhan. When Coronavirus COVID-19 emerged in Wuhan, the Chinese government were quick to roll out measures to stop the spread.
This information was then logged to intervene. Drones were used to enforce lockdown measures put in place by the Chinese government to stop the spread. Tracking tools were the most common. Facial recognition cameras can detect somebody's temperature. This is all assisted by the mandated National ID card Chinese residents are required to carry. When you purchase a mobile phone in China – you need the ID card. When you use a mobile phone application – you need the ID card. This links all information to you personally.

Location data and activity from mobile phones were used to track the places of people who had the virus, as well as notify those in the surrounding areas. Phones were also used as personal trackers to ensure that those in quarantine remained in their homes. In the weeks leading up to a target's diagnosis, a combination of human and automated data could map exactly who may have been infected from the target. Travelling anywhere would require your national ID which could then be scanned by enforcers seeking to know if you were a contagious risk to others.

Mainland China has an estimated 600 million CCTV cameras in use today which is little surprise given that eight out of the top ten camera-filled cities are in China.

Facial recognition has always been a concern but with the CCTV technology becoming so common, people breaking the law or simply concerned about their privacy just cover their faces or use facial recognition preventing glasses which can circumvent detection. China solved this issue by introducing *'gait recognition'* which uses the shape of a body and the way a person walks to identify them. Pretending to have a limp or specific feature won't stop the technology, as it will use other measures to calculate who you are[119].

Chinese law enforcement personnel are equipped with facial recognition *Smartglasses* that are used to alert them to criminals.

China leads the world in supercomputing. Lots of data needs lots of computing power.

---

[119] https://apnews.com/bf75dd1c26c947b7826d270a16e2658a **OR** https://archive.vn/SBraV **OR** https://git.io/Jvdpa

PART FIVE:
SMART AND ALWAYS CONNECTED

UNDER CONSTANT SUPERVISION

TOP SECRET//UNDER//CONSTANT//SUPERVISION//REL TO READER

We are stuck with technology when what we really want is just stuff that works.

- Terry Pratchett
  Author

SMART FEATURES IN A SMART WORLD — BUT WHO BENEFITS MOST?

Connected portable devices, television sets, audio speakers and even appliances like smart toasters and fridges within a smart home, all connected and working unanimously together; the future is sure to impose the reliance on the *Internet of Things.*

The Internet of Things (IoT) is a system of interconnected devices with the ability to transfer over networks without the need for user input. IoT incorporates mechanical and digital components to provide what most technology is marketed as "smart"

Security and privacy will always be a factor in the adoption of smart devices, but one of the overlooked factors in IoT is obsolescence.

An old fridge can be repaired by repairing or replacing internal components that have ceased working due to age, misuse or accidental damage. One only needs to travel on the main road to see a classic vehicle that has been restored to its former glory by an enthusiast, despite parts being entirely unavailable. Hobby car enthusiasts and professionals opt to keep their classics on the road even if it means rebuilding parts or having brand new ones manufactured. With technology slowly invading these industries, how long will our modern smart technology be useful? When companies cease updating buggy software and data servers that the parts rely on are shut down, the technology connected to the IoT are potentially no longer fit for purpose raising ethics of disposal and short-term compatibility.

Remember the satellite constellations? Internet broadband satellites are one of the main reasons for providing universal access to IoT applications.
With so many devices able to "make life easier" by automating life roles, it's imperative to ensure privacy is priority.

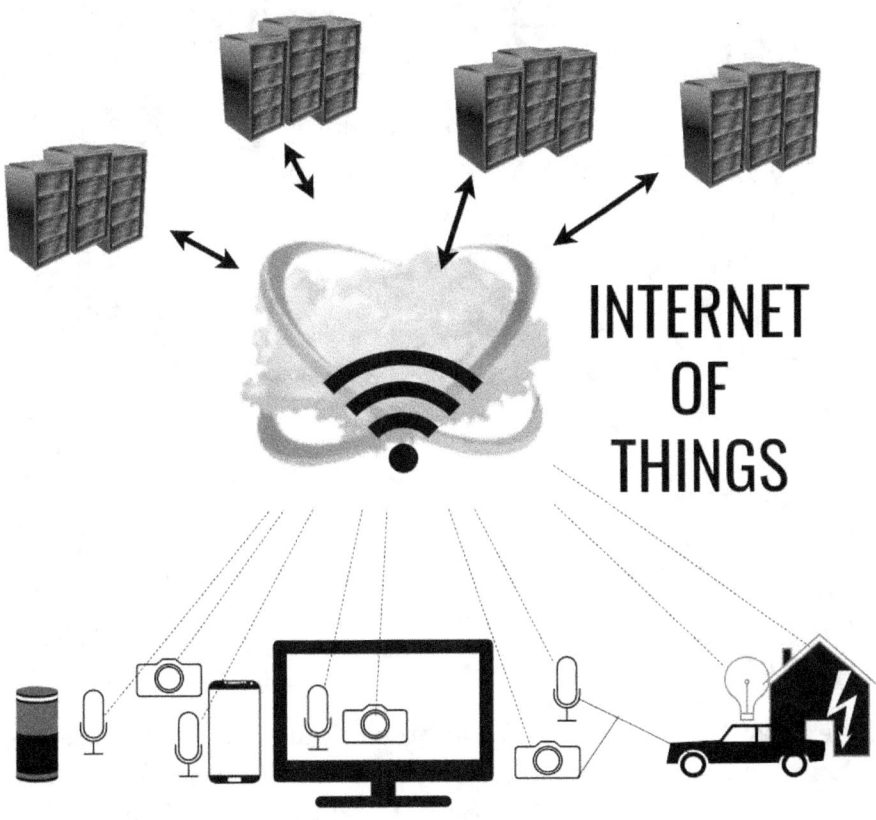

SMART CONSUMPTION

With the world becoming more and more environmentally conscious many governments and electricity providers have introduced smart meters – also referred to as digital meters.

Like most technology with the prefix *Smart*, Smart Meters are advanced versions of the power meter that is attached to the fuse box of residential and commercial properties. The purpose of smart meters varies with some simply giving energy providers the ability to read the meter remotely thus eliminating the need for employees to travel to thousands of houses and document the numbers on the gauge.
  Many smart meters, however, are used for telemetry.

This is often done using a node network or mobile network. Smart meters like the one pictured have an antenna connection internally or externally that continually or intermittently transfers data using cellular networks. Companies such as Singaporean-based company EDMI Limited sell hardware and software systems to energy providers around the world as part of a solution called AMI – Advanced Metering Infrastructure. The company has secured contracts throughout the world with countries like Australia and New Zealand, United Kingdom, Denmark and Thailand, the latter of which use *Near-Real-Time Reading*.[120]

Meters have internal storage with some manufacturers offering up to 365-days worth of information should the unit not communicate with energy company servers. The data can then be exported manually by energy company workers. Almost every smart meter manufactured contains a lithium battery so that information can be stored for roughly ten years without power.

---

[120] https://www.edmi-meters.com/solutions/advanced-metering-infrastructure/

Many critics of the smart meter have accused state governments of restricting their choice not to have the meter installed. Australia, for example, mandated the rollout of smart meters to new and existing homes in 2017 without enforcing that energy providers give their customers the choice to refuse or opt-out of the scheme. Companies such as Origin Energy state on their website: *"If you're offered a digital meter as part of a product or marketing campaign, you can choose not to take up a digital meter at that time. You can also choose a non-communicating meter, which is a digital meter with the communications functions disabled – however, this will come with additional costs to cover manual meter readers visiting your property and you'll miss out on the advantages of having a digital meter"*

The company's Frequently Asked Questions page states: *"There are many benefits to having a digital meter including no longer having meter readers visit your property, more frequent data so you can monitor your electricity usage more easily, and access to products and services. You can choose to have a digital meter without communication enabled, but this will come with additional costs to cover manual meter readers visiting your property and other services which can't be used without your meter having communications."*

When I asked three of the major electricity providers if I was able to have the meter disconnected, I was unanimously told that total disconnection would be the only option available to me if I were concerned about the use of the meter. One company even went as far as to threaten me, suspicious that I was going to damage the meter. I was told that should I tamper with the meter in any way I would be liable for all expenses and prosecuted with the destruction of company property (as customers do not own the equipment used for providing and measuring electricity)

Luckily, I had no issue with the smart meter but those who do have legitimate concerns are left without a choice. Looking deeper into the available smart meters, all the most-used meters per country have some sort of tamper detection and alarm system. Tamper events are stored in the systems event logs.

I contacted four providers pretending to request that my soon-to-be-built property be fitted with a non-communicating meter. Giving four different locations, I was informed by each company that it would not be possible in the area I wanted to be connected.

It may be extreme to suggest these devices are intended for surveillance – but privacy concerns are valid. As with any connected device, security is of tremendous importance. Property owners are within their rights to be concerned about the protected transfer of data and prospective misuse of meter functions. One of the benefits to energy providers is the ability to remotely disconnect users. This *kill switch* function has been debated as potentially life-threatening with the very real possibility of criminal interference affecting those who rely on medical devices.

Smart meters can also be used to remotely control the access and pricing of electricity. For example, a power grid may report an increase in power from a specific neighbourhood which the energy company can use as justification to increase the electricity price during this peak, possibly without the consumer knowing. Though uncommon, the use of temporary surge pricing has occurred in the United States.

Another issue often raised is law enforcement. Homes displaying "unnecessary" power usage may be accused of illegally farming marijuana or housing more people than is allowed for the size of the property. In the United Kingdom, this data has given social workers and law enforcement agencies the ability to validate suspicion of landlords renting their small apartments to larger than permitted occupancies.

There have also been suggestions that law enforcement has been able to use the information collected by smart meters to determine when a person is usually at home based on energy consumption. Police officers can then schedule raids and arrests with precision. Some locations combine smart meters with smart gas meters. The EFF has argued this can help a company reconstruct a daily routine such as when a person wakes up, showers and leaves for work.

And finally, there are common fears that the radiofrequency emissions from smart meters can be unhealthy for occupants of the household or business. The biological effects of RF emissions have been debated for decades and are subject to one's research if concerned. As far as the World Health Organisation and U.S. Federal Communications Commission (FCC) are concerned, radiofrequency emissions from transmitters used for cellular and PCS communications result in exposure levels that are typically well-below implemented safety limits.

Most countries have privacy disclosure requirements in place that give customers the right to request data that an energy provider has collected from the Smart Meter. This data usually comes without charge, with some companies such as the one I use charging a fee for data that is more than two years old and if requested more than four times in twelve months.

To test this, I contacted the company responsible for the energy sources in my area. I handed over my billing information and the numbers on the smart meter and within 24 hours received an email containing a PDF and a large CSV file with information relating to the last two years of consumption. The company told me that their metering device collected information in intervals of thirty minutes. This data is then consolidated into daily logs at the end of each month. The data export also included graphs and various averages as shown:

UOM	From Date	To Date	General Supply	Controlled Load	Generation	Maximum Demand	Max Dem UOM	Estimated Data?
kWh	31-Mar-2017	31-Mar-2017	17	0	12	3	kW	N
kWh	01-Apr-2017	30-Apr-2017	546	0	300	6	kW	N
kWh	01-May-2017	31-May-2017	673	0	246	7	kW	N
kWh	01-Jun-2017	30-Jun-2017	773	0	138	7	kW	N
kWh	01-Jul-2017	31-Jul-2017	638	0	257	6	kW	N
kWh	01-Aug-2017	31-Aug-2017	572	0	334	8	kW	N
kWh	01-Sep-2017	30-Sep-2017	584	0	323	6	kW	N
kWh	01-Oct-2017	31-Oct-2017	735	0	178	8	kW	N
kWh	01-Nov-2017	30-Nov-2017	638	0	220	6	kW	N
kWh	01-Dec-2017	31-Dec-2017	877	0	207	7	kW	N
kWh	01-Jan-2018	31-Jan-2018	807	0	213	7	kW	N
kWh	01-Feb-2018	28-Feb-2018	664	0	188	7	kW	N
kWh	01-Mar-2018	31-Mar-2018	593	0	233	6	kW	N
kWh	01-Apr-2018	30-Apr-2018	519	0	273	5	kW	N
kWh	01-May-2018	31-May-2018	544	0	318	6	kW	N
kWh	01-Jun-2018	30-Jun-2018	480	0	307	5	kW	N
kWh	01-Jul-2018	31-Jul-2018	502	0	330	5	kW	N
kWh	01-Aug-2018	31-Aug-2018	478	0	439	5	kW	N
kWh	01-Sep-2018	30-Sep-2018	469	0	349	6	kW	N
kWh	01-Oct-2018	31-Oct-2018	603	0	287	6	kW	N
kWh	01-Nov-2018	30-Nov-2018	514	0	387	8	kW	N
kWh	01-Dec-2018	31-Dec-2018	685	0	276	7	kW	N
kWh	01-Jan-2019	31-Jan-2019	657	0	270	6	kW	N
kWh	01-Feb-2019	28-Feb-2019	742	0	182	7	kW	N
kWh	01-Mar-2019	31-Mar-2019	888	0	189	11	kW	N
kWh	01-Apr-2019	30-Apr-2019	723	0	206	8	kW	N
kWh	01-May-2019	31-May-2019	616	0	310	7	kW	N
kWh	01-Jun-2019	30-Jun-2019	737	0	268	8	kW	N
kWh	01-Jul-2019	31-Jul-2019	815	0	288	8	kW	N
kWh	01-Aug-2019	31-Aug-2019	731	0	363	8	kW	N
kWh	01-Sep-2019	30-Sep-2019	555	0	382	7	kW	N
kWh	01-Oct-2019	31-Oct-2019	743	0	266	8	kW	N
kWh	01-Nov-2019	30-Nov-2019	644	0	285	7	kW	N
kWh	01-Dec-2019	31-Dec-2019	816	0	210	7	kW	N
kWh	01-Jan-2020	31-Jan-2020	922	0	188	7	kW	N
kWh	01-Feb-2020	29-Feb-2020	793	0	139	6	kW	N
kWh	01-Mar-2020	15-Mar-2020	295	0	114	5	kW	N

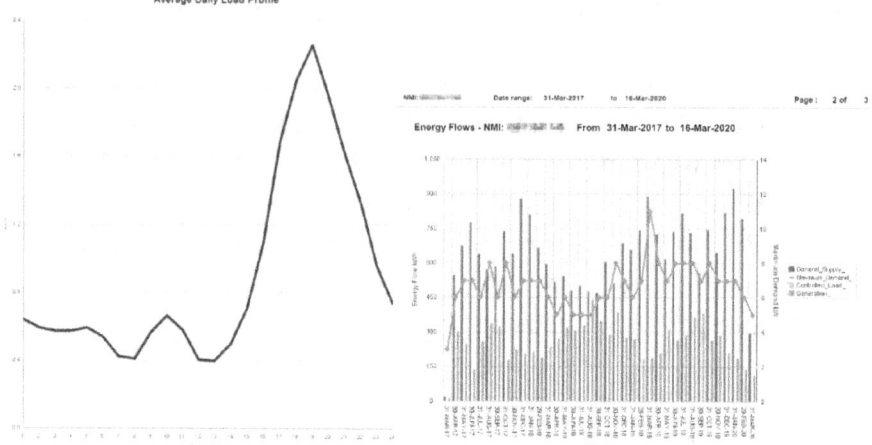

Smart Grids follow the same concept at a much larger scale. A connected smart grid can be vulnerable to cyber-attacks. Transformers which increase the voltage of electricity created at power plants for long-distance travel can be overloaded causing high voltage damage to transmission and distribution lines. If targeted, the increased voltage can also possibly lead to homes and businesses being attacked and perhaps even cause electrocution to occupants. The increased voltage may also cause fires. In the United States, hackers have infiltrated and disrupted electric grids on numerous occasions causing financial damage to the electricity provider as well as inconvenience to the users. Should this type of attack be used against hospitals, the consequences could lead to many deaths. The ability for hackers to gain access and threaten to shut down hospital power supplies may benefit exploiters seeking ransoms. Smart Grids may also be an easy target for terrorists.

In 2015, just a few days before Christmas, Ukraine was targeted by hackers who successfully compromised information systems of three energy companies and disrupt the supply of electricity. The attack is considered to be the first of its kind. A total of 30 substations were shut down affecting over 230,000 people.

The possibility of extensive network grid hacks is of great concern to national security around the world. In 2015, insurance company *Lloyd's of London* demonstrated the potential outcome of a cyberattack on America's *Eastern Interconnection* electrical grid[121].

The report claims that an attack could cost the country's economy anywhere from $243 billion to $1 trillion in damages and impact approximately 93 million people across 15 states.

---

[121] https://www.lloyds.com/~/media/files/news-and-insight/risk-insight/2015/business-blackout/business-blackout20150708.pdf

SMART VIEWING‹
BUT WHO IS THE VIEWER?

As explored previously, Smart TV's are one of the easiest ways to pry into the lives of families and individuals. Whilst not always the intention of Smart TV functionality, data can be collected by the company or by hackers. In 2013, Samsung released a patch to fix a security issue affecting their TV's with inbuilt cameras. The security defect allowed hackers to remotely activate web cameras and spy on users. Hackers could take control of the Television and access data stored in what is essentially a giant phone with security credentials such as accounts and payment information entered by the customer. Samsung's advice was to disconnect the television from the home network when features which required online connectivity were not used.

Californian television and accessory company Vizio was found to be collecting non-personally identifiable information on customers and selling it to advertisers. The company was made to pay out just over US$2 million for using eleven million of their television sets to spy on customers using ACR – Automated Content Recognition. The Video ACR collected data related to the content displayed on the televisions including broadcast, programs and commercials viewed. This data included times, dates, channels and whether they were watched live. The ACR feature had not asked users for consent when collecting data and did not make it clear that the data would be shared with analytics companies, media companies and advertisers.

Vizio has since confirmed that their devices with ACR activated collect household demographic data and digital actions such as content purchases. This would affect not only the TV itself but any devices sharing the IP address. The classic *relevant advertisement* justification was presented, with the company claiming the data is used *"to help content publishers, broadcasters or content distribution services create or recommend more relevant entertainment based on summary insights."*

The extent of Vizio's spying doesn't end there. Vizio TV's also could recognise and track what people are watching, even if it's not a channel on Television. Multiple companies have been accused of using inaudible, high-frequency sounds (digital watermarking) to devices within range to correlate relative advertising on multiple devices.

This feature is known as Cross-device tracking and advertising companies like SilverPush lead the way in tracking users across multiple devices, mostly without the user ever knowing. When a user comes across a SilverPush advertisement, the advertiser places a tracking cookie on the computer and plays an ultrasonic audio 'beacon' that is broadcast from the connected speakers. These beacons are also embedded in TV commercials which can then link users to their various portable devices without the user being aware.

SilverPush collects the data and can successfully analyse how long the TV commercial was watched for if it was skipped then how long it was watched for before the channel was changed and what kind of smart devices are used by the person watching the TV[122]. This technology can de-anonymise the user if they are using computer software or anti-tracking technologies as it can associate the user without the need for having connections to any privacy software that is being used to mask identity. A frightening scenario can involve data, locations and software use all being compromised thanks to a tiny inaudible sound heard through a nearby device. SilverPush claims that they made a *"business decision"* to discontinue their use of the technology and have since attempted to distance themselves from it, especially after the Vizio revelations but ultrasonic tracking is likely just the surface of what is possible with global surveillance.

Many mobile phone applications comprise of 'add-ons' and libraries for analytics and the prerequisites that make an application work the way it is meant to. Apps across most platforms such as Android and iOS are available to view these libraries and explore any permissions the applications may have. Chances are if the application has microphone permissions when it doesn't those permissions to function; it may be using ultrasonic tracking technology.

In 2017, WikiLeaks began to publish *Vault 7*, a series of leaked documents detailing mass surveillance by the United States' Central Intelligence Agency. These documents portrayed the government's ability to compromise mobile phones, operating systems, web browsers and even smart vehicles.

---

[122] https://cdt.org/files/2015/10/10.16.15-CDT-Cross-Device-Comments.pdf **OR**
https://github.com/BookRefine/references/blob/master/supervision/CDTcrossdevice.pdf

> "The attack against Samsung smart TVs was developed in cooperation with the united kingdom's MI5. After infestation, weeping angel places the target tv in a 'fake-off' mode, so that the owner falsely believes the tv is off when it is on. In 'fake-off' mode the tv operates as a bug, recording conversations in the room and sending them over the Internet to a covert CIA server."
>
> - WikiLeaks Vault 7: CIA hacking tools revealed press release – 7th March 2017.

The WikiLeaks documents claimed that over five thousand registered users and more than one thousand systems for hacking existed in the CIA division.
Many of the privacy violations are ignored due to ignorance, complacency or lack of information.

Two years before the *Vault 7* leaks, Samsung was already utilising personal data legally via their later-amended Privacy Policy:

> "You can control your Smart TV, and use many of its features, with voice commands.
> If you enable Voice Recognition, you can interact with your Smart TV using your voice. To provide you the Voice Recognition feature, some voice commands may be transmitted (along with information about your device, including device identifiers) to a third-party service that converts speech to text or to the extent necessary to provide the Voice Recognition features to you.
>
> In addition, Samsung may collect and your device may capture voice commands and associated texts so that we can provide you with Voice Recognition features and evaluate and improve the features.
> Please be aware that if your spoken words include personal or other sensitive information, that information will be among the data captured and transmitted to a third party through your use of Voice Recognition."

Samsung would later release a statement that the Privacy Policy in question required clarification edits and that Samsung had not sold any of the data collected.

> "In all of our Smart TVs we employ industry-standard security safeguards and practices, including data encryption, to secure consumers' personal information and prevent unauthorized collection or use."

According to the Vault 7 documents, a primary spy tool is a "fake off" mode that was developed with the UK's MI5. The CIA spying tool known as **Weeping Angel** recorded voices despite the TV appearing in standby. The means appears to be built on the EXTENDING tool by the MI5 which *"record[s] audio from the built-in microphone"*

> Weeping Angel places the target TV in a 'Fake-Off' mode, so that the owner falsely believes the TV is off when it is on. In 'Fake-Off' mode the TV operates as a bug, recording conversations in the room and sending them over the Internet to a covert CIA server.

UNDER CONSTANT SUPERVISION

1 Introduction

The EXTENDING tool is an implant designed for Samsung F Series Smart Televisions. The implant is designed to record audio from the built-in microphone and egress or store the data.

The implant is configured on a Linux PC, and then deployed onto the TV using a USB stick. Audio files can then be extracted using a USB stick or setting up a Wi-Fi hotspot with-in range of the TV. It is also possible to listen to audio exfiltration live, using the Live Listen Tool, designed for use on a Windows OS.

The implant can be uninstalled by inserting a USB stick into the TV or configuring a Death Date.

Known Issues can be found at the end of this Guide.

The EXTENDING system consists of the following components. These components can be found or generated from the "EXTENDING Settings and Installer" CD

- An **Installation Application**, which installs the implant to the target TV
- An **Implant Executable,** which runs on the target TV and records audio. This is installed by the Installation Application
- An **Encrypted Settings File**, which configures the implant
- A Linux application called **encryptSettings** which will encrypt an unencrypted Settings file, and check that the XML contents are valid.
- A Linux application called **rsakeygen** to generate rsa keys.

293

The EDG (Engineering Development Group) is responsible for the development, testing and operational support of all backdoors, exploits, malicious payloads, trojans, viruses and any other kind of malware used by the CIA in its covert operations world-wide.

The increasing sophistication of surveillance techniques has drawn comparisons with George Orwell's 1984, but "Weeping Angel", developed by the CIA's **Embedded Devices Branch (EDB)**, which infests smart TVs, transforming them into covert microphones, is surely its most emblematic realization.

The attack against **Samsung smart TVs** was developed in cooperation with the United Kingdom's MI5/BTSS. After infestation, Weeping Angel places the target TV in a 'Fake-Off' mode, so that the owner falsely believes the TV is off when it is on. In 'Fake-Off' mode the TV operates as a bug, recording conversations in the room and sending them over the Internet to a covert CIA server.

As of October 2014 the CIA was also looking at **infecting the vehicle control systems used by modern cars and trucks**. The purpose of such control is not specified, but it would permit the CIA to engage in nearly undetectable assassinations.

The CIA's Mobile Devices Branch (MDB) developed **numerous attacks to remotely hack and control popular smart phones**. Infected phones can be instructed to send the CIA the user's geolocation, audio and text communications as well as covertly activate the phone's camera and microphone.

These techniques permit the CIA to bypass the encryption of WhatsApp, Signal, Telegram, Wiebo, Confide and Cloackman by hacking the "smart" phones that they run on and collecting audio and message traffic before encryption is applied.

- *WikiLeaks Vault 7 Press Release: Analysis*

SMART AUTOMOTIVE

Automotive technology has always progressed in ways that have proven to increase the safety of drivers and passengers alike.

From the humble beginnings of anti-lock braking (ABS) to automated technologies such as blind-spot mirror alerts and collision avoidance systems (CAS), modern car manufacturers continue to homogenise safety features with every new model. There is no doubt we will see automated vehicles used in a day-to-day setting and all the fallbacks such technology may bring with it. The criticism of all these platforms is often directed at the cars weak point – the driver.

With each generation of smart vehicle, however, comes the prospects of data collection and even malicious remote operation.

In 1996 General Motors, Electronic Data Systems (EDS) and Hughes Electronics Corporation worked together to bring their expertise to a smart technology that would be intended to become the new standard across General Motors' vehicles, giving the driver security, navigation and remote diagnostics as well as emergency services. The service was called *OnStar*. OnStar uses data from the onboard diagnostics (OBD-II) module in a vehicle and built-in cellular technology such as the early CDMA network. Seen as the ultimate sequel to the giant brick phones found in early high-end vehicles; OnStar gave users access to their mobile phone (though hands-free this time around) as well as turn-by-turn navigation and even the ability to contact the emergency services in the event of a crash.

OnStar wasn't all automated – the subscription service would send data to OnStar's headquarters who could aid with stolen vehicles, roadside repairs and advice in times of crisis. Licence agreements outside of General Motors gave vehicle manufacturers like Acura, Subaru and Volkswagen the technology between 2002 and 2006. A blue OnStar button could be pressed, connecting you to a live operator who could look up an address or give you a live diagnostic check – perhaps the vintage human-operated version of digital assistants like Alexa or Cortana.

The voice-activated technology set a precedent for car owners, but with the ever-changing technology surrounding us, OnStar Vehicles manufactured between 2001 and 2008 were antiquated with the phasing out of analogue networks. The mass of microphones, cables and antennas spread throughout the analogue-only vehicles became a dead weight with the system unable to be upgraded. OnStar was no longer compatible with thousands of cars. The small roof antenna that would crumble under the elements would need to be replaced with an empty dummy and various buttons and controls within the car would now do nothing.

Despite being a subscription service, General Motors were accused of tracking driving habits, speeds and GPS data even if you weren't an active subscriber. OnStar's privacy policy stated that whilst they do sell data to third parties, all information would be anonymised.

In 2011, the OnStar Terms and Conditions were updated to say that the company could sell GPS location information, safety belt usage and other information to law enforcement agencies. The system also required users to press the OnStar button or call the company when you planned to sell or dispose of the vehicle.[123] And that the company *"may keep the information [they] collect for as long as necessary"*

The company clarified that to cease data collection, one would have to physically disconnect the system (such as cutting the wires to the antenna) In some cases, this could cause issues with other connected components.

A 2019 experiment conducted by *The Washington Post*[124] proved that data from a 2017 Chevrolet Volt could be extracted, revealing identifiable locations travelled to and even contacts. The experiment also revealed the ability to buy a pre-used system from a car wrecking yard to construct the life of a previous owner:

> *"It contained enough data to reconstruct the Upstate New York travels and relationships of a total stranger. We know he or she frequently called someone listed as "Sweetie," whose photo we also have. We could see the exact Gulf station where they bought gas, the restaurant where they ate (called Taste China) and the unique identifiers for their Samsung Galaxy Note phones."*

The OnStar system originally featured on General Motors vehicles such as Saturn, Chevy, Pontiac, GMC, Cadillac, Hummer, Buick and Saab and had over six million customers. It is unclear what control OnStar has over data after vehicle brands have been sold to other companies.

---

[123] https://www.onstar.com/content/tcps/us/20140601/terms_conditionsold.html **OR** https://archive.md/Fl4iq **OR** https://archive.vn/CDwFe

[124] https://www.washingtonpost.com/technology/2019/12/17/what-does-your-car-know-about-you-we-hacked-chevy-find-out/ **OR** https://archive.md/GcNj8

OnStar has since become a product that can be added to any vehicle with an aftermarket rear-view mirror sold as *OnStar FMV* (For My Vehicle).

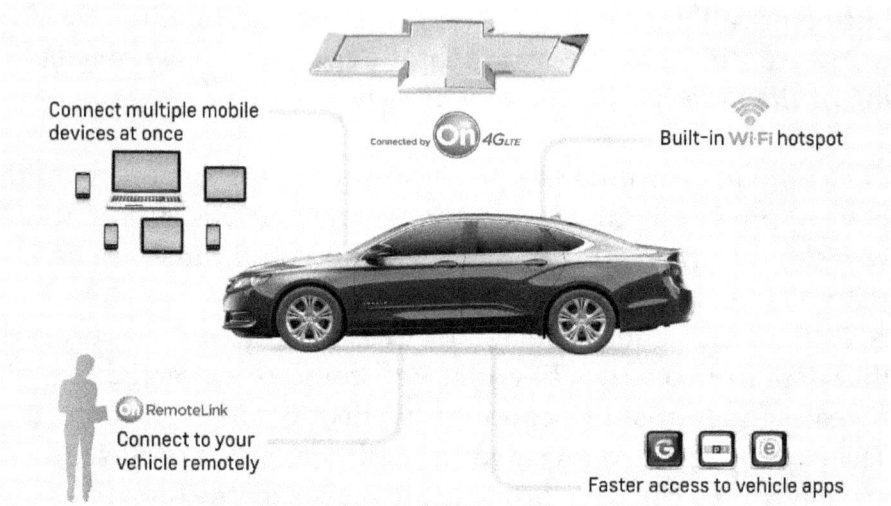

A Promotional graphic showcasing features of OnStar
© OnStar Corporation

Multiple automotive manufacturers like ***Tesla*** have integrated similar systems. Tesla vehicles store most information at a voluntary level, but data like video, location, navigation and more with their Event Data Recorder (EDR) which as the name hints, is much like the data recorder or 'black box' found in aeroplanes. The data collection can be disabled, but drivers use many of the features that may have enticed the driver to buy the vehicle as well as software updates that could be critical for the vehicles' operation.

Tesla sells a retrieval kit for around $1200US that could give customers access to limited information. The company had previously fought customers in court for access to the information stored.[125] Tesla later amended its stance[126] and provided free software to retrieve EDR with the use of the EDR Hardware Retrieval Kit that can generate reports for the owner.

According to former Tesla service workers, owners who try to analyse and modify the vehicles' systems can be flagged as hackers and punished by not receiving software updates until much-later than those not flagged.

Anonymous white-hat hacker *greentheonly* extracted data from a salvaged Tesla Model 3 that had stored unencrypted data from at least 17 unique devices and locations as well as video footage of the crash that lead to the car being sold for scrap. The GPS data shows the location of the crash and call logs that indicate a family member rang the driver moments before the accident. Despite this phone call being potentially unrelated to the accident, one must wonder if an insurance company could argue against settlement by suggesting the driver was distracted.

I asked greentheonly if Tesla's release of the EDR kit and software has made them more transparent and if it gives owners the right to access the data collected, to which he responded *"they withhold all the juicy info only providing bare minimum mandated by law it appears"*
[for the sake of easier reading, I'll refer to greentheonly as he]

---

[125] https://www.plainsite.org/dockets/3hd2fpwvp/supreme-court-of-the-state-of-new-york-nassau-county/wang-jing-vs-tesla-inc/ **OR** https://archive.vn/CDwFe

[126] https://edr.tesla.com/help **OR** https://archive.vn/DjVFn

They explained that the data is not encrypted but that it is cleared once transmitted. *"You can cut the power to the unit before transmission completes (typically 20 minutes) and then you have the ability to read the full data assuming you are not afraid to remove a BGA chip...I did it for some friends and also do it with some salvage units people send to me. Does not work 100% but often enough"*

I asked about gaining the data after a crash, to which he suggested that the best way would be to disconnect the car computer after the crash has been logged – something that may not even be possible depending on the accident. This would not be exclusive to Telstra. Many cars collect data in storage locations, some of which may be scattered throughout the vehicle.

Tesla uses camera data to identify roads and traffic lights to improve their self-driving system *Autopilot*. Tesla states they do not sell personal information to *"anyone for any purpose, period."*[127]

Poor security in many cars can give hackers remote access to the vehicle and even activate the airbags, causing the driver to crash. Hackers have been able to take control of Jeep's with connectivity features. This allowed them to track the car, shut it off while driving and even deactivate the brakes. Fiat Chrysler alerted customers to the security issue and released a patch that inconveniently must be updated by the owner or a dealer by USB drive.[128]

---

[127] https://www.tesla.com/support/privacy

[128] https://media.fcanorthamerica.com/newsrelease.do;jsessionid=16729ED84B5646CFD38F74E92E287B9E?&id=16827&mid=1 **OR** https://archive.vn/19Ncc

Wikileaks' aforementioned *Vault 7* documents mention the CIA's attempts to utilise smart car technology to remotely hack vehicles. WikiLeaks speculated that *"The purpose of such control is not specified, but it would permit the CIA to engage in nearly undetectable assassinations."* igniting the theory that acclaimed war correspondent and vocal critic of government surveillance, Michael Hastings, was assassinated in June 2013 when his Mercedes C250 lost control and burst into flames at high speed.

Whilst purely a conspiracy theory, many security experts including former U.S. National Coordinator Richard A. Clarke have stated the crash was "consistent with a car cyber-attack" [129] In 2010, 7 years before the release of the CIA documents, BBC News published a story about research conducted by the *Center of Automotive Embedded Systems Security* which revealed cars had little resilience against cyber-attacks that could cause the death of a driver[130]

Michael Hastings' final article was highly critical of the Obama administration for their surveillance systems[131]

With multiple mechanical car components now featuring electronic throttles, electronic brakes (both of which are linked with automatic cruise control), electronic steering assist, automated parking assist and other intelligent features; connected cars can be useful and secure for the users, but only if the manufacturer implements frequent security updates and the ability to disconnect all data connection and analytics without forfeiture of the cars' features.

Publications by *the Center for Automotive Embedded Systems Security* can be read at their website Autosec[132]

---

[129] https://archive.vn/isCv6
[130] https://www.bbc.com/news/10119492 **OR** https://archive.vn/V2KND
[131] https://archive.vn/dRize
[132] http://www.autosec.org

As we have proven, software solutions exist for the retrieval of vehicle data. Berla's Project iVe (eye-vee) has been used in multiple high-profile criminal investigations including the Charlie Hebdo terrorist attack, which demonstrated the potential to access devices that had been connected to an infotainment system found in an abandoned Citroën.

The digital bread trail that vehicles can supply certainly aids investigation into a crime but leaves the imagination open to misuse.

Acquisition and Decoding

IVe directly interfaces with vehicle systems via specially designed hardware. It can acquire a full or partial binary image and decode the data. It can recover deleted information from either image type. iVe can decode and parse data such as:

Vehicle/System Information
- ✓ Serial Number
- ✓ Part Number
- ✓ Original VIN Number
- ✓ Build Number

Installed Application Data
- ✓ Weather
- ✓ Traffic
- ✓ Facebook
- ✓ Twitter

Connected Devices
- ✓ Phones
- ✓ Media Players
- ✓ USB Drives
- ✓ SD Cards
- ✓ Wireless Access Points

Navigation Data
- ✓ Tracklogs and Trackpoints
- ✓ Saved Locations
- ✓ Previous Destinations
- ✓ Active and Inactive Routes

Device Information
- ✓ Device IDs
- ✓ Calls
- ✓ Contacts
- ✓ SMS
- ✓ Audio
- ✓ Video
- ✓ Images
- ✓ Access Point Information

Events
- ✓ Doors Opening/Closing
- ✓ Lights On/Off
- ✓ Bluetooth Connections
- ✓ Wi-Fi Connections
- ✓ USB Connections
- ✓ System Reboots
- ✓ GPS Time Syncs
- ✓ Odometer Readings
- ✓ Gear Indications

The iVe software listing

UNDER CONSTANT SUPERVISION

A SIDE NOTE:

I have visited car salvage yards and found that nearly all new deliveries from auction houses and insurance companies contain logbooks and registration information in the glovebox of the cars – some of which give addresses and details of the owner involved in the accident.
If you left these documents (user manual, service books etc.) in the vehicle, they will be transported with the car after the accident and if the car is deemed financially impossible to repair, you will need to ask to remove personal belongings.

The logbooks are considered part of the car and part of the sale to the party that purchase it for parts etc. You can request to see the car after the accident and to remove personal property, which may include removing the personal details from the books and storage.

If the insurer or assessor deems this not possible, you have the right to ask for them to remove your personal information from the vehicle or to redact any information about your financial payments on the car and ownership.

IN CONCLUSION‹

How much is your privacy worth? Do you have anything to hide? No? Well, you won't mind sending me your bank details, an export of your phone messages and call logs and some photos of your family, then will you?

The best thing now is for you to make up your own mind. Is it okay for companies to share your data to ensure you see personalised recommendations?

Do you have any objection to the advertising and sale of your data to provide you with free services?

Is censorship justified to protect users from the horrific words and visuals on the Internet? Should we be grateful that we won't have to use complicated filtering settings if it's beyond our control?

Do the government collect information on millions of citizens to keep the countries we live in safe?

Are those who leaked information regarding the secret programs irresponsible and misguided to assume that what our governments are doing is wrong?

You may not have anything incriminating to conceal, but does that mean you should have to reveal?

UNDER CONSTANT SUPERVISION

GLOSSARY
DEFINITIONS AND TERMS USED THROUGHOUT UNDER CONSTANT SUPERVISION

Data mining
Analysis of large stores of information to obtain new knowledge.
In the case of the US and UK spy agencies, the data mined is reported to include phone call records, emails, instant messages and other social network activity, photos and videos.

Backdoor
The phrase backdoor or backdoor access means to circumvent proper authorisation methods. In terms of the NSA, backdoor access refers to allegations that spy agencies had inserted secret vulnerabilities into encryption software for later access.

Dragnet
A net is drawn along the bottom of a body of water to collect everything. This is a term used to refer to the huge amount of information being trawled by the spy agencies.

Encryption
The digital scrambling of the source material, turning it into "ciphertext" - what appears to be a garbled stream of characters that are only supposed to become understandable if a piece of information called a "key" is used to turn it back into its original form.

Fibre-optic cables
Cables made from incredibly thin strands of glass that can transmit data in the form of light across long distances.

Metadata
Information about communication rather than details of what was said or written (such as dates, location information and the device it was sent from)

INTELLIGENCE AGENCY-SPECIFIC TERMS

HUMINT – Human Intelligence

A phrase used by spy agencies to refer to information gathered from people rather than machines. Sources can include refugees, espionage agents, diplomatic reporters and detainees.

SIGINT – Signals Intelligence

The gathering of information from electronic signals and systems created by humans or computers. This can include telecommunication, radars, weapon systems or other.

GEOINT – Geospatial Intelligence

Information that is gathered from satellite or aerial photography and terrain data. Can also be referred to as IMINT (Imagery Intelligence)

AGENCIES, AGREEMENTS AND OPERATIONS

National Security Agency (NSA)
The US government agency tasked with gathering intelligence for the country's government and military leaders and preventing foreign adversaries from gaining access to classified national security information.

Communications Security Establishment (CSE)
Communication Security Establishment is Canada's national cryptologic agency. CSE was formally established, by an Order-in-Council, in 1946 as the Communications Branch, National Research Council. In 1975, it was renamed the Communications Security Establishment and moved to the National Defence portfolio.

Government Communications Headquarters (GCHQ)
The UK government's communications-focussed intelligence agency, employing about 5,000 people.

Foreign Intelligence Surveillance Court (FISC)
A Washington-based tribunal that considers government agency requests to carry out surveillance for "foreign intelligence purposes" of suspects operating from within the US's borders.

Defence Signals Directorate / Australians Signals Directorate (ASD/DSD)
An Australian government intelligence agency responsible for signals intelligence and information security, established in 1947.

Bundesnachrichtendienst - German Foreign Intelligence Service (BND)
The foreign intelligence agency of Germany that was established in 1956.

Government Communications Security Bureau (GCSB)
New Zealand national intelligence service that was established in 1977.

Five Eye Alliance (5VEY or FVEY)
The security partnership between the U.S., Canada, UK, Australia and New Zealand intelligence agencies. Further explanations of the "eyes" feature in this book.

Special Source Operations (SSO)
A division of the NSA responsible for overseeing programmes that source their data through "partnerships" with the US and overseas-based companies.

Tailored Access Operations (TAO)
A division of the NSA, which the agency says is "centred on computer network exploitation".

Covert Network Threats (CNT1)
A division of the CSE, Covert Network Threats mission is "to produce intelligence on the capabilities, intentions, and activities of Hostile Intelligence Services to support Counterintelligence activities at home and abroad."

Army Cryptologic Operations: Operations Division
US Army Intelligence unit.

Network Analysis Centre (NAC)
A joint network technology research unit with branches in the NSA, CSE, and GCHQ.

Joint Threat Research Intelligence Group (JTRIG)
The Joint Threat Research Intelligence Group is a GCHQ unit focused on cyber forensics, espionage and covert operations.

Applied Research
Research Unit for the GCHQ.

Office of SIGINT Development
Division of the NSA, with joint partners from within the five-eye network, the SIGINT Development produces research and technology for use in signals intelligence.

NSA/CSS Europe (NCEUR)
NCEUR is a division of the NSA with a focus in SIGINT in Europe

Special US Liaison Activity Germany (SUSLAG)
SUSLAG is the NSA liaison to the German intelligence service (BND). It is the parent to the Joint Analysis Center (JAC) and the Joint SIGINT Activity (JSA).

Joint Analysis Center (JAC)
The Joint Analysis Center, in 2005, comprised of five NSA civilian analysts who are integrated into the German intelligence service (BND).

Joint SIGINT Activity (JSA)
The Joint SIGINT Activity is an NSA and BND intelligence partnership, operated from the German SIGINT facility Mangfall Kaserne in Bavaria.

Remote Operations Center (ROC)

In 2006, the NSA announced the opening of a new Remote Operations Center, the *"Epicentre for Computer Network Operations."*

Digital Network Crypt Applications (DNCA)

DNCA is a division of the NSA.

National Counterterrorism Center (NCTC)

The National Counterterrorism Center (NCTC) is a United States government organization responsible for national and international counterterrorism efforts. Part of the Office of the Director of National Intelligence, the group brings together specialists from other federal agencies, including the NSA, CIA, the FBI, and the Department of Defense.

National Information Assurance Research Laboratory (NIARL)

The National Information Assurance Research Laboratory (NIARL) is "responsible for conducting and sponsoring research in technologies and techniques needed to secure America's future information systems."

European Security Center (ESC)/European Security Operations Center (ESOC)

Under the leadership of the NSA, The European Security Center (ESC) is a *"fixed-site facility that provides provide crisis support to military operations throughout the European Command theatre, which includes not only Europe but also much of Africa and parts of the Middle East."*

European Cryptologic Center (ECC)

The European Cryptologic Center (ECC) is a branch of the NSA in Darmstadt, Germany.

Cryptanalysis and Exploitation Services is an office of the NSA.

European Technical Center (ETC)

The European Technical Center (ETC) in Wiesbaden, Germany, is NSA's *"primary communication hub in that part of the world, providing communication connectivity, SIGINT collection, and data-flow services to NSAers ."*

Global Access Operations (GAO) is a division of the NSA responsible for intercepts from satellites and other international SIGINT platforms.

Menwith Hill Station (MHS)

Menwith Hill Station (MHS) *"provides communications and intelligence support services to the United Kingdom and the United States of America. The site contains an extensive satellite ground station and is a communications intercept and missile warning site and has been described as the largest electronic monitoring station in the world."* The NSA has led US operations at MHS since 1966.

Special Collection Service (SCS)

The Special Collection Service (SCS) is a joint U.S. CIA-/NSA program that enables intelligence collection from highly sensitive places, *"such as foreign embassies, communications centres, and foreign government installations."*
The unit combines the *"communications intelligence capabilities of the NSA with the covert action capabilities of the CIA to facilitate access to sophisticated foreign communications systems."*

NSA/CSS Threat Operations Center (NTOC)

NSA/CSS Threat Operations Center (NTOC) is a division of the NSA with a "blended foreign intelligence (SIGINT) and information assurance mission."

Foreign Affairs Directorate (FAD)

A division of the NSA, the Foreign Affairs Directorate which "*acts as a liaison with foreign intelligence services, counter-intelligence centres*" and the Five Eye partners. There are different offices based on the geographic region under FAD.

SECURITY CLASSIFICATIONS

All documents that contain classified information must be marked with codes that detail appropriate control procedures. These are usually presented at the top of the document, and occasionally at the beginning of each sub-heading and paragraph. They are usually comprised of three elements, separated by double slashes.

There are three main classification levels:

```
TOP SECRET (TS)
SECRET
CONFIDENTIAL
```

After the security classification, there are a series of **Sensitive Compartmented Information (SCI)** codes that further control access to the document. These are usually code words – with some codewords not officially known by the public or detailed in leaks. There may be around 100-300 SCI compartments, grouped into about two dozen different control systems.

The most common codes are:
COMINT / Special Intelligence (SI)

This control system is for communications intercepts or Signals Intelligence and contains various sub-control systems and compartments, identified by an abbreviation or codeword.

They usually follow the code COMINT or SI with a hyphen. They include:

```
VTK: VERY RESTRICTED KNOWLEDGE
ECI: EXCEPTIONALLY CONTROLLED INFORMATION
G:   GAMMA
D:   DELTA
```

STELLARWIND (STLW)

This is a "controlled access signals intelligence program" created under presidential authorisation after the attacks of September 11th. It includes information related to the President's Surveillance Program (PSP), the Terrorist Surveillance Program (TSP) and bulk telephony and metadata collection by the NSA.

ENDSEAL (EL)
This control system is reserved for finalized intelligence products. ENDSEAL information is always classified as Special Intelligence (SI). Documents with this classification are intended for dissemination to various consumers within the Intelligence Community.

TALENT KEYHOLE (TK)
This control system is reserved for the products of overhead collection systems, including satellites and reconnaissance aircraft.

RESERVE (RSV)
This control system is used for compartments protecting new sources and methods during research, development and acquisition done by the National Reconnaissance Office (NRO).

KLONDIKE (KDK)
This control system has been developed for Geospatial Intelligence (GEOINT) produced by the National Reconnaissance Office (NRO).

HUMINT Control System (HCS)
This control system is for protecting Human Intelligence (HUMINT), which is derived from information collected or provided by human sources.

STRAP 1 / STRAP 2 / STRAP 3
These are code terms for GCHQ documents, STRAP 1 being the lowest level, and STRAP 3 being the highest. Despite being known, there are no STRAP 3 documents available to the public via leaks.

DISTRIBUTION MARKINGS

These codes are used to restrict the dissemination of information to only those with appropriate classification levels.

- For Official Use Only: FOUO
- Originator Controlled: ORCON
- No Foreign Nationals: NOFORN
- Foreign Intelligence Surveillance Act: FISA
- Five Eyes: 5EYE

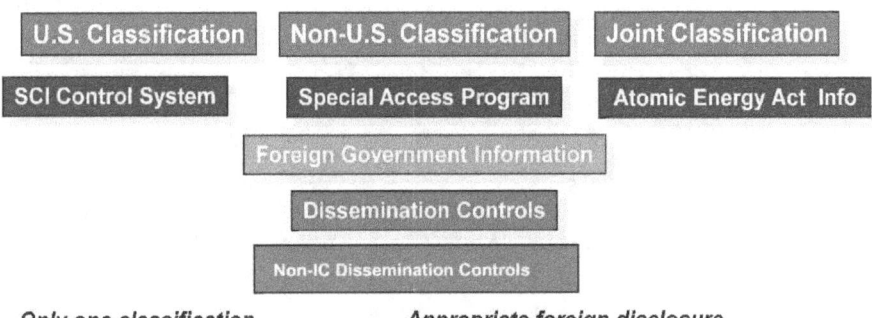

Only one classification type and value allowed

Appropriate foreign disclosure or release marking required

Classification//SCI/SCI//SAP//AEA//FGI//Dissem/Dissem//Non-IC/Non-IC

Separators
- // Double forward slash is used to separate marking categories
- / Single forward slash is used to separate multiple values within a marking category
- - Hyphen is used to link a marking to a sub-marking (e.g., SI-G or RD-SIGMA)
- " " Space is used to separate multiple sub-markings and multiple trigraph or tetragraph codes in the FGI Marking (e.g., //SI-ABD-G XYZW YYYY// or //FGI GBR JPN//)
- , Comma is used to separate multiple trigraph or tetragraph codes in the REL TO Marking

ABOUT THE AUTHOR

Born into a tech-based family and raised fascinated with upcoming technology, Cask J. Thomson spent most of his childhood tinkering with computers rather than indulging in sports and social life. Thomson and his family relocated to Australia after his father landed a new contract overseeing the merge between Hewlett Packard and Compaq.
Despite only intending to stay temporarily, the Thomson family made Australia their home.

Thomson worked as a server administrator and cybersecurity consultant before focusing on running his own publishing company alongside his design firm in Queensland.

THOMSON CAN BE CONTACTED VIA HIS WEBSITE AT
WWW.CASKTHOMSON.COM

OR
SEND AN EMAIL/HATE MAIL TO
CJ@BOOKREFINE.COM

ACKNOWLEDGEMENTS:

The reader – thank you! Especially if you didn't download the book without paying. If you did, well...I'd be a hypocrite to criticise you but hey, the publishing company is an anti-DRM and anti-copyright troll!

Everyone that has helped with the book who wished to stay anonymous. Big thank you.
Tesla security white-hat hacker greentheonly for providing information and answering my questions.
The webmaster (s) of Archive.today for providing the archive services and for answering questions relating to their service and removal demands.
Jacob Appelbaum, Lauren Poitras, Ewen MacAskill and Edward Snowden for releases.
Gildas Lormeau for the web extension Single File
(https://github.com/gildas-lormeau/SingleFile)
TeleGeography for Submarine cable information and mapping.
The Nautilus Institute for Security and Sustainability.

Diagrams without source or attribution: C.J. Thomson

UNDER CONSTANT SUPERVISION

THE EBOOK VERSION OF THIS BOOK IS FREE FROM DRM (DIGITAL RIGHTS MANAGEMENT) TECHNOLOGY THAT RESTRICT YOUR RIGHTS.
WE PRIDE OURSELVES ON GIVING OUR CONSUMERS THE CHOICE AND WE HOPE THAT IF YOU PAID FOR THIS BOOK, YOU ENJOYED IT.
IF YOU HAVE ANY COMPLAINTS OR SUGGESTIONS, PLEASE DO NOT HESITATE TO CONTACT US, AND HELP US IMPROVE!

VISIT US AT BOOKREFINE.COM
FOLLOW US ON SOCIAL MEDIA

BookRefine
PUBLISHING

GLOBAL SURVEILLANCE

FIVE EYES: AUSTRALIA / NEW ZEALAND / UNITED KINGDOM / UNITED STATES / CANADA

- YAKIMA TRAINING CENTER — **JACKKNIFE**
- SALT CREEK STATION
- BUCKLEY AIR FORCE BASE
- ROARING CREEK STATION
- SUGAR GROVE RESEARCH STATION — **TIMBERLINE**
- LACKLAND AIR FORCE BASE — FORT GORDON
- CFB LEITRIM
- CFB GANDER
- SABANA SECA BASE — **CORALINE**
- U.S. EMBASSY (BRASILIA, FEDERAL DISTRICT)
- HAWAII REGIONAL OPERATIONS SECURITY CENTER
- KUNIA REGIONAL SIGINT OPERATIONS CENTER
- RAF EDZELL
- RAF MENWITH HILL
- GCHQ BUDE — **CARBOY**
- GIBRALTAR
- FIELD STATION IN BERLIN, TEUFELSBERG
- PINE GAP JOINT DEFENSE FACILITY
- GCHQ CAT HILL (ASCENSION ISLAND)
- PYEONGTAEK STATION — **BRONCO**
- BRITISH HIGH COMMISSION NAIROBI
- GROUND-BASED ELECTRO-OPTICAL DEEP SPACE SURVEILLANCE DIEGO GARCIA
- DIEGO GARCIA TELECOMMUNICATIONS STATION — **SCAPEL**
- BRITISH EMBASSY, MUSCAT — **SNICK**
- U.S. EMBASSY NEW DELHI
- RAF LITTLE SAI WAN
- U.S. EMBASSY BANGKOK — **LEMONWOOD**
- MISAWA AIR BASE — **LADYLOVE**
- NAVAL BASE GUAM
- SHOAL BAY RECEIVING STATION — **SHOAL BAY**
- AUSTRALIAN DEFENCE SATELLITE COMMUNICATIONS STATION — **STELLAR**
- JOINT DEFENCE FACILITY PINE GAP — **RAINFALL**
- GCSB WAIHOPAI — **IRONSAND**

C. Thomson | Bookréfine Publishing · bookrefine.com

www.ingramcontent.com/pod-product-compliance
Lightning Source LLC
Chambersburg PA
CBHW071349210526
45465CB00001B/28